RIVERINE

"A SUPERB COMBAT ACCOUNT OF ONE OF THE U.S. NAVY'S MOST ELITE FORCES. . . . SHEPPARD'S WORD IS AUTHENTIC. A TRULY HISTORICAL REPORT ON A LITTLE-KNOWN PART OF THE WAR IN VIETNAM."

—Captain Paul N. Gray, USN Commander
River Patrol Force 1967–68

Lieutenant Commander Don Sheppard: Though he shared a lively camaraderie with his men, he knew that a leader makes his toughest decisions alone. But on the front lines of the river war he had two kindred spirits. . . .

Captain Robert R. Laske: An aging fighter pilot and World War II hero, he surpassed Sheppard and everyone else in aggressiveness and bravery. When he became Sheppard's commander, Sheppard soon had free rein for bold, innovative tactics. . . .

Ong Tam: A powerful village chief who had fought against the French with the Viet Minh at Dien Bien Phu, he became Sheppard's key Vietnamese ally along the Bassac River and his closest in-country friend. . . .

"A MOVING, AUTHENTIC PERSONAL ACCOUNT."

—*The Retired Officer Magazine*

"IN NAVY VERNACULAR, COMMANDER SHEPPARD'S MEMOIR CAN ONLY BE DESCRIBED AS OUTSTANDING. FOR ANYONE WITH AN INTEREST IN THE LITTLE-KNOWN RIVERINE WAR IN VIETNAM THIS BOOK IS A MUST. A TRULY FASCINATING READ!"

—David J. Wright, USN Operations Officer
Delta River Patrol Group 1966–67

RIVERINE

A BROWN-WATER SAILOR
IN THE DELTA, 1967

DON SHEPPARD

POCKET BOOKS

New York   London   Toronto   Sydney   Tokyo   Singapore

The places and events are true. The people, for the most part, are composites of the many men I served with on the Bassac. I have used no real names, but of those who were there, some will recognize a good deal of themselves, some will not. It is your choice—twenty-five years later.

POCKET BOOKS, a division of Simon & Schuster Inc.
1230 Avenue of the Americas, New York, NY 10020

Copyright © 1992 by Don Sheppard

Published by arrangement with Presidio Press

All rights reserved, including the right to reproduce
this book or portions thereof in any form whatsoever.
For information address Presidio Press,
505 B San Marin Drive, Suite 300, Novato, CA 94945

ISBN: 0-671-79691-7

First Pocket Books printing February 1994

10 9 8 7 6 5 4 3 2 1

POCKET and colophon are registered trademarks of
Simon & Schuster Inc.

Cover art by Lee MacLeod

Printed in the U.S.A.

This book is dedicated to my grandchildren. May they always have the luxury of thinking this a work of fiction.

Contents

———————◆———————

Contents

RIVERINE

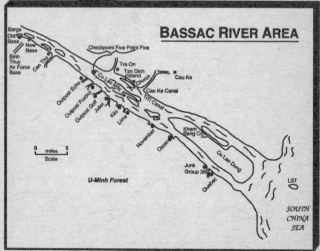

BASSAC RIVER AREA

Introduction

———————⚫———————

It used to be part of French Indochina; now it's called Vietnam. There used to be a north and a south; now it's just one country. Saigon used to be the capital of South Vietnam; now Saigon is called Ho Chi Minh City. In the old days Saigon was geopolitically the center of all events. The war of the big battles, the heavy air strikes, and the news-generating events took place north of Saigon.

The Mekong Delta, just south of Saigon, encompasses the entire southern tip of the country. The average rainfall in the delta is eighty inches a year. The delta was a sleepy place where the rice grew well and the living was easy.

In the early years of the American Vietnam War, the Viet Cong ferried men, arms, and ammunition through thousands of north–south canals and across two wide rivers into the war zones north of Saigon.

The two wide rivers split the delta. The southernmost, the Bassac, runs generally northeast to southwest; the Mekong River, to the north, runs nearly west to east.

To deny the use of these rivers to the Viet Cong, the U.S. Navy established a river force code-named Operation Game Warden. The force came equipped with thirty-one-foot, dark green fiberglass civilian cabin cruisers called PBRs,

1

which stands for patrol boat, river. The boats, right off the civilian shelves, were armed with twin .50-caliber machine guns forward and a single .50-caliber machine gun aft. They presented a formidable weapon. Two hot-rodded, high-performance, 220-horsepower GM truck diesels drove two Jacuzzi water jet pumps. PBRs had little armor, depending instead on speed and firepower for survival.

Sailors to man these boats were middle- to senior-grade petty officers—all volunteers from the fleet. Each boat had a four-man crew: a boat captain, a coxswain, an engineer/after gunner, and a forward gunner. Two boats made up a patrol unit, led by an officer or a senior-grade petty officer.

This is the story of the men who fought these PBRs on the Bassac River, and of the man who commanded them.

Vietnam,
February 1967

———•———

It was my birthday. The trip across the dateline had pushed it forward a day. Burning jet fuel and car exhaust fumes coupled with the stench of a thousand rushing bodies made Saigon's Than Son Nhut airport smell sickly sweet, like rotting fruit. There seemed to be no pattern to the scurry of people in sweat-stained clothes. I was looking for the helo port. Contradictory instructions kept me moving in circles.

Men in soiled and patched jungle combat greens sat silently on hard wooden benches, their eyes gaunt, tired, with a distant look of apathy. Civilian men in clean and pressed khaki bush jackets walked briskly by with no reaction. Women made up a fourth of the herd passing the hundred or so soldiers. Only the most stunning called forth a hint of recognition. Army MPs attempting to keep everyone moving added to the confusion.

"Excuse me, Sergeant, where is the helo port?"

"Over there, Major."

"Where?"

"Sir! Over there."

Small Vietnamese rushed back and forth, performing the labor duties enthusiastically. They were active, blending into the surroundings with no apparent notice or care for the conglomerate of blacks and Caucasians milling around them.

The gentle whoop, whoop, whoop of turning rotor blades announced the helo pad of the world's busiest airport, where takeoff intervals were measured in seconds.

"Yes, sir, Major, this helo's going to Can Tho."

"Lieutenant commander!" I corrected. The warrant officer pilots in their dark green flight suits seemed more of an age to be going to the local teen club.

The bucket seats on the "slick" Huey, UH-1, were uncomfortable and crowded with the four other passengers, but in my excitement I didn't mind.

The pilot's left hand gently pulled up on the collective between the two cockpit seats, then the whine of the engine increased and the helo slowly lifted to "light on the skids." The pilot's lips moved in unheard speech. His left hand pulled up higher and we rose hesitatingly. The nose pointed downward and we picked up speed, lifting above the other helos but staying low over the approach roads and buildings, then finally pulling high into the air and heading southeast. I was finally on my way to war; no greater birthday gift could I imagine.

It was eighty-five miles to the city of Can Tho. The open door of the helo gave me a windy view of the huge, fertile Mekong Delta—the rice basket of Asia—with its simple, flat terrain cut through by two large rivers and thousands of both natural and man-made canals and untold rice paddies. The waterway had a jungle of trees on each bank for a width of fifty to a hundred yards. From this altitude, the canals were multicolored ribbons—brown in the center, green at the sides.

I had waited twenty-six years for this ride—ever since 1941, when I was eleven years old and war news filled the radio and magazines. Oh, how I wanted to be a soldier! I tried desperately to grow fast enough to be in World War II. I had just recently forgiven the Germans and the Japanese for surrendering too soon. I still suffered from the then-common childhood disease: too-young-for-World War II syndrome. I hoped this tour of duty would cure it.

I was to relieve a Lt. Comdr. Marsh Strum as Commander, River Division 51 (COMRIVDIV 51). I had prepared myself well for this duty. Over the years no war movie or book escaped me. I read scores of surplus army technical manuals. I hung around the American Legion halls and the Veterans of Foreign Wars buildings just to catch a snatch of a war story, some snippet of adventure. I learned to play chess because someone told me it was the game of generals. I listened to the bragging and horror tales of war, believing everything. Most importantly, I had dreamed.

I joined the navy early in life, influenced by my grandfather who, so he said, had been a commodore in the British navy. The navy never let me get close to the Korean War, so they owed me this one. I hoped that I could measure up to my envisioned standard of the American warrior.

"Don Sheppard," I said, extending my hand. Thousands of little gnats buzzed around our heads.

"Marsh Strum . . . glad to see you." He wore a black beret. He looked used up, his eyes dark pools devoid of expression. We piled into a well-banged-up jeep and drove down a dusty, poorly maintained road toward Binh Thuy, a small village some five miles up the Bassac River from Can Tho. At Binh Thuy we passed a large Vietnamese military airfield on our left. Another mile or so and we arrived at the PBR base next to a tiny four- to five-hootch hamlet called Tra Noc. The people along the whole thirty-minute trip seemed friendly and unconcerned. I had expected an ambush.

The base was a surprise. I had envisioned that an advanced combat base would be rough, with bamboo huts and mud slips for the boats, and maybe, if they were lucky, a hand-hewn bamboo dock might be available. But here were the comforts of life: The men lived in an old French motel with running water and slowly turning overhead fans.

Unfortunately, the hot water heaters charged the showers with a slight amount of electricity. Uncomfortable but livable, Strum informed me.

The workshops were not bamboo A-frames with beached boats and a mechanic under the palm tree but rather modern shops with the latest tune-up, overhaul, and lifting equipment. An old converted navy barge, anchored fifty feet from shore, housed the shops. A floating pier was moored to its side to berth the PBRs, and a rickety, twenty-degree-canted floating walkway led to the beach.

On this barge were located the navy operations center (ops center) and the communications center (comm center). These two units allowed voice communications with any portion of the Mekong Delta or Saigon. I had half expected two tin cans and a long piece of string.

It was early evening as we finished the tour of the base. "Supper?" Strum asked, guiding me into the large cabana-type structure attached to one leg of the motel. Strum ordered beers and stared at me. He was very thin with a dark tan.

"You're early," he said, swigging his beer down in a gulp. "I'm not due to leave for another two months. I was surprised as hell when Saigon called and said you'd be here today. Don't get me wrong, old sport, you're welcome. Man, are you ever welcome."

"Early? Yeah, reckon I am. They took me out of PBR school at Mare Island before I ever saw a PBR. You're supposed to be dead, Mister Strum."

"You're kidding me."

"No, I was told you took a grenade in the stomach and were expected to die before the sun set. I was asked if I minded coming over without going to the school. Well you know how I had to answer that, so here I am. Teach me, Father!"

"A grenade in the stomach . . . that was old Smitty, my counterpart, up in the Rung Sat special zone out of Saigon," Strum mumbled, staring at the ceiling.

"Yeah? Well, the word got back that it was COMRIVDIV 51 that got it and since I was slated to become COMRIVDIV 51, here I am—quite frankly a little concerned that I have no idea what I'm supposed to do and what equipment I have to do it with."

"Well, I'll be damned . . . I'll be damned," he answered. "How the hell could that have happened?"

"How long you been in the navy, Mister Strum?"

Strum looked at me. "Long enough, I guess. I understand how it could happen, especially out here on the frontier."

"Yeah."

"Well, it's really not that hard, Commander. We only have one doctrine here on the Bassac and that is to stay in the middle of the river, keep out of trouble, and don't get your men hurt or your boats damaged."

"Come on, Strum, you're shittin' me!"

"You'll see . . . besides, right now the Vietnamese are celebrating the Tet cease-fire—Tet's their lunar new year. We'll hear a lot of shooting but it's all in frolic and pointed to the sky. There'll be no action for a week or so. The Vietnamese love their Tet celebrations and especially the cease-fire . . . happens around this time every year."

We continued to drink. Several officers dropped by, wishing me welcome, each one with some comment about keeping my head down or my ass covered. Each of them told me not to forget to take my malaria pills.

"You know, Don, we haven't been out here on the Bassac that long. We only came up the river in May of '66. How long's that . . . seven months ago? We didn't know what to expect. Hell, we didn't even know what we were supposed to do except interdict enemy traffic crossing the river. Before we came, there was an extensive propaganda effort directed to the Vietnamese on the river on how we were supposed to help them and be here just to make life easier. But it didn't work out quite that way.

"The people were mighty scared of us and we were mighty scared of them. Our mission was to search the sampans and junks to ensure that there were no weapons crossing the Bassac and that everyone had the proper identification papers. Hell, everyone had proper identification! We couldn't tell.

"We expected to get ambushed every time we stopped a boat. Hell, we couldn't speak Vietnamese. We got some Vietnamese policemen to start riding the boats and this helped. We never quite trusted them after we caught a few pressuring the people we stopped for money. That's all sorted out now. In the beginning we ran some offensive ops, but our casualty rates were unacceptable to Saigon.

"The Game Warden staff located here helped a lot in the early days . . . they were pretty aggressive. They're a good lot generally and shouldn't give you much trouble, but you know how it is being on the flagship, so to speak.

"I guess you know that Game Warden is the overall code name for the riverine war in-country here. It's also Task Force 116 . . . you'll be a task unit commander."

"Yeah, COMRIVRON 5 briefed me in Saigon," I replied.

"Well, things settled down after a while and we got into a routine. We got maintenance sorted out . . . got the barge working and our communications system set up. We have a hell of a problem down here with radio wave propagation. One second you can talk to God and ten minutes later your cover boat can't even hear you.

"It was our stated mission to interdict the suspected VC arms and VC troop movement across the Bassac, and the powers that be figured we could do it best from the middle of the river. That's where we're ordered to stay, and that's what we do. I suspect, though, that a few of the boys run pretty close to the beach once in a while trying to stir up some action."

Lieutenant Commander Strum looked at me as if he wanted a judgment. I offered none. Hell, I didn't know what was going on.

"You're second generation, Don; you guys have the bene- fit of what we screwed up and what we did well. The infrastructure is in place and I see you really doing well out here. I wish you luck.

"You'll find that you don't have enough boats or helo gunships to do the job right. You won't have enough repair parts. New replacement personnel will come slowly, although I've heard there's a lot of sailors in the pipeline. We've got fifty-five miles of river from here to the South China Sea to patrol and the VC can essentially cross 'bout anywhere they want to."

It grew late. We had eaten too well, drunk too much, been too serious, and forced too much laughter. I went to bed apprehensive for the first time in my assignment as COMRIVDIV 51. The overhead fan turned agonizingly slowly. Useless. The full fury of the heat closed over me, demanding sweat from every pore.

I tried to take a shower but the electrically charged water made my body quiver with each droplet. I didn't have the courage to stand under it for long. I slept poorly.

We met again at breakfast. I was drained of caring. It was 0700 and already the temperature was ninety. "You'll get used to it . . . takes two or three months," Strum advised. Then we ate in silence, the coffee giving some promise of life.

"You got the LST [landing ship, tank] down there in the South China Sea. RIVSEC 512 does a creditable job on the southern Bassac but traffic is slow down there. Most of our action is around Juliet."

I didn't know what he meant. "You ready for a boat ride?" he asked.

We stopped at the ops center and Strum looked over the night's message traffic and the patrol reports from both River Section (RIVSEC) 511 and 512. "Nothing," he said, tossing them back into an office basket. "Okay, let's go." He gave me a helmet and a flak jacket as we walked down the slippery brow from the barge to the floating pier.

"Don't get him wounded first time out," remarked some unidentified, wise-ass lieutenant junior grade in sweaty greens. I thought him impertinent and not the least bit funny. I wasn't exactly scared, but my mind was far from at ease.

"Hah! He's the last man I'd take anyplace dangerous," Marsh replied with the haughty air combatants use when talking about those who have not seen action. Marsh was a veteran. He was a true pioneer of riverine warfare. "I've already got four flak jackets on him!" he yelled back.

Our two PBRs moved smartly away from the pier. We were in the lead boat. The second boat in patrol, the cover boat, fell in automatically about two hundred yards astern. The jet pumps threw a large wake as we raced down the center of the river.

"Wakes are a problem," Marsh instructed, "until the boats get on step, then they almost disappear. We have to keep a careful watch lest we swamp the sampans. If we sink them, the Vietnamese lie about the value and Uncle Sam has to pay them ten times their worth."

Strum briefed me continuously: "Speed is an essential part of every patrol mission. The PBR is not, contrary to its sleek appearance, a fast boat. Its maximum speed of around twenty-five knots is difficult to obtain and maintain due to the heavy ammo loading and the general characteristics of a planing hull."

Strum droned on: "A planing hull must reach a critical speed—for the PBR it's around eighteen miles per hour—before it will lift out of the water onto its planing surface and obtain its maximum speed. This 'getting on step,' as we call it, becomes very difficult with a double ammo load, full fuel, a couple of cases of C rations, and perhaps a passenger or two."

It seemed the long, skinny, wooden sampans were everywhere, and we had to slow continuously to avoid them. I wondered how the PBRs ever got anywhere. The sampans had engines like those that powered lawn mowers and go-carts back in the States. But these engines had a six- to nine-foot shaft driving a small, two-bladed propeller. The whole rig was mounted on a three-foot-long two-by-four nailed across the stern of the sampan. To steer a sampan with one of these outboards, called swimmer tails or shrimp tails, the engine was pivoted to port or starboard. It could be swung perpendicular to the sampan, resulting in an extremely maneuverable boat.

"The VC put two ten-horsepower swimmer tails on their long sampans and they'll do thirty knots," Marsh said. I found it hard to believe.

We passed Can Tho, the largest city in the delta, with a population of several thousand, of which, Marsh stated, thirty percent were probably VC. The large canal through the center of town wound inland for ten miles into enemy territory.

"Man, we never go down that canal," volunteered a young gunner. "Even the RAGs stay out."

"RAGs?"

"River assault groups, a part of the Vietnamese navy. They used to ferry troops up and down the river. The ARVNs, that's the Army of the Republic of Vietnam, don't use them very much anymore, since they've got helos. Much simpler to fly in and out. RAGs don't mind—less for them to do."

"What do they do now?"

"Patrol a little up around Can Tho, mostly keep painting their boats . . . shame, too, they're good fighters," Marsh said.

The boats sped along in perfect formation, the coxswain in the cover boat following exactly the lead boat's movement. As we continued downriver Marsh resumed his indoctrination: "There," he said, pointing to a large island. "That's Cu Lao May, and that tip there is called by the code word five point five. From there on down to the South China Sea, the VC pretty much have their own way. Almost all our firefights occur between here and the mouth of the river, but mostly at Juliet."

The crew put on their flak jackets without a word; no one

wore a helmet. I, at Marsh's insistence, had my flak jacket on since getting under way. "We should wear helmets, Commander," remarked the boat captain, "but it gets so damn hot, they'll cook your brain!"

Ten hours later the patrol returned, my mind crammed with a dozen Bassac River landmarks, a hundred assorted facts, and a thousand do's and don'ts.

Commander, River Patrol Unit

———————•———————

Two days later in an unimpressive ceremony with RIVSEC 511 lined up in true navy fashion, under a hot morning sun, I relieved Lieutenant Commander Strum and became COMRIVDIV 51.

My mission was simple: Stop the VC from using the Bassac River. To do this I had a pitifully inadequate force of two river sections, designated 511 and 512. Each river section had ten PBRs and about sixty-five officers and men. The river sections were not self-sufficient and depended on base support units or a specially configured World War II landing ship, tank (LST), to keep the boats under repair and to feed and house the men.

RIVSEC 512 fought from one of these old LSTs anchored out in the South China Sea about five miles from the mouth of the Bassac. Also based on the LST were two nearly antiquated, ex-army, UH-1B (Huey) armed helicopters flown by navy pilots called Seawolves. Neither the LST nor the Seawolves were under my command.

There was also the nebulous assignment of six Vietnamese regional force (RF) soldiers to my command. These RFs were assigned to establish liaison between the PBRs and the river people before the specifically trained Vietnamese national maritime policemen were available. A sergeant named Nguyen Van Thanh led these RFs.

I didn't get much chance to talk to Sergeant Thanh while I was relieving Strum. Thanh stayed in the background and Strum didn't say much about him. Thanh was small by American standards—barely five foot four inches tall—but lean and muscular. His hair was short-cropped and when he frowned, the three-inch scar across his left cheek gave him an ugly, mean-looking face.

I also didn't get much chance to talk to Lieutenant Henry, the officer in charge (OinC) of RIVSEC 511, while I was with Strum.

"Tell me, Lieutenant, what do you see as your mission here?" I asked as he came into the small steel cubicle I called an office. It was sweltering here on the barge, with only a small porthole and a fan to cool my space.

He paused for a moment as if searching for a reply. "Do you want the textbook answer or what I feel?"

"Whichever one you're comfortable with."

"To stop the VC from crossing the Bassac."

"How you doing on that?"

"Not so well."

"Why?"

"Well . . . I guess we get along okay."

"You're begging the question, Lieutenant. Let me know what you think. We're going to be pretty close out here and I need your honest opinion, now and in the future."

"Well, we can't do our job with what we have. I mean, hell, my men are tired. They're run-down. The boats are in horrible shape. We can't get replacement parts. We can't get new people to replace the wounded or killed. Sometimes we even get short of ammo. The food is lousy. And it's always so damn hot and those goddamned bugs drive us all crazy."

"As you know I have absolutely no experience at this and I'm depending on you to help me out."

"Well, of course, Commander, but, hell, there's not much for you to do. Simon, with 512 on the LST, takes care of the lower Bassac and I take care of the upper. There's not much you need to do except maybe try to get us some new boats and some men and repair parts."

I sat back, filling my pipe to give me time to think. I could detect the problem here. "Lieutenant, fortunately or unfortunately, depending on how you see it, I'm a hands-on person. I could not be in charge here and not know exactly what's going on. The only way I see that I can do this is to be out on the river with your men. I know it will be a pain in the ass for you. I know you'll feel that I'll be interfering too much with your job, but I'll keep it to a minimum and I'll always consult with you on what I'm doing."

He looked at me for a minute, then said: "I understand, Commander, and I thank you for being up front with me. Mister Strum had the same problem with the 116 staff guys here." He smiled. "At least there's only one of you."

I got up, extending my hand. "Thank you, sir. I'll see what I can do about getting the things you need."

Just as he got to the door I asked, "What do you think about staying in the middle of the river?"

"I don't understand," he replied.

"I mean, do you think it's an effective way to do your job?"

Lieutenant Henry paused before answering. I wasn't sure he trusted me yet. "Well, I think it's good enough and it sure is less dangerous."

Next I sent for Sergeant Thanh. "Sit down, Sergeant Thanh. What is your sergeant rank? I see no stripe."

He hesitated. "I am equal to a staff sergeant, Thieu Ta."

"Thieu Ta?"

"Thieu Ta, Major . . . Thieu Ta."

"No, Sergeant Thanh, U.S. Navy lieutenant commander."

"Yes, sir, Thieu Ta," he answered, and I guessed that was that.

Sergeant Thanh sat across from me, rubbing his hands nervously. "Sergeant Thanh, I am new here. Commander Strum told me that you were a very good man and that you helped him a lot. Will you do that for me?" He nodded yes, answering that Thieu Ta Strum was a great man.

"How long will you be assigned here?" He didn't seem to understand. "How long will you stay here at Tra Noc to help the PBRs?"

"As long as Thieu Ta wants me here and as long as my men and I can do job for you. Policemen not so good— sometimes Thanh has to have good talk with them."

"Where does your family live, Sergeant?"

"I have no family, Thieu Ta. VC kill two years ago in Soc Trang. I join army and have not been back since. No family, Thieu Ta."

"How about your men?"

"They are all from Soc Trang. They do not like VC. They work for you and I work for you."

"Sergeant Thanh, I must be very honest with you. I have no experience with river warfare. I have always been on ships in the ocean. I know nothing about this type of fighting. Will you help me learn?"

"Thieu Ta," he started, then hesitated. "Thieu Ta, I have never known an officer to say he does not know something. Many Vietnamese officers know nothing but they act like they know everything. Many people die because they are ignorant and will not ask if they do not know. Thanh will help Thieu Ta as best I can."

His words made me feel better. I was out of my element here and I didn't want people dying because of my stupidity. Sergeant Thanh could be a valuable asset. "And, Sergeant Thanh, if I can help you in any way, please let me know."

Thanh's face lit up. He wasn't used to such frankness from officers. His smile told me I had an ally. "I understand, Thieu Ta, I understand."

The word *understand* triggered something in my mind. I sat reflectively for a moment. I looked toward Thanh but not at him. Understand? What did I understand? Nothing! What had to be learned? What had to be done? First, I reckoned, I'd best know my battlefield and what the boats could do. And the greatest unknown, the one thing that no amount of preparation could guarantee success for, was me. I didn't understand myself: Coward or hero—which would it be, Sheppard? Though no Spartan mother ever said to me: "Come home with your shield, my son, or on it," I hoped for the former.

"Thieu Ta . . . Thieu Ta, are you okay?"

"Yes, Sergeant Thanh . . . sorry, I was thinking there for a moment. What is your job here at Tra Noc, Sergeant?" I asked, but he did not understand the question. "My job is to stop the VC from crossing the Bassac," I explained. "What do you do to help us?"

"I try to help whatever Thieu Ta wants."

"Can you be more . . . ," I searched for a word that he could understand. I took out my English to Vietnamese dictionary, looked up *specific,* and pointed out the word.

"Yes, Thieu Ta, specific. I try to get knowledge from villages on where VC are and what VC are planning to do. Sometimes it is very good knowing . . . knowledge."

"What can I do to help this, Sergeant Thanh?"

"Trouble is that river people do not trust Americans. Many . . . please excuse me . . . many do not like Americans, many are afraid. Too many promises given, nothing happens, but VC always there. Americans not too often. Please forgive me, Thieu Ta, for speaking my mind."

I sat and watched him. He was sweating and his voice had a higher pitch. What he was saying was difficult for him. He was describing a typical antiguerrilla problem.

"It is good that you speak what you think, Sergeant Thanh. That is how I will learn. We do not have much time. What can I do?"

"Villages need many things, Thieu Ta. Can you get?"

"I don't know but I will try. Tomorrow we will visit the villages."

As he stood up to leave the room, I asked, "How do you feel about Americans, Sergeant?"

The question left him breathless. "I think . . . I think . . . Americans always go home after one year."

* * *

In the morning we were under way early. Lieutenant Henry laid on a special patrol for me. He had hinted that I might be wasting my time.

We pulled into Echo, the first outpost downstream from Can Tho. The canals on the southwest bank were named alphabetically starting with Alpha at Can Tho and working downstream one by one. The outposts and villages were built next to the canals and took the same letter codes as the canals. The island points took on numbers for identification.

Twenty to twenty-five children out of nowhere heralded our arrival. Dressed alike in black pants and loose-fitting white tops, they swarmed over the boats until Thanh yelled, then they backed off. He led the way up the rickety dock and shouted for the outpost chief. A small, childlike man sauntered out and, after a few minutes of chatter with Thanh, saluted me and walked away.

"He say he very busy now . . . we go," Thanh said. "We go next outpost."

Not very friendly, I thought. "What's the matter with him?" I asked Sergeant Thanh.

"He doesn't respect Americans, Thieu Ta."

The next outpost was at Foxtrot, marked by a huge, ugly, 150-foot chimney. The river side of the chimney was well shelled and potted with thousands of bullet holes and chipped bricks. The other side was untouched. The chimney stood alone, abandoned in an empty field next to the outpost. No one knew its history or use. They said that it had always been there.

No one met us at Foxtrot. We beached the boats and walked over to the outpost; and "outpost" it was. The scraggliest, log-walled fort depicted in the worst, grade B western movie would have been Rome compared to this filthy, mud-walled hole.

"These men not ARVN, Thieu Ta, but popular force soldiers, called PFs. They live here; this is their home," Thanh explained.

The outpost building consisted of a large triangle built of

six-foot-high mud walls. Each of the three sides was roughly two hundred feet long and the corners boasted raised guard towers.

The wall, constructed of mud mixed with straw, tapered from four feet at the base to one foot at the top. In addition to the guard towers at the corners, the wall was defended by bamboo-reinforced six-by-twelve-inch firing ports hollowed out through the dried mud about every fifty feet. In the center of this triangle were three long, garagelike buildings laid in a U-shaped pattern.

An effeminate, bushy-haired man with half-closed eyes came to meet us as we walked unchallenged toward what appeared to be the command center. Thanh introduced me. This man was the outpost chief, and through Thanh we chatted about the weather, the rice crop, and the tidal stages. His teeth were black; he never smiled and our eyes never met. During our idle chatter Thanh enumerated many things the outpost needed: tin roofing for the thatched houses, medical supplies, ammunition, barbed wire, and batteries for their radio.

None of these seemed unreasonable, so I told the outpost chief that within a week he would have all the supplies he could use, though I didn't know where I could get them.

"The government has promised many things, many times, but we have received nothing," he replied through Thanh.

These outposts were generally responsible for their own defense but would receive help from the subsector chief if available. It usually wasn't. If it were it was usually helo gunships flown by the army. To direct the helos, a flat ten- to twelve-foot wooden arrow was mounted on a swivel near the center of the outpost. Nailed to the top of the arrow were tin cans filled with greasy rags. When attacked, the PFs would light off the rags with a torch and point the arrow at the enemy, thereby showing the helos the direction of attack. One flaw: The smaller outposts didn't have operational radios to tell the subsector headquarters of an attack.

"These you shall have," I stated cavalierly, opening my mouth again when I should have kept it shut. We shook hands and he saluted. I returned the salute, then turned and started to walk away when I heard a scream.

Thanh and I ran toward the noise. It was behind one of the buildings. When we got there, several men huddled around a young man in a filthy uniform. The soldier was sitting on the ground clutching his right foot. There were two tiny holes in his big toe.

"Snake bite, Thieu Ta."

"Why aren't these men doing something?"

"What is there to do, Thieu Ta? There is no doctor. Those men there," he said, pointing at three men beating a bush, "are trying to kill the snake."

Christ! Something had to be done. How many movies had I seen where the hero saves a victim's life by cutting an *x* over the bite and sucking out the poison?

I leaned over, cut an *x* over the bite, and started sucking out the poison. I wished that my knife had been sharper. I never could sharpen a knife. It was a jagged cut. I wished his toe had been clean. The crud and manure coupled with the taste of blood drew my stomach into knots.

I continued my nauseating effort for six or seven minutes, spit out the final red glob, and wrapped my handkerchief tightly around his toe. I ordered him to be put on the cover boat to be taken to a doctor in Can Tho.

"Why did you do that, Thieu Ta?"

"To suck out the poison." My breakfast kept coming up into my throat. I kept forcing it back down.

As we started back to the boat, the three men who were chasing the snake dropped it proudly at our feet. Thanh kicked it.

"Snake not poison, Thieu Ta."

English . . . Ofttimes Misunderstood

———◆———

Bill Norwick, a young, dark-haired lieutenant, was the operations officer of RIVSEC 511. While having dinner together, he asked why I was calling on the villages and outposts. I explained what Sergeant Thanh had told me and said that frankly I concurred with him. As the conversation continued I found I had a kindred spirit. From what he was saying I could tell that Bill felt a genuine compassion for the Vietnamese people. His feelings appeared to go far beyond the ain't-it-too-bad stage exhibited by most of the people I talked to.

It seems that Bill had attended a medical college and though not graduating still possessed a fair amount of medical skill, which he put to good use. The people on the river sorely lacked medical facilities. Medicines were scarce and expensive, and doctors rarely ventured from the cities. Bill made up his own "black bag" from cumshawed medical supplies and when on patrol held constant sick call for anyone who would come to him. He treated everything from gunshot wounds to diarrhea. It appeared that he had a regular clientele. His efforts, he told me, paid off in the intelligence he received.

We discussed the shortages I had discovered during my visits to the villages with Sergeant Thanh. I told him that I was going to see what I could do. He asked if he could help.

But what we thought would be simple turned out to be extremely difficult. True, everyone sympathized and agreed that something ought to be done, but few said they would help, and fewer did.

We started with the American civilians who were responsible for taking care of these villages. "No money left—we can't get to the river villages; the monies allocated drift into different projects" was their normal, hesitant answer. Money? I saw tons of needed material lying around in warehouses in Can Tho.

It seemed that the amount of aid a village received depended upon its distance from the district town. The farther away the villages, the less they got. The Viet Cong prevented them from getting to the outlying villages was the excuse offered, which was probably true. I offered them a way to reach the river villages, but they didn't seem eager to accept. I wondered why. It disgusted me to have to deal with men wallowing in the wasteland of mediocrity.

We soon learned the game, however, and Bill and I managed to trade an old captured Chinese Communist (CHICOM) rifle for one hundred fifty sheets of corrugated steel roofing material and thirty bags of cement, plus fifty pieces of steel reinforcing rods. We loaded them on a large World War II LCM, a landing craft, medium, called a mike boat. The boat was big enough to drive a tank aboard on a front-dropping ramp. With much flourish and ceremony, Bill, Sergeant Thanh, and I delivered some of the material first to Foxtrot, because of my earlier promises, and then down to the village of Phu Hoa, code-named Golf. We chose Golf because it was the largest village on the southwestern bank.

The people were amazed; the government had finally given them something besides promises. It called for a celebration.

Large tables appeared for the crew of the mike boat and

for the escort PBR. The crew drank beer with ice while they watched chickens being killed, cut, and cooked. For Bill, Sergeant Thanh, and I, nothing less than the village chief's own house would suffice. It was crude, consisting of one very clean twelve-by-twelve room with bamboo-thatched walls and roof—a typical Vietnamese hootch. A small, slatted bed without a mattress was in one corner and a chest of drawers in the other; a three-by-five-foot table took up the rest of the area.

Photographs of Ong Tam, the village chief, covered most of the wall area. He was a thin man—couldn't have weighed more than 110 pounds. The photographs showed Tam receiving several medals from different generals and dignitaries. They showed him fighting against the French with the Viet Minh at Dien Bien Phu. They showed upon close examination the wiry, scarred body of a man wounded innumerable times, a man whose face, adorned with rimless glasses, could alternate between cold cruelty and laughing tenderness. This was a man to be reckoned with.

Ong Tam—*ong* means *mister*—rose to the occasion by breaking out a quart bottle of some nondescript whiskey and pouring it into glasses over chunks of ice. He handed us each a glass and through Thanh proposed a toast to the U.S. Army. We drank. In halting Vietnamese I told him that we were in the U.S. Navy and though the army was a creditable organization, it in no way measured up to the high standards that naval tradition demanded of us. He didn't understand, but nonetheless after that we toasted only the U.S. Navy, his village, and one another.

When the bottle was empty, he called for another. Never before had I drunk straight whiskey over ice. I felt giddy. With the second bottle came hors d'oeuvres—rotted, moldy green, whole unshelled duck eggs. Just the thought of eating them sobered me. Bill winced. Sergeant Thanh took our share and we watched as he and Ong Tam devoured them.

"What if the Viet Cong attack while we drink, Sergeant Thanh?" I asked.

Sergeant Thanh leaned over to Ong Tam and whispered

something, then they both burst out laughing. "Come, Thieu Ta, come see soldier."

I sent Bill to check on the boat crews as we walked out of the hootch into the blazing sun and down the narrow street to the edge of the village.

"See soldier, Thieu Ta?" he laughed. He was drunk. "Come . . . drink . . ."

Ong Tam had called in his soldiers from two outposts and had them stationed in a tight perimeter around the village. I felt better and a bit of a fool for questioning his judgment.

"Come drink, Ong Tam . . . Mighty Village Chief," I said in Vietnamese. My language ability was abysmal at best. I could repeat only memorized stock phrases. Vietnamese was a tonal language that twisted my tongue. Ong Tam laughed and held my hand as we walked back to his party. I tried not to let this embarrass me. Vietnamese consider men holding hands as perfectly natural and a sign of respect. For Ong Tam to take my hand and walk through his village was a great honor for me. The people clapped and bowed as we passed. I felt a little silly, but important.

Bill was just returning to the hootch as we got there. "Boat Capt'n Chambers is holding the crew down. Not too much drinking, half of 'em crapped out already. They'll be sober when it's time to go. Half of the crew isn't drinking."

"Good . . . thanks, Bill." I filled the glasses again. We finished off the second bottle amidst toasts to victories of the past and battles of the future.

"Food come, Thieu Ta!" Thanh said as an old woman cleared the mess of empty bottles, cigar ashes, and moldy duck eggshells from the table. Two young girls brought in the food on steaming plates. They were dressed in spotless *ao-dais,* the national dress of Vietnamese women. One of the girls had large breasts that seemed determined to break through the tight-fitting, high-collared white top. The long, flowing, front and back aprons of the top swished just enough to give a tantalizing view of her skin-tight black slacks. We stared. The fragrance of their bodies demanded attention.

Ong Tam gave a few soft orders and they silently served each of us, their long, flowing black hair dancing in the breeze. "Aren't they fabulous, Bill!" I whispered.

He grunted.

My drunken breath came in short bursts. I could feel a tingling in my body. Sergeant Thanh sat with his mouth gaping.

"Sergeant Thanh, you never told me anything like this lived down here!" But he didn't answer; he just stared as one of the girls walked out of the hootch.

"I see the commander thinks my sister is beautiful," the other girl purred with a soft, melodious voice in perfect English.

"You . . . ah . . . you . . . speak English!" I stuttered. Bill looked shocked. We were naval officers. The heat was already oppressive but the girl's words caused another ten-degree temperature rise in embarrassment.

"Yes, I learned at the university in Saigon."

"My . . . ah . . . name is Sheppard. Ah . . . this is Lieutenant Norwick." We both rose awkwardly from our low chairs. I would rather have crawled under them. "Of the United States Navy."

"Yes, I know. Please sit, Commander, and enjoy your food. There is more to come."

"Please, join us." I motioned to a chair that Bill was putting into place. "Forgive my indiscretion, Miss . . . ah . . . I'm afraid I don't know your name."

"Co Bac, and it is I who must apologize to the commander. Mister Tam thought this to be a funny joke." She offered her hand. It was soft and smooth, like the caress of a small kitten. "My sister, Co Hue, and I teach school here." *Co* means *miss* in Vietnamese.

Co Hue reentered the room. Bill and I stood and bowed. "She speaks very little English, sir," Co Bac said as she introduced us. They both sat.

We offered them a drink but they refused. Ong Tam couldn't keep from laughing.

We ate a type of chicken stew, made by boiling chicken

pieces in a highly spiced sauce. A bit greasy but good. There was an abundance of fresh vegetables, and the water glasses that held our whiskey never went dry.

We spoke of many things—Bill, Co Bac, and I. The weather, America, Vietnam, the Bassac, and the village. I would have liked to talk politics, the war, her feelings, but crowds and personal conversation rarely mix and I deferred the subjects.

Sergeant Thanh and Co Hue talked very seriously, his face but inches from hers and their hands interlocked. Ong Tam laid back in a kind of stupor, punctuated only by a laugh and an occasional toast to the U.S. Navy and to the obvious charms of the young ladies.

Co Bac translated the toasts in a low, halting voice. Ong Tam's words worked their way down from the raven black hair, angellike faces, and swanlike necks, but after that, no matter how long his toasts or what lewd movements he attached to them, it came from Co Bac as a "toast to the ladies." Thanh was too busy to fill us in but we imagined Ong Tam's course and destination. He eventually passed out, much to the ladies' pleasure.

The sun was getting low. "We'd better go, Bill . . . come on, Sergeant Thanh." Thanh whispered something in Co Hue's ear. She giggled. Co Bac offered her hand—I kissed it. We stepped over Ong Tam, left the hootch, and walked to the boats.

The boat captain was wiping oil on the guns. "Have a good time, sir?" he said, putting down the rag and telling someone to awaken the crew. They seemed groggy, but a quick wash in the river brought them around.

"They look like they had a good time."

"They're okay, sir, haven't had a drink in three hours. The sweating takes the liquor right out of 'em."

I, too, felt sober; my body was oozing sweat and except for a slight headache, the copious amounts of whiskey left no aftereffect.

Escorting the mike boat was slow—the trip back dull.

"You Should've Been There"

———————•———————

I would watch the boats go out on patrol and meet them when they came back. I talked to the crews. What did you see—what did you do? I could give them no advice, offer no leadership. I began to feel useless. My earlier excitement of taking command dwindled to despair. The temperature made each breath a chore. The activity of just sitting made me to sweat. I braved the electrified hot water piping four or five times a day. It made no difference if I used all cold water or not; the charge was still there.

The weather was slowly shifting from the dry northeast monsoons to the rainy southwest monsoons. For days the relentless dry winds forced driving sand and grit into everything, everywhere. The humidity crept up daily, heralding the coming rainy season.

The boats on the upper Bassac were in about one firefight a week. Down south on the LST, firefights were only once every two weeks. All were only sporadic sniper fire from the tree line. The VC would fire a few rounds at a boat and while the boats either pulled out or made a few passes, the VC would probably cross at some other point down the river.

The Seawolves were flying daily patrols trying to thwart this maneuver, but it was costly in helo time. The helos could fly only so many hours before they had to be grounded for periodic checks. This made them unavailable for firefight support. And putting all those flying hours on the helos caused them to break down much more often, rendering them ineffective as a firefight suppression weapon. Additionally, any but minor repair work had to be done by the army, and getting the helos over to an army facility caused more off-river time. We did not depend on the Seawolves. The Seawolves, however, were not under my command. I complained to the Task Force 116 staff but to no avail.

Even if we knew that the sniper rounds were a ruse, we had only a fifty percent chance of turning the right way to spot the crossing. If the VC saw that we guessed correctly, they would just wait and try it again. There was just too much river and too few boats. Our tactics had to change, but I didn't know how.

By chance I happened to have dinner one evening with Lt. Dave Williams from the 116 staff. Over the years I had learned not to talk to staff officers on anything but a purely social level. Doing otherwise always seemed to get me in trouble. I detected a difference with Dave. He seemed to understand the problem and I desperately needed someone to talk to. I mentioned what Sergeant Thanh, Lieutenant Norwick, and I were doing with the villages. He agreed that it was a good idea that they had tried before but failed through lack of follow-through. He knew of the ineffectiveness of our patrols and he knew that the Seawolf potential wasn't being realized.

"Don," he said, "you and I both know what has to be done. The Bassac must come off the defensive and go on the offensive. We tried it in the past and got bloodied, but we kept trying it. We were making some headway till Saigon made us stop."

Dave continued—he too had to talk to someone. "The people in Saigon are trying to run our war here from their air-conditioned offices eighty-five miles away. It just can't be done . . . and it's just as bad on the other rivers, too."

We were on our fourth drink at the O club. I listened, offering no comments, no questions. Dave was young to be a lieutenant commander. He was a destroyer man. We sat at a far corner table away from everyone else, yet he still spoke in a low voice, almost a whisper.

"You probably know, Don, Game Warden was conceived in October 1965, and seven months afterward, in May of '66, the first boats of 511 came speeding up the Bassac. Before the boats arrived, bases had to be built, crews had to be trained, tactics had to be developed, and supply and communications networks had to be set up. It was a formidable task and the guys worked hard."

Dave filled his glass again from the open bottle of scotch on our table. I motioned no to my refill. He looked at me with a doubting face. "You want to hear all this shit, Don?"

"Yes, Dave, I do."

"The only time the navy got into this river warfare stuff was way back in the Civil War. And no way did that operation compare to the scope of this thing. Our task was unprecedented.

"Before the boats came we set up a tremendous psychological campaign called psyops. We wanted to tell the river people why we were coming, what our mission would be . . . told them that we were coming to stop the VC from using the river to run men and supplies to the battlegrounds above Saigon. We were going to make them free.

"We asked them for their help, but the VC countered with their propaganda. They told the people that we were big-nosed killers, that we would eat their babies, rape their women, steal their belongings.

"Their message was more convincing than ours. The people were scared and didn't cooperate at all—at first. Slowly things changed but just a little bit. Our guys were careful on the river not to be too offensive. But these giant Americans with their big boats and guns ordering the people around was intimidating. I don't blame them for being frightened. Could you picture yourself in the States pulled over by a couple of tanks with huge foreigners demanding to see your identification and searching your car, and there's nothing you can do about it? Think about that!

"We tried civil action programs—you know, bringing them supplies and food and medical stores, even helping them put up new buildings—just like you and Norwick down at Golf the other day. You're reinventing the wheel, Don. I sure don't know how you managed to get the stuff."

Dave filled his glass again. His eyes were glassy and he repeated his question with a slur: "You sure you want to hear all this shit?"

"Dave, I appreciate what you're saying. I need this information if I'm to do anything worth a damn out here. Please go on."

"Well, we were making headway when the supplies dried up . . . there were no more. The VC started hitting us hard and we started taking casualties. We were running mighty short of repair parts, and we couldn't get enough men to replace our dead and wounded. We started to cannibalize what we could from laid-up PBRs. The situation deteriorated rapidly. Then came the order—stay in the middle of the river, plain and simple, STAY IN THE MIDDLE OF THE RIVER!"

He was quiet then. He got up to go to the head. I waited.

"But there's a change coming," he continued when he returned. "I understand that the pipeline is full of sailors on the way out here. I'm told that repair parts are on the way and there is a new breed coming to Saigon. We're getting a new Task Force 116 commander who hasn't had to suffer our growing pains.

"It'll be a new ball game, Don, and you're going to be one of its stars. How I envy you—I'd give my right nut to have your job right now, but I'm tired. Tired of the shit that has gone down and just plain sleepy tired right now."

Lieutenant Commander Williams pushed himself up, pressing on the edge of the table. "Hear Tanner caught the big blue sampan . . . Good man, Tanner. Bet you it was just dumb luck that he got it . . . that's all we have is pure dumb shit luck. Good night, Commander, good night. I shall be getting shocked by the water for the next twenty minutes so the bugs don't have to eat sweaty food tonight." He staggered out the door.

I walked over to my office on the barge as Tanner's patrol was tying up with the blue sampan in tow. Lieutenant Henry was watching and shouted down to Chief Tanner about what a great job he'd done. We went into my office for the debrief.

Chief Tanner was about thirty, lean and well muscled. He was a gunner's mate with ten years in the navy. We had met earlier and developed an instant rapport. He wanted to become an officer and studied every spare minute. And since I had come up through the ranks, he sought out my advice on the best course of action. Chief Tanner had come to the river from a missile destroyer. I checked his personnel jacket with the Commander, River Squadron (COMRIVRON) 5 in Saigon. It was exemplary. I had learned that he was cool under fire and was an outstanding patrol officer who exhibited great leadership.

"Great job, men," I said, passing out Ba Muai Ba beers. *Ba Muai Ba* meant *333* and that's what we called the beer. It was a French brew made in Vietnam—a strong, delicious, green-bottled beer that would knock a sailor on his ass before he knew what was happening.

"No serious casualties, Lieutenant Henry," Chief Tanner started the debrief. "Boats got a few holes but nothing bad. We were really lucky. Pure luck." Dave Williams was correct.

"We were heading back from patrol and had just passed five point five coming in on step. Commander, five point five is a checkpoint on the northern tip of Cu Lao May, the big island," Chief Tanner said, turning to me in deference to my inexperience.

"Thank you, Chief," I replied.

"Inland from Cu Lao May was always considered not too dangerous, so we were relaxing . . . not goofing off, just relaxing. I was scanning the beach on the northeast side just for something to do, and that's when I saw it. Not much but just a tip of something blue. I figured that if we continued upstream a little it might try to cross. We throttled down a bit as we watched, and sure enough the dumb bastard pushed out into the river—must have been in a real hurry. Hell! There was still a lot of light left.

"He was moving fast. We were on step and doing okay ourselves but that mother was pulling away from us. He had two big swimmer tails and they were kicking on—had to be doing thirty knots. I fired a warning shot—you know, just like we're supposed to—but the bastard kept running.

"We came right a bit so the forward guns could get a little better angle and to unmask the after fifty. And that's all she wrote. The sampan burst into flames . . . I guess one of our tracers hit the gas tank. Jesus, can you imagine six fifties firing at you and two M-60s? What is that, about five hundred rounds a minute from each fifty? That's six hundred a minute and about two hundred a minute from each M-60, for one thousand bullets a minute. Shit! We're talking around sixteen rounds a second heading for those guys.

"The VC's got balls, Commander, they got balls when they need to fight. Ya should've been there, Commander."

Chief Tanner paused a moment. The boat captains said nothing. Chief Tanner reached over and took three more 333s from the ice chest and tossed two to his men. "They got balls, Commander. Got balls. Of course we couldn't hold out that much firing for very long. We had to reload those fifties. The sampan beached at five point five, then the VC leapt for the beach and the beach opened up on us. It sounded like a couple of AK-47s . . . they got that special pop that you don't forget once it's pointing at your ass."

Lieutenant Henry interrupted impatiently. "Come on, Chief, we don't need any gunner's manual written here. Please get on with it." Lieutenant Henry glanced at me and turned away from my scowl.

"Please continue, Chief. I'm interested in gunner's manuals," I said.

"Well, Commander, we knew you guys would want that sampan, so we suppressed fire on the beach and moved in to take it in tow. I was in a hurry to get the fire out. We headed in but couldn't get close enough to put a grapnel on it. We were receiving a few more shots from the beach . . . pick it up from there, Boats," Chief Tanner finished, pointing to the lead boat captain. He took another beer.

"Well, as the chief was saying, we wanted that sampan and we had to get it fast. It was burning. I figured the only way we could pull it out was for me to swim over and attach the grapnel, so I jumped in."

"YOU WHAT?" demanded Lieutenant Henry.

"Well, we figured that someone pretty important and impatient must have been on it if the VC were going to chance an almost daylight crossing and since it was heading back across the river to the Can Tho side. Gee! I'm sorry, Mister Henry, if we did the wrong thing. I . . ."

"It's okay, Boats, I was just a little surprised. Go on."

"It seems the firing off the beach was picking up again and I heard the forward fifties on my boat open up. Those guys were shooting right over my head. Scary, but I knew that Jones on the gun was damn good. Shit, sir, I just dropped that little hook over the gunwale and swam back to the boat. Hell! It wasn't very far.

"The chief yanked me out of the water as we were backing off. Got the fire out and towed that mother home . . . beautiful, eh? Should've been there, Commander, you should've been there."

"Yes, I should've been there. It was beautiful. You guys did a great job . . . thank you," I said, shaking their hands as they walked out. "Dumb luck, just plain ass dumb luck," I muttered.

"Sir?"

"Nothing."

I was tired in the morning, my recurring dream of running after someone having kept me on the verge of wakefulness all night. I was chasing someone or something, never seeing it but knowing it was there. I kept running, and men on the sidelines were laughing, taunting me. You should've been there, you should've been there. YOU SHOULD'VE BEEN THERE!

It was my obsession with getting into a firefight that drove the dreams. As time went on I became more worried about how I would react under fire. What if I were a coward?

I was on the river every other day. By now I was confident that I could handle things and was going out as a patrol officer. I could see no reason why two leaders should be on a patrol. Where I was, I was in command. I tried all the standard tricks: drifting at night, violent course changes, towing a PBR as a decoy, anchoring close to the beach—nothing worked. I even took to flying a special command flag.

Naval officers in command of two or more seagoing units are designated as commodores without regard to their rank. Commodores fly a small, personal identification flag called a burgee pennant whenever they're aboard a vessel. This practice, which grew from the old sailing days, let the other ships know the commodore's location. Since he flew this special flag, his vessel was known as the flagship.

I would do the same. It would truly serve its purpose when we had multiple patrol operations. I had the canvas shop make a pennant for me. It wasn't fancy—just red rags and white rags—but it was good enough for my purpose, and I flew it high on a whip antenna every patrol. It caused no reaction from the VC. Maybe they weren't familiar with Navy Regulations.

I passed the enemy stronghold of Tanh Dinh Island every chance I got, perfecting my skills with our weapons. I went so far as to stick the nose of my patrol in the little canal between Tanh Dinh and the mainland, trying to get a reaction from the VC. Nothing. *Titi* means *little* in Vietnamese; that was the name of the canal and that was its size. Reports indicated that the VC 306th Battalion lived there with about 250 men. I never thought that the VC amassed in any such strength. I doubted the report.

I did other things, such as drift just off Juliet and shout obscenities at the supposedly hidden VC there. "HO CHI

34

MINH SUCKS!" I yelled through a power megaphone. Nothing. Again I shouted, "VIET CONG ARE PIGS!" Nothing. What a childish thing I was doing, but the crew of Romeo Patrol seemed to enjoy it and started filling me in on Vietnamese obscenities. I made pointed comments that could raise doubts on the marital status of Ho Chi Minh's parents. I alluded to the lack of sexual potency among the Viet Cong. I even went so far as to question the gender of Viet Cong sexual partners. I suggested that the Viet Cong indulged in copulatory activity with swine and, lacking that, they might have coitus with their female parent.

"Boy, Commander, that should've gotten some action. Juliet there is a hornet's nest . . . a lot of shit comes out of that place," said Bryan, the senior boat captain of Romeo Patrol, shaking his head. "Christ! It's almost as bad as Tanh Dinh. I reckon you're not going to make it tonight."

"You're cherry, Commander, the safest guy to be on the river with," added Willie, the forward gunner.

He meant it as a compliment but the words struck like a lash. "Yeah, cherry . . . come on, let's go home." My tenth patrol and second month in-country were over.

The next morning an order came down from TF 116 to shift river sections between Tra Noc and the T, as the LST was called. I hadn't been on the T as often as I should have been while I was learning my job. Also, it wasn't as active in firefights or intelligence reports as the upper Bassac; but nonetheless, they were my men and I was responsible for them. Lieutenant Simon, the OinC of 512, was reported to be a good man. I'd met him only once and was looking forward to getting better acquainted at Tra Noc. And I was sure that Lieutenant Henry of 511 could continue putting up with me for a few days on the T.

It was a good thing to shift the river sections. Life on the T was difficult, but more importantly, men could become too familiar with their patrol areas and this familiarity could lead to contempt and that could lead to getting killed.

I flew down with the Seawolves that afternoon. I had made a few patrols on the lower Bassac and it was boring compared to the upper. Traffic was much lighter and the landscape was mostly open fields. By this time I had flown many recon flights with the Seawolves and was well familiar with the river. I should say I was familiar with the tops of the tree lines. The growth was much too thick to see beneath them from the air. I'd read about all the fancy imagery devices that the army and air force had, but they sure didn't work their way down to the Bassac. In the overall scheme of things I guess we were small potatoes.

The next afternoon RIVSEC 512 loaded their equipment in the mike boat that had come down with 511's material, left two boats on patrol, and headed north to Tra Noc and the good life on the beach. Life on the T was at best austere. Girls and booze were all they could talk about. There were plenty of both in Can Tho, but so was the Can Tho crossing corridor.

It was approaching sunset and we had received no word of 511. Radio transmissions could be extremely poor in the delta at times and this was one of the times. We finally made contact through Saigon and San Diego, California, on the U.S. Navy's worldwide, long-range teletype communications network. The teletype message from Tra Noc said simply that 511 was in a big firefight at Juliet, with no further confirmation available. The Seawolves were down.

I waited. Where was 512? I waited in the T's combat information center (CIC), which did duty as the lower Bassac's ops center. I was on my tenth cup of coffee and twelfth cigar.

A crackle came through on the radio, then voices garbled, indistinct. "Handlash . . . Handlash, this is Handlash One. Over." It was Lieutenant Henry.

I grabbed the microphone and answered: "Handlash One, this is Handlash. Over."

"Roger, Handlash, have been trying to raise you for hours. Have engaged at Juliet with eight boats. RAGs on station now bombarding with heavies. We are disengaging now. Estimating your location. I shackle kilo point sierra unshackle. Any instructions? Over."

He had given me his arrival time in hours and tenths using a special code of letters and numbers called a KAC code. "This is Handlash. Negative instructions, keep me informed. Out." I hoped my voice hadn't betrayed my disappointment. "Sonovabitch!" I muttered to myself. "Sonovabitch!"

Any instructions? Ha! What did I know about combat? The big boys were there. What could I do? I went down to the wardroom and had supper with the ship's captain. We watched a movie; ironically, *The Young Lions*. If they ever made a movie about me it would have to be The Old Lamb.

I waited impatiently with the captain of the T for Lieutenant Henry and his ops officer, Lieutenant Norwick, to arrive. They came in at midnight and I listened. ". . . hell of a fight . . . three hours, Commander, we were engaged for three hours," they said, finishing the debrief. "You should've been there, Commander. Should've been there."

Khem Bang Co

———————•———————

I woke up early, had breakfast, read the night's message traffic, and walked down to the briefing room in the tank deck of the T. I heard the beginning of the patrol brief as I walked in. "Traffic has been light on the river for the last few days," Lieutenant Norwick was saying. "Viet Cong activity has been almost nonexistent for the past two weeks, so our buddies from 512 are saying, but we have a few rumors that they're still crossing over to Dung Island. We don't know much about Dung Island except that it's the first big island you come to heading upriver. The VC own it."

It was stuffy in the tiny combined briefing room and storeroom office that the river section had in the tank deck of the LST. There were seven of us cramped into this six-by-ten-foot closet. So many heads were in the way I could hardly see the chart. It was hard to breathe.

"Now, most of you have never been down here in the lower Bassac, so this'll be an indoctrination patrol. Take it easy and learn the river. And, oh, yes, the commander will be riding with you, so keep him out of trouble." There was some laughter. "You'll still keep your Romeo call sign down here and the RIVSEC is still Handlash One. The ops center will be the T's CIC.

"One advantage of being down here on the T is that the Seawolves are a lot closer. When you need them you call back here to CIC and they'll scramble the helos directly, rather than at Tra Noc, where you had to call the ops center first and they relayed the message down here.

"When you hear the scramble signal for the Seawolves, get off the main deck and get under cover. It's dangerous as hell when those helos lift off from such a small deck like they got here, and I don't want you guys to get hurt. Believe me, it's hairy, and you have no business up on the flight deck anyway. You can sightsee from the bridge area. Any questions?"

"Yes, sir," said Willie. "How long we gotta stay on this boat, sir?"

"Willie, you haven't been out of the fleet so long that you can start calling ships boats. I don't know. Commander?" Norwick asked, looking at me.

"I don't know."

"How about maintenance, sir? I hear it's pretty bad down here on the T. Lookin' at 512's boats, I can believe it," said Bryan.

"Climbing up that boom ladder scares me," someone else stated.

"It's a pain in the ass to reload from the main deck all the way down to the boats. I wanna go back to Tra Noc," came a voice from the pack. "There isn't even much action down here . . . and no booze."

"And no little gals."

"Quit your fucking whining, you pussies, and pay attention to the brief. The food's good and you got an air-conditioned place to sleep. Nobody's gonna mortar us out here—you're gonna live a lot longer. And look how much money you're gonna save. Hell, nothing to spend it on. And what about the T sailors? They never get off this tub," Bryan barked.

"Okay, okay, knock it off," Lieutenant Norwick continued. "Get your ass out on patrol and remember you don't know this place, so play it cool and stay away from Dung Island till you can get a feel for the place.

"I know you guys are tired from the Juliet shoot-out last night, but stay alert. Mister Jenkins, question?"

Lieutenant (jg) Jenkins was five feet ten inches tall, with the well-muscled body of a weight lifter. He was today's patrol officer and I heard that he played a great game of chess.

"Yes, sir," he replied. "What about that junk base we've heard about over on the southeastern bank? Can we get any support from them, or will they ever need anything from us?"

"I don't know much about it. Commander?" Lieutenant Norwick replied, turning to me.

"I've been there once. Not much there except a few hootches and five or six old armed junks. When I say armed, I mean an old thirty-caliber, air-cooled machine gun mounted in the bow and several Vietnamese junk sailors with thirty-caliber Garand rifles."

"What do they do nowadays?" Bryan asked.

"Well, I understand not much. The American advisors—there's four of them stationed there—told me that before we came they did some patrolling around Dung Island and out into the South China Sea, but lately we do it and they're on holiday routine. The junk sailors are going on the theory that if they don't bother the VC, the VC won't bother them. When they were active, the VC attacked them quite often. Now it's history."

"Seems ludicrous that Americans could advise anyone in junk warfare," Lieutenant Norwick commented.

"I thought it odd," I replied. "In their day the junk fleet was a ferocious lot and did a lot of good; now we've got their job. You should establish liaison with them, Mister Norwick. They're a bunch of good ole American boys who live austerely and could use some goodies from you guys once in awhile. Who knows, maybe we can save one another's ass sometime."

"Thank you, Commander, and, yes, one more thing,"

Lieutenant Norwick continued. "We have scramble codes for the helos down here. You don't just call for them like up north. There are three codes: scramble one is when you're in deep shit and need them bad to save your necks. Don't misuse it. For a scramble one those guys will bust their balls, launching under almost any condition, putting their asses on the line for you. Remember, those helos have a tough time lifting off under the best of conditions.

"The next is a scramble two. This should be used under most conditions. Use a scramble two when you're in a firefight but can pull away when you want to. Their mission here would be to inflict damage on the VC. This gives the pilots the option on takeoff conditions. But they'll be there if they can."

Willie interrupted: "I thought those fly-boys got all that extra flight pay for breezing around in those choppers."

Bryan cut him off again. "Willie, I can't believe you're such an asshole. Just shut the fuck up. You're always bragging about what a hot gun you are. If you're so damn good, we'll never need the gunships and you won't have to confuse your mind with trying to remember all those complicated numbers."

"If I can finish this up, men, we can get out of this sweatbox. A scramble three is for other than Game Warden troops in trouble. We're up to three now, Willie, and that's all," Lieutenant Norwick turned sarcastically to Willie. "You'd use a three when we're supporting other operations, such as ARVNs or RAGs or the junk force or something."

Bryan slapped Willie hard on the back, pushing him out of the operations office. "This is the last briefing you're coming to. You embarrassed me, asshole. Commander probably thinks I can't control my men . . . asshole!"

I turned to Bill as Romeo Patrol left the room. "No villages down here, Bill. What are you going to do on your civic action programs?" I was proud of him for this and for the help he gave me up at Tra Noc. I liked Bill and his easygoing way. He was one of the finest officers I had ever met; he was cool and aggressive in a firefight and his men revered him. He, like so many of my men, was a destroyer sailor. Destroyer duty is demanding and rigorous, and only the best men were sent to it.

"Wait till I get back up north, I guess. I still have my doctor kit. Those guys are right, Commander, life is a lot harder down here. Have you seen the sleeping compartments? Crowded as hell. The air-conditioning units don't work very well, either. Laundry service is rotten and there's not much fresh water. They'll miss Tra Noc."

"Talk to Mister Henry and let's see if we can get some rotation program set up. Maybe we can get a patrol up for a few days at a time, couple times a month."

"Yes, sir."

We wound our way up in silence to the main deck and out to the boat booms. They looked like giant fishing poles with PBRs for their catch.

"When you gonna get that beret ribbon cut, Commander?" Bill asked as we paused at the booms. Cutting the small circular ribbon used for hanging up the beret was ceremoniously done after a man's first firefight.

"I don't know. Christ! I've been on ten patrols already and heard only a few sniper rounds. They won't shoot at me. I think you guys are shittin' me about how dangerous this river is."

"Heard you've been running pretty close to the bank— that's one way to get it!"

"You can see better close in," I replied.

"Sure . . . you gonna fly that red and white burgee pennant of yours today?"

"Yes."

"Why do you do it?"

"Damn! Don't you ever go to the movies, Bill? John Wayne and Errol Flynn always had a flag when they went into battle. Hell! COMSEVENTHFLEET flies his flag, why shouldn't I? The only difference in our commands is the size."

"I don't see the connection. No one can use his for a

target. You're going to get it when the Viet Cong figure out what it means."

"Maybe. See you tonight, Bill." I crawled out on the boat boom for about twenty-five feet, then climbed down the shaky thirty-foot sea ladder into the PBR and threw my helmet and flak jacket into a corner. It was 0800 and the sun had already baked every piece of metal to a sizzling touch. But at least we had a breeze here on the water in the shadow of the T.

"Ready to go, Commander?" Bryan asked. Bryan was taking the coxswain's place today because his regular coxswain was wounded last night. I nodded my head; the boat crew tossed off the bowline from the boat boom and we moved away smoothly. Boatswain Mate First Class Fern, Romeo Two, in the cover boat, cast off behind us and took up a position two hundred yards astern.

"Commander, you been yelling at the VC anymore?" Willie asked.

"Nah, that shit doesn't work. You guys were just busting my ass."

Lieutenant (jg) Jenkins handed me a pair of binoculars as we left the estuary from the South China Sea and entered the river. The water turned from a bright blue to dirty brown. I put on my flak jacket.

Jenkins had been in-country for only a month but he had one firefight—infinitely more than I had. It still plagued my mind—this ignorance of how I would react under fire. I had never been tested, really tested, in my entire thirty-seven years.

"Let's take a look at Dung Island, Mister Jenkins," I said. Bryan nudged his helm and the boat eased to port. Bryan was from New York and proud of it. Most sailors by the time they make first class petty officer lose all hometown identification. Bryan was different. He was an actor before joining the navy, and most of his conversations extolled the virtues of theater life. He would never answer the question "If it was so good, why did you join the navy?"

We sped upstream, the purring engines forcing two great streams of water out the stern, pushing the boats along at a smooth, cooling fifteen knots. The mechanical clicking of the guns loading gave me a haughty reassurance—a kind of king-of-the-mountain grandeur. The wind whipped my burgee pennant in cadence with the American battle ensign flying by its side. No man was more ready for combat.

Lieutenant Norwick had been correct: Traffic was indeed light. I scanned the lower tip of Dung Island with my binoculars for any telltale signs of Viet Cong. We were two hundred yards from the beach. I was looking for any change: any difference from a hundred yards astern, any difference from yesterday, any difference from the other side of the river. Any difference.

"Closer, Bryan," I said, easing into a command stature, effectively relieving Mr. Jenkins of his patrol officer status.

"Roger." We closed to fifty yards and kicked up speed. One hundred feet behind us our wake splashed up against the shore, causing tiny waterfalls to stream from the high bank. The cover boat had a bad engine and was not as fast. It dropped steadily behind.

We were approaching the lower inlet to Khem Bang Co, a canal separating Con Coc Island from the much larger Dung Island. Con Coc Island was a half mile wide and eight miles long. The Viet Cong had owned it uncontestedly, along with Dung Island, since the middle fifties. Khem Bang Co was eight hundred yards wide at its lower end but narrowed severely as it turned around Con Coc Island, snaking north to the top of the island, where its width was barely twenty yards across. So the maps said.

It was common knowledge that the Viet Cong used Con Coc Island as a staging area to ferry supplies across the Bassac and that huge Dung Island, perhaps the most fertile and richest island in the country, was their uncontested sanctuary. Sampan and junk traffic was usually heavy on Khem Bang Co, but there was nothing we could do about it.

Our Rules of Engagement (ROE) were painfully clear: If a watercraft did not try to evade or if we didn't get shot at, there was nothing we could do. We could not fire until fired upon; they always had the first draw—the white-hatted code of the West. Knowing this, the Viet Cong did not fire at the helicopters when they flew over the canal. And our boats didn't go in.

Enemy strength around the area varied from a hundred to a hundred and fifty men; so intelligence guessed—they didn't know for sure. My experience indicated that "intelligence" never really knew anything for sure. They worked in probabilities, and nothing can have a probability of one until the event has taken place. No government troops had ever hazarded the area, and PBRs barely eased their bows into the canal entrance before coming about and tearing away.

"Looks peaceful, Mister Jenkins."

He didn't answer as he scanned the canal entrance. "Small sampan coming off the island," he reported, pointing to a boat that had just emerged from the undergrowth.

"Let's take a look," I ordered, attaching little significance to the sighting. The PBR banked and we glided into the canal.

"It's turning around!" Jenkins yelled, picking up an M-16 and firing a warning shot across its bow. There was a flurry of activity on the sampan as it frantically came about, its shrimp-tail engine churning up the water behind. "It's evading!"

"GO GET IT!" My first evading sampan. Finally a promise of action. I slapped on my helmet. I could hear the bolts fly home as the gunners double-cocked their .50s. My heart beat faster, matching the rpm's of the screaming engines. Though already at maximum speed, the PBR seemed to jump ahead in anticipation of the chase.

"Hold your fire!" I ordered. I wanted a capture. Fern, in the cover boat, was out of sight behind the turn.

I radioed to him. "Romeo Two, this is Romeo. Chasing an evading sampan . . . close it up! Over." Close it up, what a stupid order. I knew he was at max already. Settle down, Sheppard.

"This is Romeo Two. I'm trying. Out."

But just as suddenly as it appeared, it disappeared. It had gotten away back into the swampy shoreline from where it had come. I had erred. I should have blasted it out of the water. Damn! Damn! No, I shouldn't have. I didn't know what or who was on that sampan. It evaded. I could have shot. What did Bryan and Jenkins think of me? Was I afraid?

We trolled slowly past the spot where the sampan had ducked in: found nothing. It was high tide; the area was marshy, replete with low brush and overhanging mangroves. It was impossible to see more than twenty-five feet into the jungle. There were a hundred places the boat could hide.

Romeo Two rounded the bend, heading for us full out.

"Might as well look around now that we're here," I said. Bryan set the throttles at half ahead, moving toward the point where the Khem Bang Co turned sharply right to the northeast.

"How far in, Commander?" he asked nervously.

"I wanna look up the canal, then we'll go."

I fingered my M-79 40mm grenade launcher to control my nerves, flipping the safety on and off, breaking open the breech, checking to see that I had it loaded. It looked like a giant sawed-off shotgun just a little more than two feet long and a barrel just over an inch and a half in diameter. It always contained the three-inch-long projectile inside, but I always kept checking just to make sure.

I loved the M-79. It could hurl its grenade more than four hundred yards, depending on the elevation I shot.

Fern in the cover boat was nearly up to us as we moved into sight of the canal behind the island. I kept my binoculars on the canal. I could see no movement, only a twisting, narrow waterway drawing to a sharp point some distance upstream.

"Pretty quiet," I remarked. "Let's get out of here. We're pressing our luck as it is."

The PBR swung about. Again I had that dejected feeling

of being cheated out of combat. I wished for an attack. How long must I wait?

And then I saw it—a thousand yards up the canal. Only a bow, then slowly, lumbering as if it were drifting, came the rest of it: a huge junk. What looked like soldiers and a machine gun appeared on top as my PBR pulled me out of view. I hesitated.

I couldn't believe what I had just seen! A substantial movement of troops? Bait, to suck us into a trap? The maxim "Do not engage unless the risk is worth the gain" flashed through my mind.

"COME ABOUT!" I yelled. "Big junk up the canal . . . stand by your guns!"

Bryan stared at me in disbelief. Willie, the forward gunner, yelled "YAHOO, let's get 'em!" Jenkins's smile agreed.

The junk was almost across the canal as we roared into the narrow jaws of the passage. They saw us and started jumping around in panic. One man raised a rifle and fired; he missed—the bullet whipped harmlessly overhead. Willie's gun answered immediately.

This was it. I clamped my mouth shut so my heart wouldn't fly out. The adrenaline shot through my body like a cannonball. There was no doubt, no reservation, no hesitation. Little Donny was in the game.

Willie's twin .50s tore up the junk's stern as it lumbered into the undergrowth. I pumped grenade after grenade onto the beach in front of the junk, each exploding in a puff of black smoke and throwing thousands of small wire pieces into the target. Any flesh within fifteen feet of its explosion disappeared into small bloody pieces. The BLOOP! BLOOP! of each round tearing out of my 79 gave me comfort.

The Viet Cong seemed confused: Their fire was sporadic, not concentrated. My cover boat was just turning into the narrow canal. Fern had turned with me when we started to leave and had opened the distance too much.

A blast of Viet Cong machine-gun bullets raking him at the waterline welcomed him in. His guns spoke back. I could barely see him in the combined gun smoke.

We were fast approaching the junk. The fire was getting heavier. A machine gun found us; its bullets, like angry wasps, zinged toward us. We kept up a steady stream of fire. Gun barrels grew red as round after round flashed onto the beach.

The cover boat was catching hell. We had taken the enemy by surprise—they were ready for him. He was taking a beating.

"SLOW DOWN! Bryan, wait for Fern," I barked. There was the junk, only fifty yards from us. Our guns kept the Viet Cong pinned down. Our grenades and bullets shattered into the hull, tearing it to shreds.

"C'MON! C'MON!" I shouted uselessly to the cover boat. I knew he couldn't hear me.

The Viet Cong overcame their confusion, and the sporadic fire grew more accurate, more intense. I couldn't stay here long. "HURRY . . . goddamn you, Fern, HURRY!" I had stepped in front of the bull. How do I get out of this one?

Romeo Two caught up fast. When he was two hundred yards astern, I yelled, "HIT IT! GET THE HELL OUTTA HERE!" Our PBR jumped ahead but was still too heavy to get on step.

As Fern passed the junk, all his guns concentrated on it. It erupted in a violent roar, catapulting wood, guns, men, and smoke high into the air. It had been loaded with ammunition or fuel or explosives. It didn't make any difference—we destroyed it. Romeo Two had scored!

The junk, now five hundred yards astern of us, burned beautifully. My eyes and throat smarted from the acrid fumes of smoke and gunpowder. My gunners frantically rearmed their weapons. The Viet Cong guns had stopped. We throttled back. Maybe the battle was over.

Christ! In the excitement I had forgotten to call in. "Handlash One, Handlash One, this is Handlash. Engaged one thousand yards up Khem Bang Co. Request Seawolves

. . . scramble one! Scramble one! I say again, scramble one! Scramble one! Over."

"This is Handlash Two. Roger . . . wait. Out."

I could imagine the panic on the LST's CIC as the radarman on watch rushed to call Lieutenant Henry. The radarmen fought the war vicariously.

Our reprieve was short-lived. The unmistakable staccato clatter of a .50-caliber machine gun sounded from the area of the junk, and three-foot splashes walked obliquely across the water between our boats.

"Jesus!" Bryan screamed.

"GO . . . GO!" I yelled, emphasizing it with a crack on his back. I fell to the deck from the force of the acceleration.

"Jesus!" Bryan repeated.

I was pondering how to get out of here: Go back the same way we came in, or head out the other way? It would take at least half an hour to make the eight miles upstream.

Another .50 caliber from the other bank opened fire. It was behind us but its bullets churned the water around us, filling the air above with death.

We were trapped by a heavy troop concentration behind us and an uncharted, long, continuously narrowing, enemy canal ahead. I didn't even know if the water was deep enough to float the boats. Had I been wrong in attacking this junk? Had it been a deliberate trap to suck me in? Good Lord! Was I about to sacrifice the lives of ten men on the altar of adventure? Which way to go? Which order to give?

Thirty minutes of the unknown seemed infinitely better than five minutes of sure death. I leaned over to Bryan on the helm, pointing up the canal. "Keep going . . . zigzag!"

Seconds passed. The bull must have opened his eyes; bullets tore at us from the trees on both banks, but their rounds went wild. The exploding junk must have alerted every Viet Cong for miles. There was now a continuous stream of fire. I couldn't imagine how we had gotten this far with no casualties. Splintered holes decorated our sides.

The radio blurted: "Handlash . . . Handlash, this is Handlash One Actual. Get out of the canal!" ordered

Lieutenant Henry. "No help available . . . helos hard down. Over."

"This is Handlash. Roger, I'm trying. Out."

I had neither the time nor inclination to argue with Lieutenant Henry on who had authority to give orders to whom.

After eight minutes the fire let up. Zigzagging slowed us down. Fern, in the cover boat, was falling behind again. Curse those damn engines of his! The canal was getting so narrow that our whip antennas slapped the trees as we wove back and forth. Even though I knew we were doing close to eighteen knots, it seemed as though we were standing still.

I tried to analyze my feelings during the lull. I was not scared. I looked at my hands; they weren't shaking. I was not sweating. Oddly, I felt elated. I felt anxious for the next encounter. It was as if I were in the locker room during halftime. I could almost hear some high school coach saying, "Okay, the first half was good but now go out there and give 'em hell!"

Crack! Zing! A rifle shot kicked off the third quarter and a light machine gun joined the game. The after gunner slumped, screamed something unintelligible, and continued firing. His left trouser leg turned a dirty red.

My gunners hit back and once more only noise and gun smoke existed. There was no world beyond this canal. My mind could fathom nothing other than the roar of guns and the safety of my cover boat.

"Conserve ammo," I yelled—we'd been firing wildly into the trees. "Pick your targets," I shouted. Jenkins and I were firing M-79 rounds steadily ahead of the boat. We wouldn't last long at this rate.

In a few minutes the attack seemed to be over. Five minutes had passed since receiving the last fire and all the time the canal was getting narrower and narrower. Bryan's zigzagging was now almost a straight course. Three minutes more; still no fire. Was it over? Were there no more Viet Cong?

The odds were on our side; the Viet Cong could not have organized any major resistance to our passage in such a short time. Unless, of course, they had radios. I was banking that they didn't. The previous shooting must have alerted someone that something was up. Because of the immunity they had enjoyed here for so many years, I was certain no organized static defense positions existed or any patrols were out. These things clicked through my mind like a computer. If I was wrong, we wouldn't make it.

"I can't bring my guns down, Commander!" Willie shouted. "It's too narrow." The banks were so close that the forward twin .50s could not be depressed enough to hit the shore. I threw him an M-16.

"They're running . . . there, in the jungle," Willie shouted as his M-16 cut into them. The men were falling but we couldn't tell if they were shot or just diving for cover. I laid a barrage of M-79 rounds into their position, with no returned fire.

I looked back and could see splashes all around the cover boat five hundred yards astern. He was catching it from the Dung Island side. "SLOW DOWN! SLOW DOWN!" I commanded. "He's too far behind." I tried the radio but he didn't answer. He was far too busy to hear the radio over the noise.

"Commander! Commander! More clips . . . I'm almost out," Willie yelled.

Jenkins had been loading M-16 clips for the last five minutes. He was sitting calmly on the deck, methodically putting rounds one after another into the empty clips. Enemy bullets zipped about him, but he sat unaffected. I was breaking out boxes of spare ammo and passing it around. Amazing, where it normally took a wrench or pliers to open them, I was ripping off the bolts with my fingers and tearing open the boxes with my hands.

I tossed Willie four full clips. "Take it easy . . ."

Bryan tried zigzagging again, but to no avail; the canal was only the width of a two-lane road. The jungle hung low over the banks, almost clutching at the water. We could see several sampans and junks pulled up underneath the branches. We were destroying as many as we could.

A World War II jungle movie of Japanese snipers flashed through my mind. Jesus! What a stupid error. "Willie! Willie!" He turned around.

"Shoot in the treetops ahead of us!"

His eyes lit up as a childish grin covered his face. He went back to his .50s. He squeezed the triggers and the palm trees shed their upper branches. He raked from abeam on the starboard side six hundred yards ahead, shifted across the canal to the port side, and returned. On his second cycle, just before crossing the canal, a large object fell from a treetop—it looked like a man. Ten or twelve rifle rounds flew at us from somewhere.

The after gunner scanned both sides of the canal and blasted anything that moved. The green of his left trouser leg was turning into an ugly blackish red. "You okay?" I yelled. He just smiled back.

How far away was that exit? It seemed that I'd already been in this damn canal fourteen hours. Another lull—had we made it?

"Well, Commander, this little firefight's gonna cost you plenty," Bryan said.

"How so?"

"You know the custom—first firefight gets your beret string cut and you buy a case of beer for the boat."

"I hope I can!"

"Yeah! Since you got us into this, seems you should buy a case for each boat."

"Fair enough, I—" Willie's guns ended the conversation with another burst up the tree line.

"There it is! Damn! There it is!" We rounded a narrow bend and the canal entrance loomed like the Statue of Liberty. We gave out with such a shout that the boat rocked.

"We've made it—" A BURRAT! of a machine gun cut short my words. We could see nothing.

"There they are!" shouted the after gunner. He swung his

.50 around and blasted the beach off the starboard quarter. Jenkins and I started another 40mm grenade barrage. I had seen no one, only the trees.

The canal mouth grew larger; the jungle thinned out. I could see fearsome bunkers built along the banks. The Viet Cong had prepared to defend this area. Were the bunkers manned? We fired grenades into the beach in front of us. It would take a brave Viet Cong to raise his head up through the fire that we were laying down.

We fairly flew out of the mouth of the canal. We were out! And not a shot fired at us for the last three minutes; it was holiday routine. My crew beamed with relief . . . but only half the patrol was out.

I stared at the cover boat. The Viet Cong must have been saving their bullets for them. He was still seven hundred yards from relative safety—poor bastards, their boat barely visible through the smoke.

"COME ABOUT! COME ABOUT!" I yelled. "We're going back in." Bryan's face dropped two feet.

"COME ABOUT!" I barked. Bryan spun the helm and we sped back toward the canal entrance.

"Willie! When we get into the canal mouth, you shoot at the banks, just ahead of the cover boat." Everyone stared at me. We got closer and closer. I could feel the tension build again.

"Slow down," I commanded. We were just barely inside the canal. "Keep 'er here." Bryan backed the engines and she stopped.

"Okay, Willie, you bastard, you're always bragging how damn good you are. Don't screw up. Commence fire!"

He laid his guns perfectly just ahead of the frantically exiting PBR.

"Beautiful," I prayed softly to myself. He played those twin .50s like extensions of his fingers. Where he pointed, steel and tracers landed.

Just above a whisper, I said: "Hold steady, Bryan . . . steady," more to console myself than to ensure that Bryan did the correct thing. Bryan knew what he was doing. Did I?

One lurch of the boat or a bullet into Bryan or Willie could kill every man on the cover boat. Christ! Fern was slow. My crew strained to see any movement around us. At this range the most minor attack could be disastrous. The after gunner moaned, collapsing to the deck. Jenkins moved to the after gun.

It seemed to be working. The enemy fire had stopped. I wondered how the crew of the cover boat felt seeing the twin .50s pointing at them and watching them rip up the beach barely twenty yards ahead.

"Shoot straight, Willie baby . . . shoot straight!"

Fern was now two hundred yards away. I opened my mouth to order a cease-fire, but the metallic impact of Willie's bolts smashing into empty breeches told me his guns were dry. I took the bank under fire with an M-16.

One hundred fifty yards—one hundred—fifty—twenty-five. Fern barreled by us, his wake bouncing us like a toy—so close that even over the scream of his engines I could hear the cracking of his tattered battle ensign. Their faces looked bloodless, and Fern tried hard to smile.

"GO! GO, Bryan!" I smashed him on his shoulder to punctuate my urgency. He was backing down at full throttle —the canal was too small to make a turnaround. Then we were clear. He jammed the throttles forward so hard that I swear I heard the metal crack. The PBR obeyed and reached for the open river and safety. God watches over fools and PBR sailors. We were safe.

We tied up together in midriver. Our wounds were not serious. I laughed, damn how I laughed; then Fern laughed, Bryan laughed, and Jenkins laughed—we all laughed. We laughed because we couldn't cry.

We were low on ammo. The boats were shot up. The wounded had to be treated. We headed back to the T.

I had bathed in the sacred waters of combat and had emerged, reborn, a warrior. I leaned back against the armor plating, closing my eyes. The smooth purr of the engines lulled me into a state of euphoria.

* * *

The choppy seas as we entered the estuary jolted me back.

"Damn, Mister Jenkins, we're going to have a deuce of a time making the LST."

"Yeah, pretty rough. Don't worry, sir, Bryan's a good coxswain—no sweat."

"I wasn't worried, Mister Jenkins, I was making conversation."

"Yes, sir."

Linebacker II.
The Assault

———————●———————

The island of Tanh Dinh, situated about fifteen miles downriver from Can Tho, was the uncontested property of the Viet Cong. No government soldiers had been there in anyone's memory. Perhaps thirty percent of our wounded came from guns hidden in the dense jungle that covered the island. A canal varying from fifty to two hundred yards over its five-and-a-half-mile length separated Tanh Dinh from the mainland. It was the home of the Viet Cong 306th Battalion and the northeastern terminus of the Can Tho crossing corridor.

I kept bugging the commander of the local 9th ARVN Division to raid the place. He finally agreed and called me two days before the operation was to begin. I was anxious to hear their battle plan; amazed when I did. It consisted of landing troops on the middle of the island and sweeping down to the southern end. Simultaneously, another small group was to be landed on the mainland across from the downstream tip. Vietnamese RAGs were to be used to insert the troops. There would be no insertion of a blocking force.

This plan seemed incomplete. The Viet Cong, I was sure, were familiar with such tactics and upon 9th ARVN's approach they would melt away across the narrow Titi Canal, leaving only trees as opposition. Also, security was so bad with the ARVN that by now the Viet Cong knew the exact plan. This left the northern end of the island as an additional escape route.

I had heard early in my tour that the ARVN always left an escape route open to the Viet Cong. The reason, as explained, for this patently unsound military practice was to keep ARVN casualties to a minimum. The Viet Cong fought tenaciously when trapped and this would almost assure an unacceptably high ARVN casualty rate.

To me and to the frustrated U.S. Army advisors, leaving just one escape route was unthinkable, much less two routes. Sound military doctrine throughout history has always demanded that once a unit meets an equal or inferior force, this contact should be maintained until the enemy is destroyed. Casualties must be accepted and weighed proportionately; lacking this basic concept no army can win. The ARVN was not winning.

Later the same day, I attended the amphibious phase of the battle planning conference at the Can Tho RAG base headquarters, an impressive cement villa, a relic of the old French colonial days. I found the role relegated to me was that of an insignificant, main river blocking force, as if the Viet Cong were going to escape across the Bassac. It was plain that neither the 9th ARVN, the VN RAGs, or the U.S. Navy RAG advisors understood the combat potential that my forces possessed. They bypassed me. Strangely, I felt that Tanh Dinh Island was my responsibility, my target; these people were here only to help. I was not going to have a passive role if I could do anything about it.

"You're wasting my PBRs!" I protested. "I can commit twelve boats to this operation. That'll give you thirty-six fifty-caliber machine guns, twelve M-60 machine guns, and twenty-four M-79s. Not using them is ridiculous." All six men stared silently at me. "Additionally, I can commit one fire team of gunships."

"What do you propose, Major?" one ARVN officer asked. He was younger, seemingly more alert than the others.

"Lieutenant commander!" I corrected. "First, I think the entire operation is inadequate." The other Americans winced. "Secondly, I don't think that the Viet Cong will stay and fight . . . I wouldn't. You need troops in behind to catch them running. Be that as it may, it would be better to use my boats to soften up the beach before the landing, just in case any Viet Cong are still there. When the Viet Cong face our fifties, they'll go for their bunkers. Then our 81mm and 60mm mortars can shell hell out of them." I pointed to the RAG commanding officer. "Then, just before the RAGs off-load the troops, we'll make another pass. If any Viet Cong are there, we'll get them, or at least they'll keep their heads down for your men to mop up."

Surprisingly, everyone nodded in agreement. I crossed the Rubicon. My boys had a worthwhile job to do. The operation now seemed to have a better chance of success and producing worthwhile results. I defined a worthwhile result as PBRs not being shot at all the time from Tanh Dinh.

The next morning, the day before the operation, I called a planning conference. Lieutenants Henry and Norwick came up from the T.

"The name of our portion of the operation is Linebacker II. Are there any questions?" I asked at the completion of the initial firing phase briefing.

"Yes, sir! I understand the first part, on making the firing run into Titi, but the second firing run seems a bit iffy," said one of the patrol officers.

"Why?"

"Well, the RAGs will be firing and you said we'd go in right under their guns, and when they see the first boat pass that little canal downriver from Titi, Bong Bot Canal, I believe, they'll lift their fire. Isn't that a little dangerous?"

"Yes."

"Those damn RAGs just fire and fire. How do you know they'll stop in time?"

No one else spoke. The room was like a torrid tomb; only the whirring of an old-fashioned overhead fan broke the silence. My jungle greens oozed sweat.

"They'll stop," I said, mustering bravado. Hell, I've been in this business for more than three months, didn't I know everything?

Silence.

"Another thing, Commander," another patrol officer asked finally. "What about ammo? After the first run, if it's as long as you say, we'll be dry. What about the second run? What'll we do for ammo coming home?"

"A good question." I hated people who said "a good question." I wished I hadn't said it. "The base support guys here at Tra Noc will furnish a mike boat and on it will be ammo, fuel, and a corpsman. The mike boat will be stationed in the center of the river just off the southern tip of Tanh Dinh. It'll be proceeding at full speed. A PBR will come along each side and receive ammo as fast as possible. I know we've never tried it before but I think it will work. Just follow my lead. Hell, we've been doing underway replenishments, UNREPs, in the fleet for years and years. Any doubts?"

Silence answered. The mike boat coxswain grinned; he, too, would be a warrior.

I set the prepatrol briefing for 0430, went through the details of boat positioning and the mike boat ammo loading with the patrol officers, and ordered Lieutenant Henry to have his 511 boats joined up by 0630.

"You clear this with the 116 staff, Commander?" Lieutenant Henry asked.

"I've told them I'm supporting a RAG operation."

Sleep wasn't easy. Several times my mind jarred me awake with minute details spinning through my head. If I failed, it would be many months before the PBRs could hope to be given any task save that of mundane patrols. For success on the river, to protect my boys from ambushes, we had to work with the ARVNs. The VC had to know that we had the force of the ARVN behind us. The ARVN had to be shown what we could do, that we could work together.

This was my big chance to prove the worth of the boats . . . and myself. It was my plan. It was dangerous. Was it foolish? And of all the factors, I couldn't discount fear—I was afraid. Afraid, even though by this time I had emerged barely scathed from several firefights. But this was different. This was a preplanned invasion right into the enemy's stronghold; it was an untried plan. It was the home of the Viet Cong 306th. It was important.

Many things could go wrong. What if the RAGs kept firing and hit a boat? What if the Viet Cong were waiting in force, at such close range that they could slaughter us? What was in Titi Canal? No one had ever been in as far as we were going. What if a boat broke down inside? What if . . . what if . . . ?

It was still dark when the messenger called me. Breakfast tasted lousy, and my stomach hurt. "Good morning, gentlemen," I started the briefing. "Just a few more details. One, as the boats come out of the canal, they will fire between those boats still going in."

A few jaws dropped. "Is he crazy?" some undisguised whisper drifted up. I continued before any wise ass could answer yes. "Second, if any boat loses its engines, pull off the firing line toward midcanal and continue firing. The boat behind will take you in tow."

"What about me, sir? I'm the last boat . . . ," a feigned plea came. Several chuckles followed.

"Don't lose power!"

"We make the first pass at 0700, the second at 0745. The RAGs will fire for twenty minutes on both landing zones and lift their barrage just as we start the second pass. I'll be in the lead boat for both runs. After the first run, I'll rearm along the port side of the mike boat; the second boat will go along the starboard side, then we'll form a holding circle . . . simply maintain your position. If you can't rearm in time, pull off the holding line to clear water and wish the rest of us luck. Questions?"

It rained just a few drops as we manned our boats. The only sound was the purring of the diesels. I was happy to see that First Class Petty Officer Morton was to be my senior boat captain today.

I had known Morton from my first destroyer when he was a seaman and I a lowly ensign. He'd saved my career. I was the officer of the deck and had the conn. Seaman Morton was the helmsman. We were going to station astern of a carrier. On the final approach leg I gave the order for left standard rudder. "Say again!" he requested. "Left standard rudder!" I ordered loud and clear. "SAY AGAIN, SIR!" he shouted back. "Goddamn it," I yelled. "Left sta . . . BELAY THAT . . . BELAY THAT . . . RIGHT FULL RUDDER . . . right full rudder."

"Right full rudder, aye, sir," Seaman Morton replied, frantically spinning the helm to starboard, swinging the ship clear of the collision that would have occurred if he had thoughtlessly obeyed my first command.

I squeezed his shoulder in recognition as I stepped aboard. He cut the string holding down the whip antenna to which he had tied my burgee pennant. It rebounded to attention. "Nice touch," I whispered. "Ready?" He nodded yes. "Okay, let's go!"

They were late—0650 and the 511's boats were not here yet. I'd have to go in with just the seven boats from 512. Damn 511! The RAGs were moving into position. It was already blistering hot, though the sun had scarcely lifted over the tree line. A light drizzle started, and stopped as soon as it began. Huge, dark thunderclouds were forming in the distance over the tree line. Lieutenant Commander Williams had wanted to come on the operation but the staff wouldn't allow it. I could have used him.

The other six boats followed behind in perfect order. My burgee pennant cracked in the wind as we roared downstream. We must have been a real sight to the RAG sailors, for they manned the rails, staring and waving. I set my course for a point five hundred yards south of Bong Bot

Canal, the first mainland canal downstream from Tanh Dinh, and when sixty yards from shore whipped around to the north, paralleling the beach on my starboard side at thirty-five yards. We were to start firing when abreast of Bong Bot and continue firing all the way into Titi.

Our timing was perfect. There seemed to be no activity on the beach. Periodically a lone bird rose above the jungle. The tops of the palms swayed in the gentle breeze. I knew that even if the Viet Cong were there we wouldn't see them. It was so very peaceful. A good place to picnic. I kept breaking open the breech to see if my M-79 was loaded. The 40mm grenade was still there after my seventh check. In between, I'd click the safety on and off. My heart was beating faster and faster. I looked down the line; the last boat had just made the turn.

The two Seawolf gunships made a low firing pass into the area, pulled up, and swooped in again. Pulled up and swooped in again. "You got it, Handlash, thanks for the invite to your party," the flight leader radioed as they pulled off to the west over the river.

"FULL SPEED!" I ordered. The boat jumped ahead. The others followed.

I was committed. Twenty seconds passed. Bong Bot rapidly approached my starboard bow. The jungle passed in a blur of green. CLICK SHLANG!—the bolts flew home as the gunners double-cocked their .50s.

5—4—3—2—1—0700. "COMMENCE FIRE!"

The world recoiled as the noise took over every sense. An almost solid stream of tracers from twenty-one .50-caliber heavy machine guns and seven M-60s salvoed into the beach in a macabre display of fireworks.

First one boat, then two, then three crossed into Titi Canal. Gun smoke blanked vision, stung nostrils. Everyone but the coxswain manned a gun; there were no freeloaders on this trip.

Then, as an evil omen, a torrential downpour darkened the sky, blotted out the sun. The gun barrels sizzled and hissed as the rain poured over them. In seconds nothing was dry, but the firing continued. I could barely make out the second boat in line.

We were two hundred yards into Titi—the Viet Cong answered our fire. Their bullets splashed the water around us and buzzed through the air above us. I bent to get more rounds for my M-79, and a bullet tore through the canopy where I had just stood. I stared for a microsecond, detached, as if watching TV. I reached up to adjust my helmet—my right hand turned into blood. There was no pain. Odd. Morton, the boat captain, firing from amidships, cried: "I'M HIT! I'M HIT!"

"WHERE? BAD? KEEP FIRING!" I yelled. It was a useless statement. His M-60 didn't miss a beat, nor did the determined expression on his face change. His gun's trigger area was painted crimson from his blood.

Another tracer slashed by my head. I turned instinctively to follow its path across the boat. It zinged in toward the coxswain's flat, passing no more than a quarter inch in front of his eyes. "I'm blind," he screamed over the roar of the engines and the guns. I whirled . . . he clutched his hand over his eyes. I leapt for the controls, but as I touched the wheel he shouted: "I'm okay! I'm okay!" with a sheepish grin of apology.

Those Viet Cong hidden in the jungle were good. They led my boat perfectly, then shifted fire to the second boat.

Through the rain, a hundred yards ahead, the fish stakes I had chosen for the turnaround point became barely discernible. I quit firing my M-79 and watched them approach . . . easy . . . easy . . . wait . . . now!

"COME ABOUT! CEASE FIRE! CEASE FIRE!" The boat laid over on its port side, sliding around in deference to my command. We were on our way out.

My right hand started to throb. I had forgotten. I felt light-headed. My whole side hurt. My wet greens had turned black where my blood had splattered. I didn't know that red and green and water made black.

"COMMENCE FIRE! BETWEEN THE BOATS! BE-

TWEEN THE BOATS!" My PBR rocked violently from the wakes of the incoming boats, but the gunners laid their fire unerringly.

The engines screamed as we skimmed over the water, on step, out of the canal. Our ammunition gone, the boat was a full five knots faster. The rain slackened, and visibility improved to about two hundred yards. I searched for the mike boat. Lieutenant Henry had not arrived before we went in. He still wasn't here. Repeated calls on the radio failed to raise the 511 boats. Didn't he realize how important this operation was?

So many RAG boats had arrived in the area that making out the mike boat on our small, commercial navigation radar was impossible. Things had gone to hell. "Where is that damn boat?" I cursed. It was 0710. It had been a long ten minutes. Were all my boats out? Were they behind me? I could make out only two other PBRs. Damn, stupid rain!

The RAG boats' 81mm mortars commenced fire. They were closer to the canal. Surely my boats were all out. Goddamn this rain!

Jesus! I was cold! I held on to the canopy rail for support. The boat seemed to be spinning. I wanted to go to sleep; I couldn't get my hand to stop bleeding. I discarded the blood-soaked rag and replaced it with a rain-soaked battle dressing. The coxswain strained for visibility. The after gunner mechanically threw empty .50-caliber brass over the stern. The forward gunner just sat there. I stayed away from the crew. I didn't want them to know that I felt so weak.

My head reverberated as a deafening clap of thunder rocked the earth. It was gone! The rain was gone! There, a bare two hundred yards ahead of us, was the mike boat. What a beautiful sight! It was 0716. "Stand by your lines!" Morton yelled.

The coxswain eased alongside as if he were hugging a beautiful woman, and even before the lines were secure, ammo boxes were coming aboard. The second PBR was already receiving her load before I could climb aboard the mike boat. It was working—the other five PBRs held a tight line aft while awaiting their turn.

"Handlash, Handlash, this is Handlash One Two. Over!" cracked the radio. It was Bill Norwick with the 511 boats. Handlash One Two was his personal call sign. The added "two" was for the second in command.

I grabbed the mike. "One Two, this is Handlash. What is your position? Over!"

"This is One Two. I have you in sight, estimating zero five. Over!"

Five minutes, good show. "Roger, One Two. Am alongside mike boat now, will rendezvous with you zero five. Out!"

"Hurry up that damn loading!" I yelled, just to release my tension.

"Morton, get up here and let the corpsman look at your hand!" I yelled down to the boat.

"We're ready to go, Commander. It don't hurt."

"Screw it, then, let's go!" Morton was a good man. I congratulated the mike boat coxswain as I jumped onto my already-underway PBR.

It was 0725. The PBR on the mike boat's starboard side pulled off directly behind me, and the two behind him were moving smartly alongside. Steam was rising from all parts of my boat. The sun was blinding; it seemed we gurgled the air we breathed.

Bill Norwick and his boat captains came alongside. "Don't gimme any shit about why you're late!" I yelled. "Come aboard!"

Bill broke out his little-boy-stealing-cookies smile. I laughed. My hand didn't hurt anymore. I hugged him as he sat beside me. "Where's Henry?"

"He hurt himself . . . couldn't make it."

"Okay, now pay attention . . . you've already missed part of the show." I briefed as my crew furiously rearmed our guns. "Questions? Okay, fall in behind me." It was 0735, time to go.

I set my course again for the Bong Bot Canal turn point. My fully loaded boat was sluggish. The other PBRs jockeyed for position behind me. The RAG's 81mm and 60mm mortars were still pounding the landing zone (LZ). A dense smoke hung over the jungle.

"Will they stop firing in time, Commander?" some voice asked.

My binoculars did not waiver from the turn point as I answered, "I hope so." It was 0746. I was a minute late. I had to hold on as the coxswain came hard left to parallel the beach. "A little closer," I ordered.

BWAAM! BWAAM! BWAAM! The mortars were still firing. Can't those damn fools see us entering?

"Commence fire!" I yelled. Steel and flame leapt from our barrels.

BWAAM! Another 81 flew over our heads.

I screamed over the radio to the RAG advisor: "Gray Fox 25, this is Handlash, Handlash. Get those fucking mortars turned off. Over."

"Handlash, this is Gray Fox 25. Roger, I'm trying. Out."

Once the RAGs started firing, the American advisors had a deuce of a time getting them to stop. They had assured me that they would—I hoped they could.

The jungle zipped down the starboard side. All boats were firing. Trees fell like wheat under the scythe of an avenging giant. Bushes vanished. Steaming mud splattered under the death rays of light from our constant stream of tracers decimating the thick mangrove sanctuary of the enemy.

Blood from my hand oozed through the dressing onto my M-79, forming a sticky mess before globbing into a pool on the deck.

BWAAM!

"Those bastards!"

BWAAM! The jungle off my starboard bow erupted; mud and branches inundated my boat.

"Screw 'em! We're getting out of here! COME ABOUT!" I screamed. We were still a hundred yards from the turn point. The boat skidded as she turned. The others followed.

As my boat sped out of the canal entrance, the troop-ladened RAG boats were three hundred yards from the beach and closing fast. They were coming in too soon! It would be tight for the last PBR.

With wild screams the ARVN ran ashore. Silence greeted them. It was a walk in the sun. The Viet Cong had gotten away again. We had no blocking force behind the tree lines.

Back at the mike boat, Morton and I had our wounds dressed. My hand felt like a thousand tacks had jammed into it. My index finger and thumb were a mess. I had pulled shrapnel out of my hand all the way back to the mike boat. I felt weak from the loss of blood. A little food would set me right. Except for a few men receiving minor shrapnel wounds and various-sized holes in the boats, we had gotten away clean. Did we do any good? The ARVN found no bodies. A little blood, but no bodies. They had heard only their own shots.

It was 0932. By monitoring the ARVN island sweep frequency, I learned that the assault force that landed at the center of the island had made light contact and was slowly moving south. Where were those damned Viet Cong? I knew: They were sitting back in some village drinking Ba Muai Ba beer and laughing.

After rearming and fueling again from the mike boat, I set up a five-boat blockade on the Bassac River side of Tanh Dinh Island and sent the others back to normal patrol. I didn't think the blockade would do much good, but I wanted to be around just in case any action developed. I lost faith in the operation when the ARVN received only light contact on the island and the mainland. Security was notoriously bad with the ARVN. Strong indications were that the Viet Cong had spies in every unit and they kept the enemy well informed of impending operations. "Where the ARVN went the Viet Cong didn't" was a popular ditty among the U.S. Army advisors. It seemed to prove true here.

Tomorrow morning, or the next day, there was to be

another landing on the center of the island and I was to act as a blocking force for the troops sweeping south. Tomorrow was far too late to do any good. Hell, it was too late now. The ARVNs were putting on a good but utterly useless show.

I assigned my boat the northernmost station, just off the top of Tanh Dinh Island. Arriving on station I tied up to the PBR that I had put there earlier, just in case the Viet Cong tried to pull out in that direction to the north.

"Commander, you should have seen it!" reported the boat captain. "Hundreds of sampans came pouring out of Titi Canal. Hundreds, just hundreds. They're all strung out between here and Tra On. Look at them lined up on the beach. I couldn't even start to check them all. All women, kids, and old men. Where in Christ's name are all the men?"

"Halfway between here and Saigon, I imagine."

"Sounded like you had a good show down there."

I gave him a quick rehash of the action, then relieved him with a well done. He saluted, tossed off the lines, and gunned his engines toward home.

Now the long hours of waiting. The adrenaline drained from my blood; I was weak and cold, tired and hungry. My hand hurt and was bleeding again. We were out of sterile battle dressings. I was dizzy and my stomach growled. I ate a can of cold C rations—lima beans and ham. It started to rain again. Today was the first rain in six months and no one had ponchos aboard. Wet and cold, I shivered uncontrollably.

"Morton, I'm going to rest a minute in the chief's quarters. Call me if anything happens." I lay down. It was cramped and stifling in there. I used my helmet for a pillow. Things stopped spinning. The guttural growl of the engines turned into a soothing purr. All was quiet.

PWOOW! PWOOW! PWOOW!

"Commander! Commander! We got one trying to get away!"

PWOOW! PWOOW! Hot .50-caliber brass shell casings came pouring down, burning my arms, neck, and face.

"WHERE?" I demanded, stumbling into the coxswain's

flat. "Where are the troops? WHERE IN CHRIST ARE WE?" I looked around but could recognize nothing. The noise from the forward .50s shattered my head. I realized that I was shouting. "Where's my goddamned helmet?"

"We're about a quarter way down the island. You okay, Commander?"

"YES! Yes, any other PBRs around?"

"A sampan's been going in and out from the island like it's trying to get courage to cross. When I fired a warning shot, it ducked in," Morton reported.

I hoped this wasn't a trap. I put my binoculars on the spot the tracers were hitting. Nothing. We were almost there. I became more lucid as the wind blew away the fog in my head. "You think it's a trap, Morton?"

"I don't know."

"CEASE FIRE!" I yelled as we zipped by the spot. Morton hit the horn we used as a cease-fire alarm and the forward .50s quit. All was quiet.

There it was—a bullet-riddled sampan beached in the undergrowth. "Come about! We'll take another look." With a blurring motion the coxswain twirled the wheel, banking the PBR to port, sliding around as smoothly as on the rim of a crystal goblet. We raced back the other way.

There was a slight movement in the undergrowth. We pitched violently as we crossed our own wake. "STAND BY YOUR GUNS!"

A flame shot out of the jungle, followed by the staccato BURRRAT! BURRRAT! of a heavy machine gun. The water under our bow churned. He was leading us and found his mark. Christ! The boat was beginning to look like lattice. We were only twenty-five yards from the beach. CHRIST! All four guns of the PBR barked in answer. I fired six M-79 rounds during the fleeting moments as we passed the bunker. I reached for the mike to call for help. The after gunner was still blazing away as we passed. Then from ahead another burst of fire and again the jungle threw death at us. Two emplacements. Sheppard, you fool! You stupid fool! You've been sucked in!

"BREAK OFF! BREAK OFF!" I screamed to the coxswain as we raced to midstream.

I ordered in the two nearest boats from the blockade and called to Tra Noc for a scramble two on the Seawolves. Then, thinking that maybe they were still airborne from their earlier strike on the mainland, I called: "Any SEAWOLF this net, any SEAWOLF this net. This is Handlash. Am engaged quarter mile down northern tip Tanh Dinh. Over. Over!"

The radio was silent. I called again. Nothing! Where were those goddamned helos when you needed them? I tried again.

"SHIT!" I shouted. "SHIT! SHIT! SHIT! Come about Morton! We're going in."

The PBR screamed as she leapt to the challenge. I could hear the other two PBRs on the way. As we closed the position, bullets splashed ahead of us. They were firing wild and much too soon.

"Hold your fire . . . easy . . . stand by." I could see the forward gunner's hands, his knuckles white as they strangled the trigger grips. Great beads of sweat dropped from his thumbs, poised a microinch above the triggers. He was ready.

My plan was to hold down the enemy fire with the .50s while Morton and I shot 40mm grenades into their bunkers. The .50s couldn't touch them as long as they stayed down. Only the grenades could drop into their positions. I gave a final call for air support. Nothing. We were alone.

"Commence fire!" The forward gunner had ten shells in the air before my mouth closed.

"NOW!" I yelled and the coxswain swung parallel to the beach, all guns opened up in a broadside. I shot a continuous stream of 40mm's into where we thought the enemy hid. We shot at his muzzle flash. But he didn't stop firing. Stupid Viet Cong; didn't they know my plan? Can't they ever cooperate?

The other two PBRs joined us astern. We came around

and repeated the firing run. They still kept firing. Again, I tried in vain to raise the Seawolves. Two more firing runs, both closer to the beach. We were now making the runs at only twenty yards. Both positions kept up their fire. This was absurd; the Viet Cong always quit firing after the second run.

I whipped around, and the other boats followed. It now became a personal thing—I had to silence those machine guns. I studied each man's face as I hurled the boat back into attack. If they were excessively afraid, they didn't show it. Each had that glassy stare that men under stress so often get. As for me—elation; I was living every war movie I had ever seen, every adventure story I had read and every tall tale I had ever heard. I was no longer that fat kid down the block—you know, the one who couldn't run very fast and didn't know how to catch a ball.

Again, I followed the same plan. My right hand began to bleed again from the concussion of the M-79. It hurt like hell. Morton, though he said nothing, was obviously in pain. The battle dressing on his hand was dripping blood. He never let up on his fire. I could hear the forward gunner cursing as one of his guns jammed. Even the coxswain was firing an M-16 with one hand while he drove the boat with the other. Enemy tracers whizzed around us, but only a few hit. The Viet Cong deep in their bunkers could not fire accurately. They weren't even aiming their guns. Why weren't our grenades killing them—did they have overhead protection? Damn them, they were probably shooting through narrow slits. I needed a mortar or a recoilless rifle. Only a lucky shot would get them. We must be getting low on ammo.

As we pulled out to midstream to reload, a thick cloud of smoke from the gunfire lay over the kill zone. I heard the WHOOP! WHOOP! WHOOP! of helicopters and there, overhead, were eight of them circling my position. My heart leapt . . . here was help. I dove for the radio—they were army birds—and frantically tuned in their frequency.

"Down there . . . Over" is all I heard.

"HELOS OVERHEAD! HELOS OVERHEAD! This is Navy PBR call sign Handlash directly below you. Over."

"Roger, PBR Handlash. This is Maverick Lead with flight of eight. Looks like a ball down there. Can I be of assistance? Over."

"Maverick, this is Handlash. Affirmative! Have two, I say again, two machine guns under that smoke in well-bunkered positions. One is heavy. I say again, one is heavy. Been at it for three zero minutes with no luck. I'll mark the target with tracers. Over."

"Roger, Handlash. We're low on ammo. Will make one pass and send half home for reload. Over."

"Roger, Maverick. Follow me!" I turned to the coxswain but he was already heading into the target. "HOLD YOUR FIRE!" I yelled to the forward gunner. Overhead the helos jockeyed into their single-column attack positions and started their run-in. We were two hundred yards from the beach. Bullet splashes dotted around our boat.

"Handlash, this is Maverick. Got their muzzle flash spotted. Commencing run now, now, NOW!"

WHOOSH! WHOOSH! WHOOSH! The first helo's rocket flashed over our heads, smashing into the jungle. The splashes around the boat stopped. I swung parallel to the beach and without firing the .50s started the grenade barrage again. The second helo fired, then the third, then the fourth, then the fifth. The rocket explosions hid the entire area from sight. I made a slow pass at seventy-five yards. I didn't know how good those helos were and I didn't relish being shot by one of them.

As the sixth helo made its pass, tracers shot up at him. We aimed at where we thought the tracers were coming from.

"Back her down! We'll stay here," I ordered. "Keep a close eye." I radioed to my two cover boats. "If you see anything, SHOOT!" The boats astern fired ten more rounds of 40mm; the tracers stopped. The seventh helo rolled in for its run. WHOOSH! WHOOSH! What a pretty sound that was.

ZZING! ZZING! Tracers zipped over our boat. "Let's get the hell out of here!" I braced against the acceleration as the coxswain jammed the throttles forward. The firing stopped as the eighth helo pulled up from its attack.

I hove to in midstream to watch the show. Four helos flew off south toward their base while the other four continued their firing runs. For forty minutes the firing went on, then the first four came back and relieved the four that had remained overhead. The Viet Cong started shooting at them on their first firing pass. Tracers flew up about every second run.

We finished our lunch of C rations heated on the exhaust manifolds and reloaded our guns. I lit a cigar that had somehow remained dry and took deep puffs. "Morton, that heavy in there sounds almost like a fifty but not quite. Ever hear anything like that before?"

"I think, sir, that it might be a Russian DAK-38."

"The rate of fire seems a little slower. We ran into one of those down at Dung Island a couple weeks ago."

"Yes, sir, we heard about that. The DAK-38 actually fires a 12.7mm round, fifty-one caliber. It can fire about one hundred twenty-five rounds a minute but is grossly underpowered compared to our fifties. Our fifties can fire almost three times as fast and more than twice as far."

"It can still kick us in the ass pretty hard." Morton was a gun enthusiast. We had often chatted about his hobby on the long night watches at sea. Morton was a crack shot and had been assigned to our destroyer's mine-clearing detail. Here he was responsible for shooting at the exposed horns of a floating mine with a rifle to blow it up. He never had the opportunity.

"It can sure do that," Morton answered. He was scheduled to be promoted to patrol officer when the next vacancy came up.

"Let's go now! Nice and slow, we'll sneak in from upstream." I figured that if we came in slowly and close to the beach we might get them while they were firing at the helos. I briefed the cover boats by PBR number; both replied they were getting low on ammo. I didn't even know who was back there covering my ass.

The army Mavericks were good. They varied their attacks continually to throw off the Viet Cong gunners and to hit the bunkers from different positions. We had drifted very close to the shore. They were there, the bunkers, thirty yards in from the beach. I could see their muzzle flashes as we drifted slowly past them. We took careful aim and fired at the slit just as a helo rocket exploded in the same place. The bunker seemed to disappear. "Go!" I yelled. We kept firing as we sped out of range.

The helos made two more runs and received no fire. We went in trolling by the bunkers. All was silent.

"Maverick, this is Handlash. Looks like that's the ball game. Thanks for your help. Over."

"Roger, Handlash. Thanks for the excitement. Give us a call anytime. Out." The helos formed up and flew away.

It started to rain again. I was cold and tired; no muscle seemed free from pain.

"Only a hundred fifties left, Commander, and about ten M-79 rounds," Morton reported as we returned to station. He was rebandaging his hand. Each crewman looked like he was in a stupor. It was getting dark. We had been under way sixteen hours. Sixteen hours of unknown productivity, only perhaps and maybe.

The relief boats were a welcome sight. I wasted no time in briefing the new blockade commander.

"Jesus, Commander, they told me you're cherry to be on the river with. That's a lie," Morton said, looking at me with a skewed grin.

"Let's go home, Morton!"

Linebacker II.
A Child's Cry

———•———

I slept till noon the next day—woke up in a pool of sweat but nonetheless felt good. Things must have been quiet during the night and morning or the ops center would have notified me. A check of the ops center confirmed only light to sporadic contact on the island. This meant that the troops heard a rifle shot once in a while. The ARVN always swept an area in single file. It's little wonder they had only light contact. I often thought that one company of U.S. Marines would be more effective than ten companies of ARVN.

The PBR patrol had detected nothing. The ARVNs had refused to investigate the area of the DAK-38 after the Maverick strike. Not in their tactical area of responsibility (TAOR), they said. The ARVN had withdrawn from the island sometime during the night without contact. Surprise, surprise.

The ARVN were going to sit tight today and go in tomorrow to finish the sweep. It seemed a waste of time, but they were doing it for me so I went along with it. I saw nothing for me to do today. Morton was okay. His crew was ribbing him about his lack of sex life because of his shot-up hand. We had about ten wounded all together but none were serious and all would be back on duty in a day or so. We had been lucky. Some boats were in pretty bad shape, though. Both the T and base support at Tra Noc voiced complaints about the lack of repair parts again. Mostly the boats simply needed fiberglass repairs.

The men, hopped up over the fights, told their stories repeatedly to anyone who would listen. Not many of the crews were that interested; they all had their own stories to tell. I briefed the Task Force 116 staff a couple of times and no one but Lieutenant Commander Williams seemed interested. The staff was against the entire operation and went along with it just to humor me, the new kid on the block. They wanted to tell me their stories. I listened but I wasn't interested. I had my own stories now.

I tried to write after-action reports but my hand wouldn't hold a pencil. My yeoman, my only staff member, wasn't worth a damn at shorthand or dictation so I figured to hell with it. I'd write them tomorrow or the next day.

I talked at length to Lieutenant Simon, the OinC of 512, to get his views and opinions. He had been unable to make the operation and felt bad about it. He seemed a good enough chap. In truth I'd rather not have the OinCs with me on operations such as this. They felt too protective of their men and lived under the memories of the old days and the orders from Saigon about the middle of the river and no special operations.

So did I, of course, but I hadn't had my head pounded with it yet. I was getting away with this operation so far. I wasn't sure that Saigon would approve when they found out the extent of it. I had not really outlined the whole operation to anyone but Lieutenant Commander Williams and he had said, unofficially, that it was great but stand by for a blast from higher headquarters. I had told the 116 staff only that I was supporting a RAG operation south of Tra On.

Seemingly, I was living on the fringe of my authority, but no one told me I couldn't run support operations. It was the responsibility of every naval officer to carry out his duties as he saw fit. No one officially told me anything but to obey the ROE. In this operation I had done this specifically and according to the book.

The ROE said that to take an area under fire you had to have the permission of that area's district chief. I had this from him when he was acting in his role as the subsector military commander. Each political leader wore two hats in Vietnam, one as the civilian leader over his geographical area and the other as the military commander over the same area.

The country was roughly divided into large governmental units called provinces, equal to a state in the United States. Militarily these provinces were called sectors. The province chief–sector chief was equal in rank to a lieutenant colonel, and ruled over his province and sector simultaneously.

Down from this was the district chief–subsector chief, equal in rank to a captain, with his area roughly equal to a county in the States. Most of my dealings in this operation were with the subsector chief of the district where Tanh Dinh Island was located.

Next in the pecking order were the village chiefs; here they stopped having dual titles. The village chief was comparable to a mayor and had the rank of sergeant, with very little outside authority. Still further down was the hamlet chief, or outpost chief, as he was sometimes called. Corporal was the best rank he could achieve and he lived a miserable life.

The ARVN did not report to these political-military subdivisions but to the ARVN military commander in the area. The ARVN, supposedly mobile, could theoretically be used in any part of the country but were pretty well entrenched in the provinces in which they lived. When the ARVN operated in a particular district, they kept the district chief advised.

The province-sector chiefs controlled their troops, the regional forces (RFs). The RFs would be comparable to a non-call-up state militia in the United States. In theory, the

ARVN lacked authority over the RFs. Sergeant Thanh was an RF from Ba Xuyen Province.

The village chiefs had their own troops, called popular forces (PFs), which were placed in the various villages and outposts. Ong Tam was a village chief and controlled about fifty PFs. The district chiefs rarely called upon the PFs for any military support; consequently, the village chiefs ran their own show. The down side was that the PFs received almost no support from the district level. That is why we found the villages and outposts in such horrible shape for supplies.

The U.S. Army advisors were located with the provinces and districts. At the province-sector level a lieutenant colonel was assigned. At the district-subsector level a major or captain held the billet. There were no advisors at the village level, and the ARVN had a completely different structure of advisors.

It all seemed so complicated but I wondered how we in the United States would organize if a huge guerrilla war raged in our country, across our states. It worked for the Vietnamese.

Lieutenant Simon set up a special patrol for me at 0400. I would use these two boats plus the two on normal patrol around Tanh Dinh to support the ARVN sweep. I had a huge steak and three beers for supper, went to bed early, and managed to read two and a half chapters of *Alice in Wonderland* before falling into a deep, restful sleep.

The small district town of Tra On was just visible in the morning gloom as we tied up to the rickety public dock. I walked with Sergeant Thanh to the subsector command post (CP) in the center of town just off the public square. This was where the American advisors lived and worked. The district chief lived a few hundred meters away in an old French colonial villa. A few RFs were giving scant attention to security.

"Good morning, Major Shellon," I formally addressed

the somewhat sleepy major as I walked in. "How goes the war?" Sergeant Thanh waited outside the door.

"Oh, okay. I guess the troops had a nice outing day before yesterday."

"Why are you guys still manning the CP?" I asked.

"Shit, I don't know, Don. Sector says man it and here we are wasting our lives away."

"Any casualties, Shelly?"

"No, none that I know of at least. I doubt it; 9th ARVN hasn't had a casualty in years, except a *punji* stake or two. Want some coffee?"

"The 9th ARVN pisses me off. What time is the Normandy invasion?" I asked.

He laughed as he got up from his makeshift desk and sauntered over to a map nailed to the wall. "I hate those damned black bugs," he groaned, crunching as many as he could. "They stink like hell when you kill them."

"That's why they're called stinkbugs, Shelly. I thought they were standard army issue. We don't have any at Tra Noc."

"Shit, I think not. Those bugs can't take high livin'."

"Thanks," I said as he handed me the too-many-hours-old coffee. "What time's the landing—wheh!—you guys drink this shit?"

"Standard army coffee. Tastes great to me."

"We pour crap like this in our crankcases. What time they going in?"

"About 0800 here to here," he answered, pointing to two black arrows grease-penciled in about halfway down Tanh Dinh Island. "Your boats catch anything?"

"Only women, kids, and old men. How many troops going ashore?"

"About a hundred. You sailors really rape the women you find in the sampans?"

"We'd rather eat the babies," I replied. "That old story still going around?"

"No, I've just been here a long time. Only a few more

months to go before my year is up, then DEROS,* Tra On. I might extend, though. This beats slogging around with a bunch of hop heads up north. I'd be back in a year. What happened to your hand?"

"Cut it trying to open a bottle of fine wine for supper. What time will the general be in?"

"Don't know, maybe noonish. He likes to fly over his troops to give them inspiration. Your call sign still Handlash?"

"Damn well it is."

"Well listen, keep your ass down, Commander. Some of the Maverick boys were telling me about that little shoot-out you had with a twelve point seven DAK-38. Anyone hurt?"

"Not on our side."

"Listen, Don, Captain Gordon is due to DEROS out of here soon. He's not seen much action. Do you think you might take him out once and let him shoot some Cong for Christ?"

Captain Gordon was Shelly's assistant. "I'd be proud to, Major."

As I walked back to the boat with Sergeant Thanh, I felt lonely. Early mornings always depressed me; I've always felt that I was an intruder on the day. Silly feeling. It was very quiet; my boots made a clicking noise on the cobblestones. A few early produce merchants were setting up their stalls. They didn't seem to mind the smell of stale urine. I wondered why all the towns and villages smelled like outside toilets. Maybe, as one advisor told me, it was because Vietnam was just one big urinal. I imagined it was more likely the rotting vegetation.

I loosened my .38 revolver in its holster. Chief Gathy had given it to me when he rotated out of country a few months ago. Chief Gathy was like an old China hand, even though

---

*DEROS: date (of) estimated return (from) overseas. This was normally a year after one entered Vietnam.

the real old China hands disappeared in the late 1930s. Chief Gathy had been in Vietnam many times and for many years and was as close to being an old China hand as you could get. He was with the junk force before he came to the PBRs.

He had an uncanny sense about what the VC were planning. His favorite trick was to put himself ashore in an outpost when he suspected a VC attack. When they did, he'd call in the PBRs and have them hose down the area. He spoke fluent Vietnamese and taught me a tremendous amount about river warfare.

The Smith & Wesson .38 Police Special was unmarked and untraceable. I don't know where he got it and I didn't ask. This juvenile touch of mystery intrigued me. I managed to get an English World War II canvas holster from a group of visiting Australians. I thought the combination gave me an air of being cool, somewhat different. Childish? Yes, I knew, but it set me off from the pack and I preferred a .38 pistol to a .45 automatic anyway. He also gave me an old .45-caliber "grease gun" in perfect condition. Time enough to be mister straight-line naval officer when I got back to the fleet.

I envisioned lurking Viet Cong behind every doorway. Could I shoot a man face-to-face? Sergeant Thanh was not that comfortable. I noticed his eyes searching every dark corner and alleyway. I went nowhere on land without Sergeant Thanh.

My Bravo Patrol met Charlie Patrol in the middle of the river just off the center of Tanh Dinh. "Quiet all night, Commander," the patrol officer reported. "One rice convoy about 0600 but that's it. Everyone knows the ARVN's gonna hit today. No one's sticking around I guess. Great show day before yesterday. We were scared as hell but it was a great show! Think we did any good?"

"There are a lot fewer trees back there. How you fixed for fuel?"

"We been driftin' a lot . . . we're good for several more hours. Lieutenant Simon said to conserve. Said you might need us."

I briefed all four boats on the operation for today. "It's simple, we're just going to make a few passes by the LZ and hose down the beach. Once the VNs are ashore we'll orbit, waiting for call fire. A walk in the sun. Charlie One and Two will follow behind my cover boat at one hundred yards. Piece of cake, gentlemen, piece of cake."

We made one fast nonfiring pass by the LZ, then pulled out into midriver. It was 0750 as the RAGs were moving into position. The rain two days ago had soaked the land and turned the air into a virtual river of humidity. My lungs hurt from inhaling the steamlike air. Our clothes looked as if we had swum in them.

"STAND BY YOUR GUNS!" The words always kicked off my adrenaline. With a flair the gunners double-cocked their .50s as the coxswains jammed their throttles forward. Two great streams of water jetted from the stern of each boat as we turned and raced to the beach.

Huge white birds alternately rose and fell from the tree line to the sky. They always seem to disappear after the first rounds go off, or maybe after the first shot; I just didn't notice.

It was 0755; our guns roared on the first pass. We rolled in firing the second. At 0810 the RAGs were still out of position. I ordered a third pass. The center of the LZ was a huge dead tree lying over in the water. We were to fire two hundred yards on either side of it. I'm sure the VC knew exactly where the center of the LZ was.

The initial point upriver was a uniquely beautiful pink and blue flower cluster; downstream a rotten palm. "COMMENCE FIRE!" I ordered as the flowers came into my binocular view. Our .50s answered before I finished the word "fire." The flowers disappeared as a 40mm grenade exploded into the center of the cluster. The tracers laced across the water, jumping onto the beach as the gunners found their range.

I continued to scan the beach as the fallen tree came into sight. "GOOD LORD! CEASE FIRE! CEASE FIRE!"

A sampan loaded with children had just pushed off the shore from beneath overhanging mangroves. I screamed "CEASE FIRE! CEASE FIRE!" again and again but the guns wouldn't stop. I couldn't be heard over the thunder of the .50s. I leapt for the horn. It didn't work. I threw my helmet at the forward mount, then twirled and threw my binoculars at the after gunner. They looked at me in surprise. "CEASE FIRE!" I screamed again. "On the beach a sampan full of kids . . . over there . . . over there," I pointed.

They strained to see.

My cover boat! Oh my God! He was almost in firing position. I grabbed the mike as they opened up. I was yelling cease fire, cease fire, but I knew it was useless. Nothing can be heard once all the guns are lashing out. I could only hope that the coxswain would notice that we quit firing and would do the same. Their bullets were now tearing into the very overhang that hid the sampan.

I ordered the helm hard over starboard. They'd have to notice we were pulling out. The coxswain's duty was to follow the lead boat. The firing stopped on my cover boat. "CEASE FIRE!" I radioed again just as Charlie One opened fire. Their guns still defied my order. "CEASE FIRE!" and Charlie One stopped.

"This is Bravo Two. Roger. Out," my cover boat answered.

"This is Charlie One. Roger. Out."

"This is Charlie Two. Roger. Out."

"Bravo, Charlie, this is Handlash. Sampan full of kids on the beach. Wait . . . break, break. Gray Fox 25, you copy? Over."

"This is Gray Fox 25. Affirmative. Over."

"This is Handlash . . . break, break. Bravo, do you have them in sight? Over."

"This is Bravo. Negative . . . WAIT! . . . affirmative, I have sampan in sight. Request instructions. Over."

"This is Handlash, wait . . . break, break. Gray Fox 25, request you break off landing. Over."

"Regret cannot, Handlash. I have no control at this point. Over."

"Roger, Gray Fox, I am going in to pick up that sampan. Do what you can . . . break, break. Bravo, go in and get that boat. Bravo Two, Charlie Two, you copy? Over."

They rogered in turn as they heeled over, heading for the beach. I strained to see any activity. Was this a trap? It would be our ass! I ran my boat in front of the RAGs, hoping it would slow them down, keep them from firing. Gray Fox 25 must have had some control; they were slowing.

Bravo One's bow disappeared in the undergrowth; the gunners were tense on their weapons. I headed back to the scene. What in God's earth was taking them so damn long? Patience, Sheppard, patience.

"This is Bravo . . . got 'em!" the radio cracked. They backed out with the sampan in tow from the bow.

"Roger. Charlie Two, follow me. Out." I whipped the boat around and headed for the LZ without waiting for Charlie Two. We sped past the destroyed cluster of pink and blue flowers and opened up. Charlie Two fell in astern and started firing. The river assault group with their ARVN troops were almost to the beach. At the fallen palm tree I came around again and kept firing until we passed where the flowers had been. The previous wakes of our two speeding boats rocked us unmercifully.

The RAGs came right behind us discharging their troops. We had completed our mission. I headed for the two boats moored together in midriver. As we tied up alongside, I stared in disbelief. My body shuddered at the sight. "Quick! Bring your first-aid kit," someone demanded. Morton leapt to the other boat in response. The crews frantically worked on the ill-fated occupants of the bullet-riddled craft.

The crimson red of fresh blood colored the entire inside of the sampan. A man's body lay in the bottom. His face, or what had been his face, looked up. He had no head, only a chin and lower lip; his left leg was gone below the thigh, and what had been his innards covered the rest of him. The smell of the dead man's released feces fouled the air.

In the bow, sitting like a statue, was a naked, ugly little girl of about seven—her eyes wide and blank, her hands clutched tightly over her ears while her sweat oozed over her blood-splattered body. The grotesque, vacuum-eyed upper half of the man's head filled her lap; his separated scalp plastered her chest.

There was that sweet, sickly smell of death about. A forward gunner lay on the bow with his head over the gunwale, retching violently. I fought to hold my vomit.

I bent to help lift another little girl into the PBR. In her hip was a yawning, raw hole the size of a cantaloupe. I could see the twitching, blood-soaked muscle fibers and the corrugated brown of her intestines and stomach. We tried vainly to stop the bleeding. She seemed to smile as she died, lying there on the engine covers among the empty brass .50-caliber shell casings that had killed her. Thanh and several of the men cried as they bent to their grisly task.

Here, Sheppard, here is your glorious little war, here is the work you do. Here you stride ten feet tall. The giant butcher of the Bassac.

Two boys about ten years old sat silently in the stern of Charlie One's PBR. One had battle dressings around his head and left arm. The other had a tourniquet and a battle dressing where his right leg had been. They each held a stick of gum that one of the crewmen had given them. The boy with the bandaged head muttered over and over in Vietnamese: "VC come . . . VC come . . . VC come . . ."

"THANH . . . THANH! Over here," I called, motioning him away from his ministering to one of the little girls. "Talk to the boy, Thanh . . . what happened? Find out what he means."

The dazed, ugly young girl made no protest as a sailor gently lifted her into a PBR. A crewman filled his helmet with water as she was placed on the engine covers. He tried to gently wash off the man's scalp, but it wouldn't go free. "SHIT!" cursed the boat captain, forcibly yanking it off and throwing it in the river, alongside his vomit.

"Thieu Ta! Boy say Viet Cong come two, three days ago. Kill mother. Kill father. He say Viet Cong put them in sampan. Man in boat Viet Cong. He say he push them in front of green boats. Then bullets come. That's all he knows."

I bent over and spit on the man's body.

"Get them into Can Tho. We'll take your patrol until you get back," I ordered Charlie's patrol officer. I leaned over and kissed the ugly little girl with the wide eyes and wept as I stepped back into my boat. My daughter was the same age.

"And bring some ammo. We got some shootin' to do. KICK 'ER IN THE ASS! Let's get the fuck outta here!"

The wind across the bow blew away the stench, but not the memory.

Linebacker II.
Titi Canal

———————•———————

Time passed slowly as we patrolled Bravo's station. I intercepted a call from an army helo reporting several sampans with men aboard crossing over from the southern end of the island to the mainland. He requested instructions; his answer from the ARVN CP at Tra On was, "Watch them."

Ridiculous! More Viet Cong getting away. I called the CP on the radio and told them to drop six bits: Going down in frequency .75 megahertz was a fast and dirty way to dupe the enemy if they were listening. Captain Gordon's voice answered back on the new frequency: "Roger. Go . . . Handlash."

His lack of proper radio procedure bothered me. The navy is always precise about how they use the radios. Except, of course, for the aviators. This preciseness is extremely important because it helps cut down on confusion and lack of understanding. The most overused word is "roger." It means only one thing: you understand. It doesn't mean yes and it doesn't mean you'll do something; it means only that you understand.

"Over" means that you want a reply from whomever you're talking to. "Out" means that you do not want or request a reply and that your message is complete. Whenever I hear someone say "over and out," I cringe; it means go ahead and answer me back but I won't be listening. "Wilco" means I understand and will comply. The movie talk of "roger wilco over and out" is a foolish redundancy.

I informed Captain Gordon in code that I was going to go to the southern tip of Tanh Dinh to investigate the sampans. "Wait. Out" was the reply.

I watched Bravo Patrol in the distance. They were low in the water, slugging toward us with our ammo.

"Handlash, this is Ironblood. Over," the radio broke in.

"Ironblood, this is Handlash. Interrogative plan. Over."

Ironblood was the call sign of the senior RAG advisor in Can Tho. I again sent in simple cryptic voice code that my intention was to investigate the sampans at the southern tip of the island. "Wait. Out" was the reply I received. The RAG had such few operations that I guessed he was along for some vicarious excitement.

While we waited, Bravo came alongside and we replenished our ammo. It seemed that Ironblood was taking a long time to reply. I imagined that he was conferring with the ARVN commander. Finally, he answered affirmative. I didn't really need his approval, or 9th ARVN Division's, but it was a courtesy. If I had had enough ammo, I would not have waited but gone directly in after the helo report was received.

I verified the troop position, then came back up on the Bassac River common frequency. In the KAC code I informed the ops center of my intentions, instructing them to have Handlash Two dispatch the patrol on the Juliet side to rendezvous at the southern tip of Tanh Dinh. I gave the same instruction to be passed to Handlash One on the T.

Radio wave propagation was superb today. I had been listening on the RIVSEC 511 frequency for a while and knew that they were in a minor firefight off Dung Island.

Each PBR had two U.S. Army FM transceivers. One was normally on the RIVSEC frequency and the other on the Bassac River common, which meant that any boat could talk to any boat or Seawolf. The army was on different frequencies, but we generally knew them and could switch over if necessary. The jet fighters used UHF and we could not talk to them except through the forward air controllers (FACs).

I heard both calls go out from the ops center and in minutes the orders to the boats. Both patrols answered "on the way"; they had been listening.

We sped downstream. It would take at least fifteen minutes for my four boats to get there. Lieutenant (jg) Jenkins with Sierra Patrol from the T was waiting when we got there. They must have started heading this way when they first heard the transmissions. Jenkins was a real tiger. He'd been with me on my first firefight in Khem Bang Co. Foxtrot from the Juliet area came scooting around Cu Lao May minutes later. They too had been listening. What marvelous sailors these men were.

"Now watch your ass," I briefed, "and don't shoot farther upstream than my boat. We're going into Titi up to where the troops landed. They're moving north, so anything is fair game from my boat down. You, Sierra and Foxtrot, stay close outside Titi. In case we get in trouble you can save our ass." They looked disappointed and good naturedly whined that Charlie and Bravo were my favorites.

With four boats in a column we entered the canal at full speed. My plan was to stay at full speed all the while we were in the canal. A PBR that was stopped or at slow speed was a mighty juicy target in a narrow canal.

"We're not too late!" I yelled over the engine noise. "Look at the traffic!" Two small sampans had just ducked into the jungle on the mainland side and one was in the middle of the canal. I guessed that they hadn't seen us enter. My heart pounded at the thought of combat, which momentarily allayed my consternation about entering the narrow canal.

"Fire a warning shot!"

The bullet sliced the water just in front of one of the sampans. Where did the ricochets go?

"It's a young woman, Commander! She's all alone."

"Bring 'er alongside." I wanted a capture. With a quick command the other three boats took up flanking positions.

"Damn you, bitch!" my boat captain shouted. He and Thanh were trying to hook onto her with a grapnel.

"What's the trouble?"

"She's too maneuverable, sir. We can't get close."

The woman was a good sailor. She jockeyed her sampan inside our turn. Every time we turned into her to get closer, she flipped around her shrimp-tail motor, coming out on the outside of us.

I scanned the beach with my binoculars; several men were running around, and one or two had rifles.

"Watch the beach!" I said to the boat captain, handing him my binoculars. The men on the beach were pointing at us and yelling at each other. "If they make a move, cut 'em down."

I leaned over the gunwale toward the woman. She looked at me, glancing up at the gold oak leaf painted on my helmet. She turned ashen white.

"Come here, we won't harm you," I said in what I construed to be my most soothing Vietnamese. This woman must be important or we would be catching it from the beach by now. What had I gotten into?

She screamed and started to cry. She was a beautiful young woman about nineteen years old.

The activity on the beach seemed to increase. What was going on here? She tried to escape. "CUT HER OFF!" I ordered. The coxswain gunned the engines, whipping around in front of her.

"STOP! STOP!" I yelled, but she wouldn't stop. I drew my .38 and held it with both hands, pointing it directly at her. She stopped.

"Thanh! Tell her to come alongside."

"She no listen, Thieu Ta. Kill her!" he replied.

We were deep in the Viet Cong territory. She had to be someone really valuable for the men on the beach not to take us under fire. She stayed just out of reach, no matter how we maneuvered. I didn't dare bring up another boat.

One barely moving boat at a time was target enough. I told the boat captain to order the 511 boats to go south to the tip of Tanh Dinh in case we had to fire at the island.

"Tell her I'll kill her if she doesn't come here!" I pulled back the hammer on my .38. Her tears magnified to a wail. I couldn't stay here, surely those men on the beach would do something. They were milling around and shouting. I could hear them, but neither Thanh nor I could make out what they were saying.

"Goddamn! Commander! Our ass is out on a limb. Shoot the Viet Cong bitch!" the coxswain pleaded.

The men on the beach had disappeared. I took careful aim; things were getting tight—I had to do something. No one on the PBR spoke. I could feel their eyes boring into me.

She quit crying. I spoke again, "Come here, come here. I'm Thieu Ta of the United States Navy; I won't hurt you."

She spit at me. Her expression turned to hate. "Shoot! Shoot, Yankee bastard," she screeched in passable English.

My .38 grew hot in my hands. She pulled open her black blouse, exposing her breasts. "Shoot, fuckee number one. Shoot, Yankee bastard. You name Sheppard . . . we know . . . you die," her voice screamed from a hate-distorted face. The mention of my name sent shivers through my body. They know my name. Jesus Christ, they know my name!

Through the rear notch of my sights, the front post lay perfectly centered, pointing directly at her now smug, smiling face. My hands were steady, as in a vice. I could feel my pulse smashing against the pistol.

Why didn't one of the Viet Cong fire at us? I wanted the Viet Cong to fire at us. Why didn't she try to escape? Why didn't she start crying again?

DO SOMETHING! DO SOMETHING! my mind screamed.

"Shoot me, Yankee bastard."

"Kill her, Thieu Ta," Thanh whispered.

FIRE! I ordered my finger to fire. Squeeze the trigger, I ordered. End this foolhardy mess. Fire! Fire!

"Kill her, Thieu Ta," Thanh whispered again.

My grip on the handle tightened until pain filled my entire body, but my trigger finger wouldn't move. Slowly my mind turned her face into that of the dead little girl.

"Kill her, Thieu Ta," whispered Thanh, standing so close I could feel his body heat.

I lowered the gun, gently releasing the hammer, and threw a pack of cigarettes at her. I looked at Thanh's disgusted face and felt sick inside.

"MOVE OUTTA HERE!" I vented my wrath. "Son of a bitch!" Her sampan sped for the island.

"Thank God!" someone said. "Thank God."

The whine of our engines was a refreshing sound. "How'd she know my name, Thanh? How'd she know?" I sat on the engine covers. Every bit of energy drained into my feet. The other three boats joined up astern as the woman beached her sampan and rapidly disappeared into the jungle.

Thanh stared at me in disgust. "Everyone know your name, Thieu Ta. Why you not shoot?"

I couldn't answer. I had come within a heartbeat of being an executioner—a murderer. I imagined that tonight, around a campfire, somewhere a beautiful young woman would be sharpening punji stakes or assembling a booby trap. She would be passing out Lucky Strike cigarettes as she told the story of the cowardly Yankee Thieu Ta Sheppard, and they would laugh.

We moved at twenty knots up the canal to the first island, a distance of two miles from the canal mouth, then reversed course and sped back to the entrance at the same speed. My fears dictated this high speed, but we were going too fast to see back into the dense jungle. When we came about again, I ordered slow speed. I didn't even know what I was doing back there.

Now we could see what was going on. We were making bare steerageway, about three knots, and the gunners sat tensed, their guns cocked. Silence revealed our fear.

"See anything?" I asked no one in particular, the high pitch of my voice betraying my fear.

"No, sir, I reckon we're too late," the boat captain answered.

"Yeah . . . how many sampans you figure are pulled up there on the beach?" I had never seen so many empty sampans in one place.

"Fifty or so. Big junk under the trees; guess the Viet Cong bugged out."

"Yeah. It's sorta spooky, isn't it?" I said.

"Large pucker factor, I'd say. Rather be out on the river," the coxswain replied.

"Me too, but this is where the action's going to be, if there is any!"

For an hour we patrolled slowly up and down the canal, expecting an ambush at any moment, but all was quiet. An occasional lily pad floated downstream and birds screeched, but no human moved. My eyes became sore from the sweat dripping into them and from the constant pressure of the binoculars against them. My arms grew tired from their weight.

The coxswain continually worked the wheel and throttles to keep the boat on a steady course at this slow speed. The gunners never took their fingers off their triggers.

No breeze stirred the stagnant, moisture-laden air. The sun seemed to focus all its fury directly onto our boats. God, it was hot! To touch metal was to burn your hand.

"Be snow on the ground back home," someone said.

"Quiet!" I ordered. The strain was tremendous. No man had a dry spot on his greens.

I couldn't take the strain anymore. I picked up my microphone. "Handlash Sierra. This is Handlash. Bring your boats in and relieve us. Over."

"This is Sierra. Roger. Out."

Within ten minutes Lieutenant (jg) Jenkins arrived with Sierra and Foxtrot. We pulled out of the canal at top speed and I took my first full breath of air as the coxswain throttled back and dropped into Sierra's blockade station on the main river.

"SHIT!" exclaimed the after gunner. "Fuck that place!"

I shared his sentiments, though not voiced with equal eloquence. "Which C ration has the cheese in it?" I asked.

"B-1, Commander! We got all the meat heating on the manifold."

I could never remember the coded numbers on the box tops that identified the variety of the contents. Each box had the name of the main meat dish printed on top and a series of letter-number codes told what other goodies it contained.

"You guys got a kerosene stove? Some fish and rice would taste good," I commented.

"Don't figure any fishermen will be out today with all this ARVN bullshit going on," the coxswain answered. "It looks like good ole C rats, Commander."

Many boat crews bought fish, rice, chicken, and vegetables from the sampans or in Can Tho before going on patrol. They could whip up a delicious feed to break the monotony of C rations meal after meal, especially when laced with a goodly portion of *nuoc mam,* a very tangy Vietnamese sauce. We discouraged the practice of buying food from the VC, but not very forcefully. There was always the fear that they would poison us.

We ate C rats, which personally I liked.

The senior RAG advisor's voice broke the silence of midriver. "Handlash, this is Ironblood. Intend to join your inner canal patrol. Over."

"This is Handlash. Roger. What is your position? Over."

"This is Ironblood. Heading for upper canal entrance now. Over."

"Interrogative. Do you intend to transit canal? Over."

"Affirmative. Over."

"Damn it!" I shouted. "One boat will get its ass shot off."

"Ironblood, this is Handlash. Recommend you come via the main river. Over."

"This is Ironblood. Negative! Out."

I didn't know why Ironblood wanted to come through the canal. He knew the danger. I thought it stupid to do so, but he must have had a good reason. He was in overall command of the entire naval element of Vietnamese RAGs, and indirectly of me.

"Sierra, Sierra, this is Handlash. You copy Ironblood? Over."

"This is Sierra. Affirmative. Over."

"Roger, Sierra, take your boats and go up the canal to meet Ironblood. Over."

"Handlash . . . ahh! . . . this is Sierra," he said after a pause. "Say again. Over." I repeated the message. I knew damn well he had heard me the first time.

"This is Sierra. Wilco. Out."

"Come on, Sanders, we're going back in!" I said.

"Shit!" said the after gunner. Again I shared his sentiments.

"Ironblood, this is Handlash. Interrogative you copy my last to Handlash Sierra? Over."

"Handlash, Ironblood. Affirmative. Over."

"Ironblood, Handlash. We'll do the best we can to support you. Request you reconsider. We don't know what's in there. Over."

"This is Ironblood. Negative. Thanks for support. Out. I say again, OUT!"

"Handlash One, this is Handlash. Scramble one. I say again, scramble one. Over." The radios were working so well today that I called directly to the T.

Instantly back: "Roger, Handlash. Regret two zero wait time. Over."

"Roger One, do the best you can. Interrogative. Do you know the situation? Over."

This time it was Lieutenant Simon's voice: "Roger, Handlash, we're doing our best. Seawolves previously alerted. Have ordered Tango to your posit. Over."

"Thanks, One. Out." Simon was on the ball.

Well, fuck Ironblood, I thought. He's sitting in one of those iron monsters that the RAGs used and was in little danger except for rocket fire. Why in Christ's earth was I sending boats to help? He didn't even ask. What an asshole I was.

"Shit, piss, fuck," I heard from the after gunner. I set up the same patrol pattern as before with my four boats. It was still ghostly silent. I worried about Sierra. No PBR had ever run Titi Canal before.

Back in the summer of '66, almost a year before, when the PBRs first came to the Bassac, a few patrols eased their nose in, but they got shot up badly. That ended the incursions, and since then the Viet Cong on Tanh Dinh usually played hell with any boat passing the island. They even had the audacity to put up a sign reading: "If green boats want to fight, come behind island." The sign now hangs in the officers' club at Tra Noc, but we had heeded it for a year.

Ten minutes passed.

"Handlash! Handlash! This is Sierra. Drawing heavy fire from island. Over." I could hear his .50s in the background.

"CEASE FIRE! CEASE FIRE! SIERRA! Friendly troops on island. I say again, CEASE FIRE! Over."

"Ahh . . . Roger, Handlash. Fire's pretty heavy. We're about halfway through. Over."

"Roger, Sierra. Sorry. Out."

What a rotten command to have to give. Why hadn't those damned ARVNs cleaned out those Viet Cong? What a useless army.

"Handlash, this is Sierra. We're getting it again. Shot up bad . . . two wounded. Out."

I felt helpless; I should have gone instead. I could have kicked myself in the ass. Damn those ARVNs. Damn you, Sheppard.

"Handlash, this is Sierra. Getting it again. Just passing a big white church on the starboard. Lotta activity. Out."

The waiting was unbearable—five minutes, ten minutes. Twice I thought of speeding up there to help him but rejected it both times as stupid. What could I do? He'd be out before I could get there. Damn! What in Christ is keeping him? Fifteen minutes.

"Handlash, this is Seawolf Seven Six. Two minutes out. I have situation . . . break, break . . . Sierra, your location three minutes. Hang in there," came the characteristic squishing transmission from the gunships.

"Roger, Seven Six. This is Sierra. You'll be coming in hot . . . good to see ya. Out."

I could see the fire team making their passes as they climbed high each time to swoop down again. Ten minutes passed. "Handlash, this is Sierra. Clearing canal now . . . break . . . RAGs are here extracting the troops. For info, Ironblood did not enter canal and is moving out with the RAGs. Request instructions. Over."

Ironblood didn't even tell me it was over. He had put my boats in harm's way for nothing. They had been patronizing me for three days. I felt like an ass—a stupid, clumsy ass.

After a damage report from Sierra I told him to send one boat to take his four wounded to Can Tho, take what ammo the boat could give him, and to join me soonest. By this time Tango had arrived from downriver. I was glad to see that it was Bill Norwick. I instructed Seawolf Seven Six to go back to the T, rearm, and return.

I called the ARVN CP at Tra On again and reminded them of the abandoned Viet Cong sampans I had reported earlier. They had obviously forgotten.

"Roger. What about them? Over," they replied.

"What about them? Jesus Christ!" I yelled to the wind.

"This is Handlash. Request permission to destroy them. Over." I tried to keep the disgust out of my voice. It irritated me that I had even asked. I didn't need their permission. What if they refused? Screw 'em! I'd destroy them anyway. That colonel or general, whatever asshole is up there now, wasn't the civil commander in this area. Damn! Why'd I ask? I'll never do that again. I could always say we were taking fire from the area.

"Roger, Handlash. Use your discretion. Out." What a mealymouthed, fucking answer. In other words, they were taking no responsibility if things went wrong.

I briefed the boats: "Now, for those of you who haven't been in there, about four junks and thirty to thirty-five sampans are beached on the mainland side. What we're going to do is line up, make one slow-speed pass, and destroy every one of them. Look close now! Many of 'em are camouflaged; some pulled way up on the bank.

"Boat captains! Ensure—and make damn sure!—that one man in your boat keeps an eye on the opposite bank. We don't want to get ambushed from behind. And one more thing, take it easy on ammo expenditure—we may have to fight our way outta there. You guys pick one sampan each and blast it good. Don't waste ammo on every one of 'em; there's more boats coming up behind. Any we miss going in we'll get on the way out. We'll wait until the Seawolves get back. They'll hose down the area ahead of us just in case the bad guys are still around. Questions? . . . Okay, move out."

Our nine boats moved slowly in column formation back toward the canal. Seven Six returned, made two firing passes over the area, then orbited midriver. We entered the canal.

"Hold your fire," I ordered my gunners, "until we pass the first twenty sampans." The PBRs were about fifty yards apart. Only an occasional screech from some jungle bird broke the silence. A gentle breeze came up, smoothly rustling the palm trees. A mother hen and four chicks pecked their way across an opening in the mangroves. Behind them came a fat, mud-covered pig. Small white birds flitted from tree to tree. Large, vivid white and blue flowers hung from the lower branches.

We saw thatched hootches built close together, and mud bunkers placed about every forty yards along the bank. I wondered in which of these lived the Viet Cong who killed those children's parents? Which one housed the man whose thirteen-year-old daughter placed the bomb in the Tra On marketplace a few months ago, killing thirty-nine villagers? My memory again ripped the scalp from the little girl's chest.

"COMMENCE FIRE!"

I flinched from the noise. The bank churned from the .50s; two sampans disintegrated before my eyes. The chickens scurried in panic. The pig just stood there, grunting in the mud. My gunners were having a field day. I looked down the line; every boat belched smoke and tracers.

We came upon a junk, and all four machine guns on my boat cut into it, but it remained. The PBR behind me fired, as did the third, fourth, and fifth. But as the sixth PBR, Sierra One, opened fire, the junk erupted in a violent fireball, shooting about a hundred feet into the air. Sierra had hit its hidden munitions. It renewed my faith.

My boat captain kept changing the crewmen's positions so all could have target practice. Never before did we have such a wonderful training aid. Never before did we see such direct results of our efforts against the enemy. This, in part, made up for the hundreds of ambushes that constantly plagued our boats. The debt was being paid—one debt being my right hand, which hurt so much that I couldn't fire my 79 without pain thundering through my entire right side.

I came to the end of the line of sampans and made a wide turn to port to allow all the other boats to join behind before I started the second pass.

"Ain't that pretty, Commander!" exclaimed the after gunner. "Man, we ain't never had a turkey shoot like this before." His trousers were polka-dotted a dull crimson from the dried blood of the little girl.

The bank was a shambles of destroyed sampans. The gunners had done their work well. No piece larger than two feet remained and these were soon reduced to splinters as an occasional burst finished the job.

"ALL UNITS, this is Handlash. Well done, let's go home. Out." Seven Six made a pass as an encore.

What had I proven? Did the ARVN respect our power? Did they realize now what a potent force the PBRs were? Fuck, no! The entire operation proved nothing. Did the ARVN use us incorrectly? Did I offer enough? I don't know. The only known Viet Cong KIA (killed in action) was the one in the sampan whom we killed by accident. The ARVNs never made contact. They had two wounded by punji stakes; we had seven wounded by gunfire. I should have shot the woman—gunned down the men.

True, there were forty or more junks and sampans the Viet Cong would never use again. But they could be replaced easily. How did my wounded feel about this "devastating" blow for democracy and the Western ideal of freedom? What about a crippled boy and a dead little girl?

"SHIT!"

The little white birds were returning to the trees. . . .

The Bassac
Interdictors

———•———

I stayed off the river for the next several days, rereading old afteraction reports. There was no strategy to our efforts. We were being purely reactive to the Viet Cong, and since we fought where and when they chose, it was obvious that we weren't hurting them. I felt that my men had a high potential for aggressiveness, but it was not being used. Why? I talked to the patrol officers; there must be a reason. I knew from Linebacker II that they didn't lack courage or drive.

Their answers were the same: They felt constrained by the order to stay close to the center of the river and pull away from a firefight. Maybe they were right, but I didn't think so. I poured over the operation orders again. They said that "normally" a patrol should stay in the center of the river. Normally was my out. It said that a patrol "should," not "must," pull away from enemy fire and call in support. The writers of the op order simply espoused the safe way to do it. The op order also said, in so many words, that a patrol officer should pursue the enemy aggressively.

I knew the answer: We must hit the VC hard before the crossing even started. We needed an overall plan for the Bassac. We needed a strategy and the tactics to carry it out. I called the patrol officers together. "Our mission is to keep the Viet Cong from using the Bassac. We are to interdict any enemy supplies and men trying to cross, and attempt to pacify the so-called friendlies we come in contact with. Gentlemen, this is not happening. We are not carrying out our mission. The Viet Cong cross almost at their pleasure and at best we are a mere annoyance to them. The little sampan shoot we had at Tanh Dinh last week will probably just be an inconvenience. They'll just confiscate more from the people."

Faces dropped. Stares of anger came up at me.

"I know you're probably thinking, who's that sonovabitch up there whose been here a few months and has the gall to tell us we're screwing off. Well, be that as it may, from now on we have to figure a better way. I'm sure you're sick and tired of searching sampans and junks all day and finding nothing. Of course we won't find anything, except perhaps what some crook or black marketeer might be trying to get away with.

"Conventional wisdom says that the VC are receiving arms by junk or trawler to the southern coast of Vietnam. They move north through the U Minh forest across the Bassac and Mekong rivers, then deliver the supplies to the Saigon battle areas up north.

"This makes sense and is how I'd do it. We've got the Market Time operation checking all the junks and trawlers they find in the open oceans, but so far they've yet to make a big haul.

"This isn't surprising; we know how easy it is to get across the Bassac here. The VC are extremely clever and have been doing it for years. The Ho Chi Minh trail is still functioning, though the best of the U.S. Army and Air Force have been trying to shut it down for years.

"As you guys know, the VC are dedicated and ferocious fighters. They are patient and thorough and sometimes, I think, bulletproof. And the present government in Saigon doesn't seem to be the type to engender much love and loyalty from the people.

"Where does all that leave us? It leaves us with our same

old job of interdicting them here on the Bassac. Bassac interdictors I guess I could be called."

We were sitting in the officers' club and I had bought plenty of beer for everyone. The 512 boats were in such bad shape from their heavy use in the last several days that a day off the river had to be called. We were also low on ammo and were awaiting a resupply LST from Saigon.

"What I'm getting down to, gentlemen, is how we can do better." I took a huge swig of beer, waiting for the reaction.

Silence, then a little whispering at the tables. Chief Petty Officer Tanner spoke first. "As I see it we gotta hit 'em where they live, we can't wait for them to cross. We have to stop them on the beach." I made no reply.

"The chief's right," a young first class petty officer spoke up. "We can't be sitting on our ass in the middle of the river and expect to catch anything. Besides, I think it's a helluva dangerous place to be and boring as shit . . . oh! sorry, Commander."

Morton, now a patrol officer, stood up. "We should pop into those small canals once in a while just to let 'em know we're not patsies," he said with a little reluctance, staring at the more senior officers in the club. "And something should be done so that the Seawolves are available more often. Hell, they seem to be doing everything but supporting us."

"Doesn't the commander think that's . . . ah . . . mighty dangerous, sir?" said a lieutenant junior grade named Lange. Beads of sweat formed on his forehead, and he held his hands in his lap, squeezing one another.

"Yes, I know," I replied in a soft voice, trying to ignore him. Lieutenant (jg) Lange was a recent U.S. Naval Academy graduate. He had obviously done poorly at the academy, because his first assignment was to the amphibious fleet. The front-runners at the academy went to destroyers or submarines or into aviation. Amphibious ships or service ships, such as oilers, were not combatant vessels and therefore not considered career enhancing. Lange was a whiner and a spit-and-polish officer who always addressed me in the third person, even after I told him to knock it off. I had little tolerance for his type. I wondered how he had been selected for PBRs. We usually got only the best.

He kept it up. "The brass'll eat you alive if they find out you're going against the op order."

I looked at him, trying to keep the disgust out of my voice. "Read it again, closely! Besides, that's my problem, Mister Lange. I'm paid to take the bite."

"But I . . . ah, we . . . are the ones who'll get shot at."

"If you'd care to, sir, I'll cut a set of orders this afternoon and you can spend the rest of your tour on staff in Saigon. You won't get shot at up there," I said, this time not masking the contempt in my voice.

"Well, I think taking the offensive is a damn fine idea. It's about time we got off our ass and started hitting the Viet Cong," a young first class petty officer spoke up. "I've been doing it myself every chance I get, but I've been afraid I'd get my ass in a sling. Another thing, the order on conserving ammo in a firefight just don't seem right. We should have as much ammo as we need."

"I'm sorry, I didn't know we had an ammo problem until yesterday. I'll take care of that." I turned to Lieutenant Simon. "Any comment, sir?"

"Let's go for it," he replied, a thin smile emphasizing his point.

"We're going to have a lot of casualties. It's easy to hit a PBR next to the beach," Lange whined. I ignored him.

"Here's how I see it, then. On every patrol I want you to dash up one of the canals and dash right out again. Make sure it's done randomly. Canal running could get dangerous."

"Jesus Christ!" someone said.

"On this canal bit, take it slow. I think that it might be extending the op order a bit. We'll see how it works out."

"You know, Commander," Chief Tanner spoke up again, "I've done it twice in the last three months, and they've never got me. We've caught a few sampans loading up and destroyed them. I didn't tell anyone . . . thought I'd get in trouble."

"I've suspected that most of you have been pulling this off for some time, but now we're going to have a concentrated effort. I want everything, I repeat everything, reported. We must make damn sure that no patterns are formed."

Most of the men seemed excited as they shifted around in their chairs. They looked like tigers waiting for the cage door to open.

"I'm going to start keeping score on firefights and the number of kills and the amount of enemy equipment captured or destroyed. I'll publish it every month. It's about time you guys got credit for your work, and a few medals." More smiles. "The navy has never been much on medals, but you guys deserve them. I'm going to make damn sure you get them.

"We'll adopt the name the Bassac Interdictors, and our motto will be 'close and kill.' Anyone who doesn't want to play the game, let me know. There are plenty of jobs you can do without going out on the river. If you don't want to go with the program, please see Lieutenant Simon after the meeting . . . no stigma attached." No one moved. The room was silent again. "If any of the crews don't like it, same thing applies."

"That'll be the least of our worries, Commander," Chief Tanner said. "They'll love it." It pleased me to hear that. I hadn't known how this little speech would go over. I was nervous about it, but their enthusiasm was all the acceptance I needed. I knew I was doing the right thing—I hoped. The first dead PBR crew might change my mind. I'd be there with them; no one would be able to say I pushed instead of led.

"And stay out of Titi—that's a no shitter. We've got plans for that place. Okay, gentlemen, that's it!" I opened the cage.

Then I sat back and watched. The patrol officers took the bit in their teeth and exhorted their men every briefing. They went on patrol with new gusto. The firefights increased as the boats took the offensive; we had two and three a day instead of the normal two a week. Our wounded rate climbed. More and more boats came back shot up. Our ammo expenditure rose astronomically, but so did the Viet Cong's.

To spur on the men I became bold to a point of near recklessness. I was invincible. I lived only to be on the river, only to engage the enemy. One day was the height of foolishness: We were hitting a particularly persistent machine gun down by Juliet. No matter what we did, we couldn't silence it. No Seawolves were available and I couldn't get any artillery to blast it. Common sense would have demanded that we pull out and let it be, but all my big talk wouldn't let me get away with it.

We made another pass, a sweeping turn, and roared into shore, beaching our boats right in front of the nest. Both forward .50s kept up a steady stream of fire while the rest of us pumped close to a hundred rounds of M-79 grenades into the area. The Viet Cong machine gun didn't fire again. And to crown my stupidity, Thanh and I got out of the boat to search the area.

The bunkers at Juliet were formidable. There were three of them. The large one, about six feet across, was made of clay and straw, about three feet thick at its base and tapering to one foot at its top. Three gun-firing ports a foot from the bottom were four inches wide on the outside opening to two feet on the inside. These gave the VC a fine field of fire and made it almost impossible for our bullets to hit them from the river. The dried clay and straw was impregnable to anything but a five-inch shell or a direct hit from a mortar round; we had neither. Even a 2.75-inch rocket hit from a helo probably wouldn't penetrate. No wonder the VC always kept firing.

The top of the large bunker had thick logs covered with the same clay compound for overhead protection. The other two were small replicas of the first but had no overhead protection. Our 40mm grenade could take care of them. The only true vulnerability was the rear. How could I take advantage of that? Singapore fell in World War II because the British had their guns pointing to sea and could not turn them to stop the Japanese advancing from the land. Lesson?

Thanh nodded at the three-foot tunnel entrance in the rear of the large bunker, pointing to himself and then toward the entrance. I shook my head no and pointed to the river. We'd been here long enough. I was scared. As we withdrew, I pulled the pin from a concussion grenade and tossed it into the tunnel entrance. The loud, low rumbling of the confined-area explosion made me feel good. I thought I heard a scream.

The entire maneuver was stupid, the risk hardly worth the gain. I was trapped by my words—my actions had to bear them out. I was a child in an amusement park—a bloody, deadly amusement park.

Things started going well: a contingent of U.S. Navy SEALs reported for duty and started operating (a mixed blessing); there was a promise of more helicopters coming with their own repair facilities; new faces appeared wearing new jungle greens; repair parts trickled in; three replacement boats arrived; the rainy season would start soon, and the weather was cooling off.

Earlier I had hinted to the men that they might write their mothers and congressmen, telling them of our shortages and how lives were in danger because of it. I'm sure that the letters exaggerated, but they got some fast action. The Saigon headquarters was insisting that there was plenty of ammo and supplies in Vietnam. Theoretically there was. The brass in Saigon counted the supplies as in-country when the ships arrived at Saigon; unfortunately, the congested harbors prevented the ships from unloading. The troops in the fields were short but the country wasn't. I guess that some heads rolled, but we started getting everything we needed. I don't know how the rest of the U.S. forces made out, but we did beautifully.

And I met Capt. Robert R. Laske, U.S. Navy.

Captain Laske was an aging fighter pilot, well muscled and five feet ten inches tall, a hero from World War II and Korea and, lately, from command of an aircraft carrier.

Rumor had it that he was an ace with several Japanese Zeros and Korean MiGs to his credit. I wasn't sure. They said he had been shot down five times. Also rumored in the back bars of officers' clubs was that he failed promotion to admiral because of his insistence on bold, innovative tactics and procedures—not an easy cross to bear.

Four months ago I would have been awestruck by his credentials and reputation; now I needed no heroes. I was my own criterion. Captain Laske had become commander of all Game Warden units in the delta a few weeks before, but I had paid little attention.

One afternoon, he called a meeting of his staff and asked me to attend. Shit! What a waste of time. Then I heard him say, ". . . the patrols must be more aggressive, they've got to get out of the middle of the river."

I heard nothing else. His words were a reprieve. No longer did I have to live knowing that I was operating on the fringe of my authority. I left the conference room fifty pounds lighter—he had handed me a blank check.

Now I had someone to lean on. I wasn't alone anymore. I don't mean to imply that my responsibility was lessened one bit or that I could sluff off by quoting his words. But I had a sympathetic ear in court, a man who thought as I did. Later events proved that Captain Laske far surpassed any of us in aggressiveness and fighting spirit. He became an inspiration to everyone who met him. When my spirits were low, a word from him cheered me. A slight rebuke tore me apart.

Thanh and I continued our liaison with the outposts. Each time we visited one we harped on them to be more aggressive. We brought them supplies and building materials, which I now found easier to get, since I traded captured Viet Cong equipment for them. When the outposts were low on ammo, I resupplied them from my cornucopia. The PFs did not have the standard M-16 or M-14 automatic rifles that the Americans used but rather the old M-1 Garands and the big, cumbersome Browning automatic rifles leftover from World War II.

It was difficult getting the .30-caliber ammo for them, but

our barter system worked well, plus a little secret money I had control of from a "mysterious" source.

Early on I had met the civilian advisor of the Can Tho city police force. We became good friends and, though he always maintained that he was just a dumb flatfoot from the Midwest, his personal weapon—a 9mm Browning automatic pistol—belied his words. The 9mm automatic was the standard weapon of the CIA. Every one of them carried one; nobody else did.

We often discussed our problems—mine being mostly a lack of reliable intelligence, his, the lack of mobility. I questioned why a "police advisor" needed mobility, and he just laughed. He thought my plan of trading supplies for intelligence or buying it was a good idea. I corrected him on the buying part; just supplies and ammo, I said. He smiled, saying he'd see what he could do.

I thought no more of the conversation until a week later, when a clean-cut young man in a khaki bush jacket and dark sunglasses walked into my office and handed me an envelope. It contained 200,000 Vietnamese piasters—about $1,700 worth. I looked at him quizzically.

"Don't ask," he replied. "And someone will replenish that monthly," he said, turning around to leave.

"You want a receipt?"

"Just your conscience." I saw the butt of a 9mm Browning automatic pistol tucked in a shoulder holster as we shook hands.

The PFs were mistrustful at first but we slowly won them over. I could feel an actual camaraderie building between us. I needed them—they didn't really need me if they maintained the status quo—but I needed them. I needed an intelligence network and only in the villages was it available. I needed their assistance in hitting the bunkers from the land side, but I knew that this would take a long time. I reasoned that a bullet from one of their guns killed a Viet Cong just as dead as from one of ours.

Wherever I went, Thanh went; and he walked tall. When

we were together in the villages, he talked as if he wore my gold oak leaves. It got to a point that whenever we visited an outpost, the outpost chief would break out an honor guard and expect me to inspect, which I proudly did.

The first time it happened we were at Foxtrot. I saw several PF soldiers milling around but thought little of it. When we started to leave, they lined up at attention. I thought it odd, but attached no significance. As we left, I walked behind them, not wanting to disturb their formation. At the gate the chief saluted me with an agitated look of distress and chattered to Thanh.

"What's the matter with him, Thanh?"

"He say Thieu Ta too ashamed of his men to inspect them. He lose much face."

Christ! I blew it. I stood straight marching back toward the troops. I must redeem myself. At each man I stopped, looked him up and down, then sidestepped to the next. A marine drill instructor would have been proud of me. The PFs looked ridiculous with their oversized American helmets and their World War II M-1 Garand rifles that were easily two-thirds their height.

At one man—mustering all my recollection of how John Wayne did it—I yanked the M-1 Garand rifle out of his hand (God, let it be clean), snapped open the bolt (bruising the hell out of my finger), and pointed the butt skyward to look through the barrel (it was clean).

"Very good, soldier!" I barked in Vietnamese, tossing the rifle back to him and continuing down the line. The chief beamed. We saluted. Thanh and I marched out of the outpost.

We visited Golf more than any village. Ong Tam, the village chief, controlled three nearby outposts and all their men. Juliet was in his area. To win him over would bring them in. Also, it seemed that Co Hue and Co Bac would always show up for the chitchat. They were nice to look at. We became good friends, Co Bac and I.

I wanted her for an agent. She was a schoolteacher, and children see and hear many things. And children talk. One night she asked me if I would give her a ride into Can Tho from Golf. On the way, I asked her if we could use the schoolchildren to get information. At first she said no, then later said maybe. I dropped the subject and sat on the engine covers.

"Does the commander mind if I sit by him? It is cold."

"No, of course not, I'm sorry . . . here," I said, extending my hand as she sat next to me. Her leg and thigh pressed firmly against mine. She didn't feel cold. Little flames pricked my skin where our bodies touched.

"Is the commander angry with me for not reporting on the Viet Cong?"

"No! Ah . . . no, of course not." I tried to keep my breath from betraying the physiological manifestations that were taking place. I wanted to move away but she was so damn soft.

She laid her hand in mine. I was glad it was dark. I could imagine the story the crew would tell about this. I was relieved to see the lights of Can Tho come into sight. My attempts at conversation had been awkward and sophomoric.

"Good night, Co Bac," I said.

She stood demurely on the pier, waving as my $75,000, well-armed, combat-ready, eight-ton fiberglass junior-high-school hayride pulled away. "Chao, Commander."

"Chao . . ."

About nine months before, work had started on a new base a mile or so down the river toward Can Tho, almost right across from the big Vietnamese air force base at Binh Thuy. Work had progressed slowly, but the base was finally taking shape. Unfortunately, money ran out and so did the civilians. The base was ninety percent completed. That didn't sound bad to me until I found out that the last ten percent of a project such as this consisted of little things, such as installing electrical fixtures, painting, hanging doors, installing locks, installing laundry and galley equipment, checking out power systems, and so on.

The navy solved this problem, as they solved so many others, by simply putting the average sailor to work on them. For instructors, they moved in a small contingent of Seabees. It was amazing—a barely satisfactory Seabee is worth three civilian workmen. An outstanding one is worth perhaps ten. Under Seabee tutelage and hard work, the base took shape rapidly.

The new base held the promise of tropicalized barracks—a vast improvement over the cement rooms we now lived in. In these barracks, air could circulate freely because the walls were mostly screen and louvers and the ceilings were high and open. The plumbing would be American, and no longer would a shower be a thing to dread—we might smell better. We would have more modern repair shops and the finest kitchen equipment. Office space would be streamlined and not a hodgepodge of isolated rooms.

Security would be improved by the addition of watchtowers and a high fence. New communications equipment promised better control of the boats and helos, plus faster message service from Saigon (a dubious plus). In all, it would be a significant improvement in our standard of living. We would also have our own helo pad and aviation repair shops.

The war was falling into place for me. I finally felt that I understood what was going on. The Bassac divided into three areas of combat: Tanh Dinh Island, Juliet, and Dung Island. The Juliet and Tanh Dinh Island complex was the Can Tho crossing corridor—a classic guerrilla logistics effort.

Dung Island was a mystery to me. We never received any hard intelligence of any major crossing activity. There were no extensive canal networks on the northeast bank of the Bassac leading to Saigon, as there were around Tanh Dinh. Nor were there many canals on the southwestern bank or any villages of any size on either side of the river. Also, from a crossing point of view, the Bassac was extremely wide between Dung Island and the mainland to the northeast. The Seawolves detected nothing on their patrols. The land on both sides of the river was flat and open. But the Viet Cong shot at us. Rumor had it that Dung Island was a training camp and an R&R center.

These three areas of combat accounted for ninety-percent of the action. Of course, the rest of my TAOR had to be patrolled, too, for there was no assurance that the Viet Cong would confine themselves to these three areas; often they did not.

The war was where the enemy shot.

Juliet

———◆———

In the dancing light of early evening could be heard the low rumble of the coxswains warming up the engines of Delta Patrol. Heavy thunderclouds formed to the south, and periodically a flash of lightning tried to prolong the day.

Unassociated voices drifted up to my office. "Don't forget the coffee." "Yeah, okay, how about me getting some sodas?" "I don't think they have any ice." "Hey! . . . got any oil?" "Gotta match?" "My ass and your face." "Fuck you, Smith!" "Best piece you'd ever have." "Knock it off, Maxwell . . . load that ammo." "Tote that barge . . ." "No one likes a wise ass." "Sorry, Boats." "You guys, don't forget kerosene for the stove." "Hey, Hanks, I hear your whore's got the clap." "Can't have, she wears white socks." "Don't pull the plumbing out!" "Damnit! Knock it off and get those PBRs ready." "Sorry, Boats."

Chief Tanner, the patrol officer for tonight's sortie, sauntered into my office, which did double duty as the briefing room and intelligence center—both quite poorly.

"Evening, Commander. Killed three thousand of those black bugs on the way over here."

"How do you know?"

"Counted 'em."

Lieutenant Simon, the briefing officer for tonight, walked into the room with the two boat captains. "Hot as a mother tonight," griped Taylor, the boat captain of the cover boat, Delta Two.

"Probably rain like hell before we get back. I hope so anyway. I hate this damn heat . . . and I hate the smell, too, always like sweet, rotting garbage," Chief Tanner said to no one in particular.

"Wear a surgical mask, Chief," I answered sarcastically. We were informal here on the Bassac. Verbal exchanges were far more familiar than if we were shipboard or, I guess, any other place in the navy. We were pretty close here on the Bassac, sharing the same hardships, the same danger. We didn't need to act as though we were on an Annapolis drill field. As it turned out, one was familiar only with those he respected. This applied to both officers and men.

I was a mustang; I had come up through the ranks. This was my style of leadership. I had joined the navy as a seaman recruit when I was barely eighteen and had gone through officer candidate school (OCS) ten years later.

"Okay, you guys, listen up," Lieutenant Simon started. He stood in starched greens at the large, 1 : 50,000 scale map of the Bassac area glued to the wall. Lieutenant Simon exhibited an almost paternalistic devotion to his men, and he took great pains to give them the best briefing possible. Though he never gave them fight, fight, fight talks, he nonetheless encouraged aggressiveness. From his attitude and questioning I knew that he felt ambivalent about the current tactics on the Bassac. He knew that they were successful—agents had attested to that—but they were dangerous. I suspected that Lieutenant Simon wished for the good old middle-of-the-river days.

"Standard communications plan . . . and, damnit, watch your security violations. We're getting blasted by those security guys sitting on their air-conditioned asses in Saigon monitoring our radio transmissions. They say we're giving too much information over the air, so watch what you say and use your KAC codes for messages to the ops center."

The KAC was a classified booklet that allowed someone in the field to communicate by using the numbers substituted for words. The KAC codes changed frequently so no pattern could be established. They were cumbersome to use and in a firefight you just didn't have time. Our thoughts were that if you're in a firefight, the VC knew where you were anyway. I was an offender myself—not using the KAC codes. It would be best if we used them.

Taylor interrupted: "I'd like to get those bastards out on a boat in a firefight sometime and see how much fuckin' KACing they'd do!"

"BE QUIET, Taylor! All you do is goddamn bitch," Chief Tanner snapped, raising his voice and rapping his fingers loudly on the desk.

"Sorry, Chief," Taylor replied, screwing up his lips.

"Never mind, Taylor," Lieutenant Simon broke in again. "Those COMSEC guys are just doing their job. You do yours and try to use the KAC. Delta has the southern river fork from five point five to kilo. Bravo will be on the other side by Tanh Dinh. You'll be relieving Charlie.

"Got some info that there might be a big crossing at Juliet. Of course, we've heard that for the last three nights, but we can't pin it down. Keep your eyes open; you'll be in the hot seat. Supposedly it's good info this time. If you don't get in a firefight, whip past Tanh Dinh and put a few rounds into it. We're catching a lot of shit outta there lately and—"

"Damn, Commander," Chief Tanner interrupted, turning toward me. "How many wounded we pull outta there lately? When they gonna do something about that shithole?"

He said "they," but he meant me.

"Well, Chief, it's been about sixteen in the last month or so. We're putting a little op together right now."

"Well, you can count me in," he replied.

Lieutenant Simon continued with a little bite in his voice from all the interruptions: "That's all I have . . . oh, yeah, one more thing. Some weird flags are flying again. I agree that Ho Chi Minh is probably a bastard, but you can't fly flags to that effect. Only your battle ensign and the commander's burgee pennant are authorized. Yeah, I know it's not you guys but knock it off anyway. And wear your flak jackets and helmets, understand? Wait . . . I'll give you your latest KAC." He bent over to take the booklets out of a small safe and handed them to Chief Tanner. "Any questions?" he asked perfunctorily.

"Well, yes we do, sir," Chief Tanner said as he got up and walked over to the blowup map of the Juliet area. "You know, Commander, you're always asking for ideas and plans to fight this war . . . hell! There ain't any textbooks, you know that. Well, the guys from Delta and me were having a beer the other night and talked about it. We'd like to try that old towing-a-boat trick, but this time we figure we got a better angle." He paused for effect.

Lieutenant Simon had an "oh shit" look on his face.

"We know it's never worked before, but now, with, as you say, a big one brewing at Juliet, maybe we can pull it off. We figure the problem in the past was that we never fooled the VC that two boats were proceeding away after one of the boats was dropped.

"We've been practicing for a while and we got it down."

"How? What do you mean?" Lieutenant Simon asked. He had started pacing in front of the briefing map. He kept glancing at me. Questioning.

"Go on, Chief Tanner," I encouraged.

"The trouble is the sound. We've worked it out to run one of the engines on the pullaway boat at a different speed, with one engine cover removed, while simultaneously reducing the speed on both of the engines. We've tested it and it works."

Chief Tanner and the two boat captains looked at me, then to Lieutenant Simon. Silence. I was going to wait for Lieutenant Simon to make the first move. Thirty, forty seconds passed. Lieutenant Simon just stared at the Juliet area map.

Lieutenant Simon was a good man, a good officer, but he often tried to play it too safe. I don't think he particularly liked me or approved of my tactics. Being based together made it cumbersome for him because I played such an active part in his day-to-day river activity. I could appreciate his problem. I faced the same thing with Captain Laske's staff, although not Captain Laske himself. I could feel the resentment they had for me as my men and I played hero while they could only watch.

All the staff officers were volunteers. They had come to fight, and all they did was watch and make reports to Captain Laske and Saigon on what my fellow river division commanders and I did. I was the focal point of their frustration. To complicate matters there were far too many of them for the little bit of meaningful work they had to do.

Lieutenant Simon glanced at me. I nodded yes. Silence.

"You guys know that there could be a lot of VC back there and the ambush boat could really get it," Lieutenant Simon finally said. His lack of commitment had been driving me crazy. "Whatta you think, Commander?"

"Your call, Lieutenant Simon."

"OKAY! But for Christ's sake be careful. At the rate we're going we can't keep enough boats up as it is, and we're down to only nine crews instead of the thirteen we're supposed to have."

"There's sure enough officers around here, though," Taylor offered.

"That's enough, Taylor," Lieutenant Simon barked.

I'm glad Lieutenant Simon agreed to the plan. If he hadn't, it would be the last time these guys would offer anything. I wondered whether, if he hadn't, I would have countermanded his decision.

"So that's what you guys have been doing, eh?" I commented. "I was trying to guess what the games were just off the dock for the last few days. Just remember, it's clear and open here by the base . . . the sounds of the engines will reflect differently from the jungle riverbank."

Chief Tanner glanced at me as he and the two boat captains walked out. "Got it covered, Commander," he said, winking.

"Hey, Taylor," I yelled after them. "Good luck on the chief's test tomorrow!"

"Got that covered, too," he replied.

Lieutenant Simon and I walked over to the O club. "What's the movie?" I asked.

"Don't know . . . whatta you think, Commander?"

"About the movie or Delta?"

"Delta."

"Could get messy down there. Who did you say was on the other side, Bravo?"

"Already thought of it. I'll have them stay to the lower end of Tanh Dinh just to be close," Mr. Simon replied.

"C'mon, I'll buy you a drink. What do you think of Chief Tanner?" I asked.

"A pretty good man, though a little too aggressive. I think he should take it easy out there, and I've told him so. The patrols think he's great. He always takes care of his men and has a good record."

"He tells me he wants to go to OCS. Do you want to recommend him? I understand he studies every free moment he has."

"Yes, sir, I think we should."

"Write up something and I'll sign it."

As Delta moved away from the pier the movie on the patio was just starting. It was a war story—training films we called them—about some British major taking kayaks up a German river to blow up a ship. As I sat he was just cocking his beret at a jaunty angle, telling his men how dangerous it was going to be. I should have gone with Chief Tanner and his jaunty-angled beret.

A couple of hours later I walked over to the ops center. Lieutenant Simon was sitting there. "Any word from Delta?" I asked.

"No . . . guess the plan didn't work. Had some rain; moon's up now—be pretty light down there for an ambush. How was the movie?" he replied.

"Pretty good . . . a little phony though. No one's stupid enough to try to run an operation like that. You seen it?" I asked.

"Yeah, I liked it. You seen it, Rankin?" Lieutenant Simon asked the watch officer, but before he could reply the radio blurted in.

"Roger, Bravo, cover me. We're pulling out."

"Pulling out? Bravo, cover me? What the shit's going on?" Lieutenant Simon yelled.

"I don't know, sir," Lieutenant (jg) Rankin pleaded. "I haven't heard anything over those radios for two hours . . . reception is rotten tonight."

"Handlash Delta . . . Handlash One Actual. Request status. Over," Lieutenant Simon radioed out with that calm in his voice that professionals reserve for when they're really uptight. When Lieutenant Simon said the word "actual" in his call sign of Handlash One, it meant that it was actually Lieutenant Simon himself instead of just his control station.

We waited. "Shame the Seawolves are down this evening," I said just for something to say.

"Roger, Bravo, hose her down, hose her down . . . no, we're okay. Got the loudmouth in tow. He's not saying much. Over."

We heard no reply. We waited.

Then: "Handlash One, this is Handlash Delta. Coming home . . . op textbook quality. Delta Two's got four hurtin' . . . not critical . . . request ambulance. Over." Chief Tanner's voice came in calmly as if he were just chatting.

"Roger, Delta, this is Handlash One. Do you desire to make Can Tho for medevac? Over," Rankin answered, his tone just as indifferent as Delta's.

"Negative . . . negative . . . hometown's the best. Tell the Interdictor that it worked. Estimating five zero. Out."

I doubted that the radio wave propagation was that bad. The patrol officers would shift frequencies on their second FM transceiver so that they could discuss things and not let the ops center know. They knew that everything they said over the regular net would eventually get back to Lieutenant

Simon or me or, worse, Captain Laske's staff. I'd more often than not done it myself.

We waited. There was nothing we could do. The U.S. Air Force ambulance arrived from the Vietnamese air force base and they waited. The air force had a much more extensive dispensary than we had, and they took care of our wounded, including flying them into Saigon if necessary.

Captain Laske came into the ops center, which was really his command post; we were just users. He asked for a brief and Lieutenant Simon told him all that he knew, including the original ambush plans. Captain Laske looked at me. I nodded yes. "Good aggressive planning, Lieutenant Simon."

"Handlash One . . . Handlash Delta. Kilo tango dash bravo five . . . sierra sierra dash tango one. Over."

"Roger, this is Handlash One shackle echo whiskey."

A disgusted voice came back: "This is Delta . . . wait. Out."

I gave Rankin a scowling stare. He was grandstanding for Captain Laske. Chief Tanner had used the KAC code to tell us that he was passing Can Tho and would be arriving in fifteen minutes. Rankin had asked him to use another set of identification codes to authenticate his identity. One gave out two letters and received two in reply that linked to the original two. It was fast and efficient but hardly needed now. He recognized Chief Tanner's voice.

Chief Tanner was being sarcastic when he used the KAC code in the first place. It was even compromising, because if the VC had the electronic sophistication to follow events, and if they had agents to observe PBR movements, they could bust the KAC codes in minutes.

We'd already given the communications security (COMSEC) boys enough good stuff to let them finish out their night in glee. My superiors in the chain of command and I would receive a full bullshit report in the morning.

"Here they come," someone yelled.

Maxwell, Smith, and Hanks sat on the engine covers of their towed boat. I could see their battle dressings even in the dim light of our electric bulbs slowly pulsating from a sick generator we had to use.

Chief Tanner on the lead boat made a perfect landing, and the corpsmen were on the boat before it even tied up. Lieutenant Simon and I were standing on the dock. Captain Laske stayed on the barge; he didn't want to interfere. Taylor was standing in the coxswain's flat, staring at the lights, his left arm bandaged.

"It worked, Commander. We're shot up a little but it worked. Goddamn, it worked!" Chief Tanner said, coming up to us.

"How many wounded, Chief?"

"Well, it looks worse than it is. My coxswain got one in the leg—minor, and the after gunner's arm got burned from the barrel on his fifty . . . and I'm thirsty as hell."

It started to rain again. I glanced up at Captain Laske and motioned with a thumbs-up that everything was okay. The base support people were already lifting Taylor's boat out of the water as we walked off the pier and to my office. I fought the urge to question them but it had to wait—these men were still suffering from residual shock.

We sat in my office in silence drinking cold beer for perhaps five minutes. "It worked, Commander, it goddamned worked. We did some powerful interfuckingdicting tonight," Chief Tanner finally said.

"Tell us about it, Chief," Lieutenant Simon answered.

Taylor still sat there in a sullen silence, an angry scowl covering his face.

"We were hauling ass to station . . . it was completely dark by then and a few drops of rain were coming down. As we approached five point five I called Taylor in the cover boat to come alongside. Just as he did, those assholes from Charlie coming off station came whipping by us at top speed. Our boats smashed into each other and threw my coxswain against the armor plating. That's how he hurt his arm."

"That's why those boats always look like shit. No one

cares a damn about things here anymore," Taylor blurted out, giving Chief Tanner a withering stare.

"Typical boatswain's mate shit," Chief Tanner responded. "Well, I asked Taylor if he still wanted to go through with this and he said yes. I—"

"I didn't think anyone was going to desert me either," Taylor broke in with disgust.

"What's your problem, Taylor? You sure sound like you got a burr up your ass," Chief Tanner replied. "You got anything to say, Taylor, spit it out right fuckin' now!"

"Forget it, Chief. Me and my boys can take care of things."

Lieutenant Simon looked at me. We had a problem. "Go on, Chief," he said.

"It was 2230 . . . moonrise would be in a couple of hours or so. I took Taylor on a long tow and carried out the procedure just like we planned. Taylor, you take it from there."

Taylor didn't answer right away. He was a big talker, often talking way too much, and was always in some kind of trouble over his mouth. "Come on, Taylor, what happened after Chief Tanner took you in tow? Were the engine sounds convincing from where you were?" Lieutenant Simon almost demanded.

Taylor just looked at Lieutenant Simon with a blank stare. "Goddamnit, Taylor, you okay? Do you want to go to the hospital?" Lieutenant Simon said, reaching for my phone.

"No . . . no, sir, I'm okay." He paused again, then started in a rapid-fire delivery: "We passed Foxtrot and Golf and I knew that Juliet would be coming up fast. The chief's boat sounded just like we practiced—just like two boats. We passed Hotel and India . . . Juliet was coming up next. My boys looked a little tense. Can't say I blame them; I didn't feel so chipper myself.

"The chief pulled in close to the beach. We were sloppy on our response, since, of course, we had no rudder. It's hard to tow a PBR that ain't got a rudder. Just before we got to

Juliet, Maxwell on the forward fifties cut the towline. We could hear the chief's boat pulling away and it sure did sound authentic. We eased out the anchor and gave her plenty of line.

"We were all alone, Commander, all alone," Taylor said, then paused again.

"Go ahead," I urged.

"I hated the waiting. Every sound was magnified. My guys were breathing so hard that I swore the entire Bassac could hear us. Maxwell, on the forward guns, looked cramped and uncomfortable. You know, that forward mount just ain't made to sit in for a long time. But that's where he had to be.

"Maxwell is a helluva smoker. I imagined he was hurtin'. Smith, at the helm, was comfortable, sitting on the little fold-down stool behind the armor plating around the coxswain's flat. He kept fondling the throttles like he had the urge to push them back and forth. I could hear low, murmuring Vietnamese voices from the beach. I wondered if the other guys could hear them. Could they hear us?

"I knew that Hanks on the after gun was uptight. Someone told him that little flying bugs always clustered around the Viet Cong. If it were true, there must have been a helluva lot of VC out there. Hanks really believed it . . . it was no joke to him. Hell, Commander, I've tried to tell him it's stupid but he still believes it. How can a bug determine a man's political affiliations? I asked him. But he still believes it."

I could see Chief Tanner becoming more irritated. He was tapping my desk with his fingers. I reached out and put my hand over his. He raised his eyebrows in disgust, nodding toward Taylor. I wanted to scream at Taylor to get on with it. Lieutenant Simon sat back, seemingly unconcerned with the long diatribe.

"I don't mind telling you, Commander, I was mighty uptight. I couldn't see anything, not even with my starlight scope, and that's usually pretty good. I was blind out there. Ask the chief. Dark, wasn't it, Chief?"

"Yes, it was dark out there, Taylor," Chief Tanner said

soothingly, paused, then in a burst: "For Christ's sake, Taylor, get on with it. I'm tired as hell and I want a drink."

"Okay, okay . . . but the commander wants the whole story, don't you, sir?"

"Go on, Taylor," I replied.

"Well, that's when we heard them . . . very low voices. I inched back to the after gun and alerted Hanks. He'd already heard them. I crawled back forward and had Smith alert Maxwell on the forward mount.

"Then I heard the dip of oars and the muted thud of wood hitting wood. It was coming straight from Juliet. The tide was pulling us and the anchor rope was taking a strain. I wanted to scream, man. Sorry, Commander, but it was tough waiting. Then we heard a sampan engine start up from somewhere inside Juliet." Taylor continued smoking, lighting one cigarette after another. His voice rose in pitch as he talked. "Then the first sampan lit off its shrimp-tail engine. We still couldn't see 'em but they were close enough. I was just going to open fire."

Chief Tanner sat back, cleaning his fingernails with his survival knife. He was trying to keep his cool and stared at Taylor impatiently. The chief knew that Taylor had to talk. Had to get it out of his system.

"Then it happened . . . WOW! A huge bolt of lightning crashed down and it was like daytime. You saw it, Chief, didn't you?"

"Yes, I did, Taylor . . . go ahead," Chief Tanner answered again in a calm, low voice. He was one cool sailor. I envisioned him on the bridge of a destroyer.

"There they were pretty as you please . . . two of 'em only thirty feet away heading right for me. Were they surprised. We blasted 'em with everything we had. Both their engines were going now and they were moving fast into us. We started taking fire bad. Then the beach opened up and goddamn I didn't know what to do. I screamed at Smith to back down the engines and for Maxwell to cut the anchor. Me and Hanks just kept firing. Hanks was new to our Delta crew but he's good with the gun and he kept blazing away.

"We got one of the sampans. Its coxswain fell over the shrimp-tail outboard and canted the damned thing to the right. The sampan kept turning in tight circles.

"Maxwell couldn't get the anchor loose and the coxswain kept backing down the engines as Maxwell kept hacking away at the anchor line with his knife. Chief, there was nothing I could do but keep firing. I . . . was alone . . . I . . . where were you, Chief?"

"I want you to know, Taylor," Chief Tanner's slow voice broke in, "I want you to know that after the first shot I was on my way back . . . hauling ass back to you. I couldn't have been more than five hundred yards away from you when it all started. Now go ahead and for God's sake cut it short. The commander doesn't wanna know all that shit—"

"Well actually, Chief, I do. Don't rush yourself, Taylor, just go on," I said, nodding to Lieutenant Simon to get the bottle of scotch I kept in my filing cabinet for moments like this.

To ensure accuracy, it was important to debrief as soon after an incident as possible. The longer you wait the more distorted the story becomes. Not because a man consciously changes it but rather the mind plays tricks as the ego moves in to embellish the story, or shame takes over to protect a questionable act, or, worse, the story grows out of proportion for self-aggrandizement.

All four of us had a heavy shot of the scotch as Taylor continued. "I knew that two sampans were there but I couldn't make them out very well. It was so confused and I knew I was taking hits from Juliet. I just kept firing my sixteen, reloading and firing. I kept screaming at Maxwell and Smith to do something. I saw Hanks on the after fifty fall, get up, and fall again. I yelled at Maxwell to fuck the engines and help me but he was already firing his sixteen at the sampans. Chief, I didn't even know what was going on anymore." Taylor paused, taking another swallow of scotch. "Where were you, Chief?" he pleaded.

"I was there, Taylor, go on."

"Finally, I heard the forward fifties start and I felt better. We were trapped and I couldn't get loose. I saw the circling sampan coming right for us. I fired point-blank at a VC firing right at me. I swear to God the slugs were going right through him but he didn't fall. The sonovabitch just kept coming. His whole sampan was on fire and a body was hanging over the side but he kept coming. He threw something at us . . . it was burning and landed aft and exploded into flame, right by Hanks.

"I dropped my sixteen and rushed back, but Maxwell beat me to it with a poncho, slapping out the flames. I could hear Hanks screaming. I picked up my sixteen and started firing again. The burning sampan seemed to drift away, still blazing. Then the other sampan just disappeared, just blew up. Poof! . . . it was gone."

Taylor stopped. Only an oscillating fan broke the silence. Taylor stared at me, then at Chief Tanner, then at Lieutenant Simon. He appeared to be looking for verification. "I ain't shittin' you, it just blew up . . . disappeared!"

"It was me, Taylor, it was me. As I said, after the first shot I came about and headed back, pedal to the metal. The whole scene was lit up by the fire you started in the first sampan. We had an easy shot at the second one and my boy on the forward mount took it out with only two short bursts. We were right on it, Taylor. We blasted Juliet with everything we had. I couldn't do anything with the first one because he was just too damn close to you. Your rounds were going everywhere."

"God! I'm sorry, Chief, I just didn't know where you were. So much noise, and the fire. I'm sorry, Chief. Sorry."

We sat silent again. "What happened then, Chief?" Lieutenant Simon asked.

"Well, that about wraps it, sir. I kept up the bullets going into Juliet until I figured everyone had bugged out. Then I eased over to Taylor's boat, helped put out the fire in the stern, cut his anchor line, bandaged them, and towed 'em home. Mighty short patrol."

My phone rang. Lieutenant Simon picked it up. "Commander Sheppard's office. Yeah . . . yeah . . . well, yeah, thanks. Appreciate the information. Bye."

Simon hung up and turned to Taylor. "Your guys are okay, Taylor. A few scratches and a couple of burns. . . . Just a little more, you guys, then we'll let you go. What did the sampans look like?"

"Like the blue one we got outside. Long and skinny and it had two shrimp-tail outboards. Could those mothers move," Taylor replied, rubbing his bandaged left arm.

"That arm okay?" I asked.

"Sure," he replied. "Just a scratch."

"Yeah, sure . . . go ahead, Taylor," Lieutenant Simon said.

"It looked like there were only two men in each sampan, but they were mighty low in the water, like they were carrying a lot of cargo. It happened so fast that I'm really not that sure."

"That's about what I saw, Taylor. It looked like a classic large-scale crossing attempt. They didn't make it this time," Chief Tanner said with some measure of finality.

"You got anything more, Commander?" Lieutenant Simon asked, turning toward me.

"No . . . thank you, Chief . . . Taylor. Good job tonight."

Chief Tanner smiled at me as he got up to leave, taking the last few swallows of his scotch. In the tone of voice that only respected chief petty officers can get away with, he said: "Well, Commander, we did some mighty powerful Bassac interdicting tonight, eh?"

"Smart ass! . . . Say, Taylor, you gonna be able to take the chief's test tomorrow?" I asked. "If not, I can fix it for you to take it later."

"Piece of cake, sir, piece of cake."

Taylor and Chief Tanner walked out together and I could hear Taylor apologize again for doubting him. "I'd ride with Delta any day," Chief Tanner replied.

Blockade

———————•———————

To exploit Delta's hit I established a blockade of the canals on the Juliet side of the river from just south of Can Tho to south of Cu Lao May. This encompassed the Can Tho crossing corridor. I reasoned that the Viet Cong had to come out of one of those canals if they wanted to cross. The Viet Cong had a well-established route here and though they could change to another location, it would be time-consuming and cumbersome. If Delta did interrupt a major crossing, the pressure would be on the VC to attempt another, which, under normal conditions, would not be difficult for them.

If I kept a boat in the middle of the river outside each canal, the Viet Cong would be reluctant to cross until they became desperate. Then they would have to fight.

It would take eight boats and would be hard on the crews and the maintenance people, but I considered it worth a try. I assigned the bottom three stations to RIVSEC 511, from the T, and the upper four, plus the roving blockade commander station, to RIVSEC 512. RIVSEC 511 was to continue a two-boat patrol on the lower Bassac. With some grumbling from the OinCs, the boats went to station and there they sat.

After a few days, the blockade settled down to a routine. The boats went, waited, and returned. The reliefs staggered every two hours so as not to lose the continuity of the blockade. Days passed; nothing happened. No Viet Cong crossed. No Viet Cong fired at us. I took blockade commander about every third day. It was a boring job. Traffic had come to almost a standstill. The up- and downriver traffic routed itself to the other side of Cu Lao May to avoid the constant search by each boat.

I started hearing complaints from the men about the lack of action. Maintenance complained about having difficulty keeping enough boats in an up status. The OinCs complained that their crews were overworked and needed more rest. The Game Warden staffies made sly innuendos that I employed my boats inefficiently.

Even from Saigon came rumors about wasting time and hazarding the boats. But I waited. Each day, I pressed home the point that the boats were to remain on station. They were not to assist another boat in a firefight unless it was an emergency. I insisted that any boat coming under enemy fire withdraw and engage only perfunctorily at a distance. I demanded that blockade integrity be maintained. I demanded that the boats remain on station, moving around. I didn't want us to be an easy sniper target. I demanded that the blockade commanders rotate their boats from station to station to show constant movements.

The first week passed into the second; the second into the third. Not so much as a lone sniper round passed overhead. Nothing happened with the Viet Cong, but something happened with us: Morale dropped. A few fights started at the enlisted men's (EM) club; uniforms got sloppy. The men bit at each other. On the river, heat was our greatest enemy; it ate away at our endurance, at our composure, at our very sense of self. Boredom filled any nook the heat missed.

Three weeks passed into four. One night five sniper rounds teased the boat at Juliet. The boat captain returned one thousand in angry answer. I chewed his ass for it. I gleaned the intelligence reports to see if there was any hint of an ammo shortage to the north. None at first, but then a remark here and a hint there indicated that the Viet Cong in the northern provinces might be hurting for ammo. Also, reports came in that unfamiliar troop movements were occurring along the river. I reminded myself again never to trust intelligence reports.

Whenever I was the blockade commander, Thanh and I visited the outposts. They told us stories of troops massing and ammo stacking up. I didn't know whether to believe them. They knew of the blockade and my hopes. The Vietnamese strive to please. If they thought it would please me to hear these things, they would tell me. Whether they were true or not carried no moral ramifications.

I had been keeping the U.S. Army advisors informed on the operation. I went to them again and told them what was happening. The time was ripe for a grand sweep of the entire area. The American advisors agreed; the Vietnamese did not. I just couldn't make them understand. The Vietnamese were so fragmented in their RF, PF, and ARVN corps and division command structure that they were virtually administrated into inaction.

I couldn't even get the Juliet area designated as a free-fire zone. This designation would allow us to fire at will into the area after checking with the district chiefs for permission. Here, unfortunately, we would have to call two districts for permission. This calling in was important because the sectors could be running an operation in the area. Remote, but possible. Tanh Dinh was a free-fire zone controlled by the Tra On subsector, and they never ran anything. We had carte blanche from them to fire into Tanh Dinh and Titi at any time.

I had the misfortune of having my hottest combat area extend over two provincial boundaries. Neither province wanted to commit troops to these frontier areas. The 9th ARVN Division, who were also responsible for this area, said that it was just too far from their headquarters and more important operations.

The air force said they'd like to help but only division

level and province chiefs could authorize preplanned air strikes. The province chiefs and the ARVN Division commanders used their helos and jets for their operations, such as they were. There were no American troops operating in the Mekong Delta and no subsector artillery support batteries could range to Juliet. I had failed again to get support.

I made up my mind that never again would I run an operation predicated on the help of any forces other than those that I personally commanded. I wanted every American on the Bassac under my control. I wanted to run the PFs in the villages. I wanted to know every time a sparrow's wing fell.

"Thanh," I barked one day, "how can I get the PFs to run operations with us?"

He laughed. "It would be very difficult. Only the village chiefs can control the PFs. Why would they want to run operations and run out of bullets? They need all they have just to fire into the jungle at night," he answered. I knew that the outposts came under harassing fire by the VC about twice a week.

"Bullshit! We're getting plenty of ammo to the outposts and Golf. What's the key, Sergeant?"

"You know, Thieu Ta, they want fancy weapons: M-79s, M-16s, M-60s. Can you give?"

"No, but for any operation, I'll lend them as many as they need. How's that?"

"I think good."

"We'll tell them that if they'll operate with us, they can use our guns and never again will they want for ammo, batteries, medical supplies, or anything else I can get. Ong Tam is our friend, isn't that true?"

Thanh smiled that damned sure-rich-Yankee-sure smile of his, answering, "Yes, Commander." Walking out of the room, he added, "That will help, Commander. We must speak to Ong Tam before you go home to the United States."

My last offer was simple. They never ran any operations on their own, but I thought it would be a meaningful gesture.

I could furnish a cache of M-16s and M-79s to Ong Tam. It would be illegal, but just by surveying out the weapons as combat losses, stating that they were dropped into the river during a firefight, would let me amass enough for Ong Tam to be a big man in the village. Some staffie in Saigon might think we were pretty sloppy and catch on sooner or later, but fuck 'em. I had a war to fight.

I wondered why Thanh called me Commander instead of Thieu Ta.

Without ground support I realized that I couldn't exploit the alleged buildup of troops. Every day the intelligence reports gave new indications that the Viet Cong up north might be running low on ammo. Were they? Or was my ego just reading it into the reports? I'm sure it was. From the west bank, reports still came in of large, unidentified troop movements. The Can Tho crossing corridor was becoming a growing boil; each day brought it closer to a head. I could sense the tension in the villages. I could see the stress on the faces of the many who knew but would not tell. River traffic trickled to a stop.

The boil festered.

"Pull the blockade" came unasked-for counsel. "Pull the blockade; you're going to get it."

"The boats are falling apart, Commander. Pull the blockade."

"Goddamn, Commander, when we gonna get some action?"

"Sorry, Commander, we just can't give you any troops. Pull your blockade."

Captain Laske said, "Don't falter. You'll win."

The boil was ready to erupt.

The firefights started—one or two at first, growing to four and five a day. The boats were catching hell. One day all eight boats returned from the blockade full of bullet holes and wounded. The blockade commanders rotated the boats at Juliet so that all hands got their share of death row, as it was now called. Lieutenant Commander Dave Williams was right there taking his turn. He was a great asset, not only by filling in as an aggressive blockade commander but also by deflecting the verbal flak from the staff.

As fortune would have it, the Seawolves were up during this period, and every firefight they were overhead, working the area with their guns and rockets. What a comforting sight to see those birds roll in, unleashing their sting against the bunkers.

The Viet Cong could wait only so long to move their supplies and men. The fighting in the north demanded replenishment. The supplies coming in by sea to the southern coast of South Vietnam had to move north. Only the Can Tho crossing corridor offered the Viet Cong an established, well-manned, and organized route.

Was this my fantasy? Was I such an egomaniac that my mind created things that weren't there? NO! damnit, it wasn't. They had to cross here. And here, by God, I'd wait.

The wounded rate climbed. Manpower was becoming a problem. I sat for hours staring at the map of the Bassac. I made artificial limits for myself. The next firefight, I'd pull the blockade. It came to pass, but I didn't. Well, next wounded, I'd pull it. It came to pass, but I didn't. Well, I'll wait for the next intel report. It came, but I didn't leave. Any hour I felt that the Viet Cong would try to fight their way across. And if they did, they would lose. I instructed the blockade commanders that when the big push came, they were to pull in all but the two end-station boats and fight it out.

My police advisor acquaintance stepped up the surveillance and inspections on the big vehicular ferry that crossed the Bassac from Can Tho to the northeastern bank. They started to catch more contraband weapons, to arrest more suspicious-looking men. He was having a field day, but it quickly dried up.

The blockade was by now down to seven boats—the best we could do out of both river sections. I even had to secure the normal patrol that 511 was maintaining on the lower

Bassac. We were having trouble maintaining repair parts. We couldn't last much longer. As a boat came in out of commission for a major component, it was cannibalized to repair other waiting boats.

"Am I doing wrong, Captain Laske?"

"You've got quite a reputation in Saigon, Interdictor."

"Good or bad? . . . 'Interdictor'?"

"Interdicting—isn't that what you do? Some think you're insubordinate and dangerously insane and should be relieved. Others think you're just what we need in the delta."

"What do you think, Captain?"

"You're still here."

What we were losing in boat availability we initially made up in crew morale. These were no longer days of inaction. The men talked constantly of the big push and of what a field day it would be. They all hoped—well, at least most of them hoped—that when it came, they would not be stuck on an end station. I overheard one crew making a deal with another to trade stations if they got stuck during the rotation at one of the ends.

My men did not possess a death wish; they were ordinary sailors who, for a short period in their lives, were somebody. They controlled a slick, powerful fighting machine that let them play out the fantasy of the American hero. Americans are nurtured on hero worship: the folklore of the western gunfighter, the hot fighter pilots, the derring-do of the PT boats, the revolutionary war, the Indian wars, the Alamo, ad infinitum. Now these men were part of it.

We lived in a precarious paradise. Of the thousands of rounds fired at our boats, only a very few hit, and of these, significantly fewer struck a man. Our biggest concern was the shrapnel caused by a bullet hitting the armor sheets around the coxswain's flat and the two sheets placed vertically on the engine covers. We also knew that even fewer of our bullets hit the VC.

We were mismatched foes. The VC had armor-piercing rockets that, whenever they hit, usually went right through our fiberglass hulls without exploding. We had only heavy machine guns and light rockets that just bounced off their bunkers. If the situation became reversed, we'd all be dead in a week. I was hoping to change our side of the equation.

Since the bunkers were impossible to penetrate with our .50s, and since it was difficult for the VC to shoot accurately through the firing ports of their bunkers, we were usually at a noisy standoff. The firefights, though, were having a telling effect. To minimize our exposure, the boats were now moving at top speed randomly around and between their stations. This consumed so much fuel that we usually had two boats at a time off station, refueling and rearming at Can Tho.

The long trip back to the T was too tiring on the crews from 511, so we berthed them at Tra Noc. This caused crowding and too much extra work for the maintenance people. I tried to get the T moved upriver but failed. I did the next best thing and moved some of their maintenance people to Tra Noc's base support. Everyone was working his ass off except me; I just agonized on the validity of what I was doing.

I found out what war is: responsibility—a grinding, constant, day in and day out responsibility that just didn't go away. A responsibility that ate away my self-confidence like a cancer, making me question every decision, every action I contemplated, exhausting me to the very marrow of my bones.

The constant action was telling on my men. They lost their bravado. They came back gaunt, staring, tired. They sat in the club drinking. Too many wounded buddies were rushed to Can Tho. Too many firefights. Too many hours on the river. Too little room to maneuver. Too few boats.

Logistics would be the weapon that destroyed the blockade. Eight more hours! In eight hours, at 2015 if nothing significant happened, I'd pull the blockade.

Then the break came! A U.S. Air Force FAC's Cessna O-1E light aircraft was flying around with nothing to do; his primary mission of supporting an ARVN operation had been cancelled. He was without a job and had a full section of loaded jets, called fast movers, at his disposal.

It seems that just the night before, a few of my officers had been over at the Binh Thuy Air Base O club having dinner and a few drinks. After five or six drinks they began to bemoan the lack of support the air force and army were giving us. They were boisterous, almost spoiling for a fight. A couple of FAC pilots decried their mission of bombing trees for the ARVN. They commiserated. The result—the FAC would check in with the PBRs when their primary mission aborted. It happened the very next day.

The blockade commander was one of the FAC drinking buddies from the night before, and, as luck would have it, the FAC had been completely briefed between their gin and tonics. A few curt words of greeting passed as the FAC swung low over the tree line.

"Can't see a thing," he reported, pulling up high over the river.

"Try again, we know they're in there," the blockade commander half pleaded.

"Roger that." The O-1E of the FAC skimmed the treetops, searching out the enemy. Odds were against him seeing anything; with an FAC overhead, the Viet Cong hid. They knew the fury that he could bring.

"Sorry, Handlash Unit, there's nothing down there. Gotta go home. See you later. Over."

"Thanks anyway. Out."

The light plane turned inland to the south and disappeared. Five, ten minutes passed. Then, like a shell, the FAC buzzed low over the trees, palm leaves slapping his landing gear.

"GOT 'EM! GOT 'EM!" he shouted over the radio. "About a hundred fifty! Shifting frequency. Out!"

Machine-gun shots from the jungle followed him as he pulled up and circled back over. From somewhere, barely minutes later, four F-4 fighter jets arrived.

What can be said about a jet air strike? They arrive, the

area erupts into a flaming holocaust, and they leave. The noise is deafening from their engines and bombs and the ERRRRRRRRRIT! of their 20mm miniguns blasting down, with several thousand rounds of bullets each pass. When they drop their 750-pound cans of napalm, two to an aircraft, the explosive detonates high in the treetops, raining flame and fire to the ground below. Like a brilliant volcano, it lights up the area for hundreds of yards, even in broad daylight, and then all is silent, save the crackling fires and an occasional scream.

The air force lanced the festering boil.

The FAC swung in low again. "OKAY! Handlash Unit, you owe me a drink; there's about a hundred twenty-five dead ones down there who won't cross. Over."

"Roger. Thanks, Shotgun. Regret I can't give you a BDA [bomb-damage assessment]. We'll pay up tonight. Out."

That night Thanh and I would make another reconnaissance run and decide what to do with the blockade. One hundred twenty-five Viet Cong was a good score for our effort. I secretly hated to have the air force get credit for them, but, after all, they were the ones who got them. I arranged to go out on the 2000 patrol and went to my room to get a few hours' sleep.

I lay there in a pool of sweat, ambivalent about the kill. The facts were there—more than a hundred Viet Cong were dead—but my troops and I had played only a gathering role in the whole show. We were simply the wall that stopped them, the ones who herded them to where the great white hunter stood. We could but cheer as he raised his rifle, felling the beast.

God bless you, air force; isn't it all the same? What difference does it make who administers the coup de grace? A dead Viet Cong is a dead Viet Cong—by napalm or .50 caliber. But we had waited so long. Is this how the line feels every time the quarterback makes a flashy touchdown? Am I going mad? What is it with me—must I grandstand every play? Is this supposed to be your own little war on the Bassac, Sheppard? How many men would you have sacrificed to your ego in order to fight the 125 if they had decided to force their way across? I felt ashamed; I felt like a childish fool. The sun was casting long shadows across the Bassac. The whir of my fan grew dim. Disappeared.

"God bless you, air force."

The river returned to normal. Sampans moved up and down and the Viet Cong crossed behind us.

The People

————————•————————

Boat availability improved as the maintenance crews finally got a chance to work on them. Within a few days our patrol schedules were almost back to normal. A few new men arrived each week from PBR school to replace our casualties and those men who reached their DEROS (Date of Estimated Return from Overseas). The manpower shortage slowly eased. Lack of repair parts and the lengthy procurement time was still bothersome, but ammo was no longer in short supply. Thank you, Moms. We got along.

Since our PBR base was the headquarters of the Game Warden operation, we had a seemingly unending stream of visitors from Saigon. Each wanted a briefing and a PBR ride. Both were time-consuming and monotonous, but guests had to be accommodated. Though initially I found the visitors cumbersome, I realized that they had a genuine interest in what we were doing and only wanted to help. I began to feel sorry for them. They wanted to be in the war; they wanted a piece of the action. Most of the officers in Vietnam were volunteers. Most of them had dull, mundane desk jobs: REMFs (rear area motherfuckers), rear echelon commandos, barracks troopers, and rear support personnel. I could hardly blame them for coming out to where the war was, hoping for a little action.

Even from Washington, D.C., they came. To get the big picture, they said. Silly me, I thought the people in Washington had the big picture. If they were coming to our microcosm for the big picture, I wondered what in hell Saigon and Washington were doing. All kinds of people came, with all kinds of titles. The most ludicrous was four civilians showing up from some small, southern Illinois town to get the businessman's view of the war.

The worst ones, the ones none of us liked, were the "hometown" reporters. These were the guys who contracted with several different, usually small, local U.S. newspapers to write stories about "our boys in the war." Each time one of them came around, they expected us to parade out all the men from the areas they represented so that they could interview them. It seemed a little phony to me and the men didn't usually care for it. The reporters' stories were often distorted and crude and full of half-truths. It didn't take me long to put a stop to it.

Not to be confused with the "hometown" reporters were the bonafide war correspondents. Unfortunately, all reporters carried the title of war correspondent, but the difference between the two was immediately apparent. Instead of asking for a parade of men from towns X, Y, and Z, the professional war correspondents asked only to go out on patrol, and they were welcome. Not only were they amiable chaps, but in a pinch they would man a gun, and another gunslinger always helped. The stories they wrote were true and authentic, not what some kid said while sitting at the bar sipping a beer. I held these war correspondents in the highest esteem.

Many visitors asked about our drug problems and general state of morale. I replied that there was no drug problem and morale was great when we had action. Most did not believe me. We had read about and heard stories of the problems the army was having up north, but since there were no U.S. troops around us, all we knew was what we read in the papers. The thought that any of my men would frag an officer was unthinkable—ludicrous.

What most of the visitors didn't realize was the quality of the men we had. All PBR sailors were prime volunteers and went through grueling qualifications to be allowed to volunteer. For the most part they were mature, middle- and senior-grade petty officers. They were the cream of the fleet. They all had their reasons for being here, and the navy took care of them with great incentive programs.

The officers were elite. Each knew that a successful tour of duty meant rapid promotion and choice assignments. The screening was extremely rigorous and demanding. An example of this was in the prison-camp phase of our survival training. There, if an officer showed any weakening, he was immediately removed from the program—no second chance—and the instructors, rightly so, were real hard asses. How did Lange get through? Was I missing something?

Another indication of the quality of the men showed in the reporting of wounds. An enlisted man wounded twice rotated home. An officer could receive three wounds before transferring out. Because of this the men asked that wounds not be recorded after the first one. If the man went into the hospital, there was no choice. Many wounded who should have gone to the hospital received treatment by our corpsman, which was left unrecorded. This was the mettle of the Bassac Interdictors.

Such was the war at the home base. When things got too bad, I would go on patrol; when they got worse, I simply shifted my flag, which meant my burgee, to the T and operated from there for a week or so.

But nowhere was I completely free of the tentacles of the Game Warden staff. As time passed the situation degenerated. I don't know if it came from the flamboyance of my men or from the tight-knit camaraderie we enjoyed and the staff could not. Or maybe because I was such a smart ass. Although the staff could not easily get to me, they could harass my men.

I was on the T to get away from Tra Noc for a while and to run a few patrols on the lower Bassac. On the T all fresh water had to be made by distilling seawater from the South China Sea. Evaporator plants on board ship work best when the outside water is cold. As the outside water temperature increases, the efficiency of the "evaps" decreases dramatically. The water temperature of the South China Sea is about eighty degrees Fahrenheit. The T didn't make much water.

The ship's water-starved laundry couldn't clean and press very many PBR sailors' clothes. And with the rationed water, few men could take a shower or even shave. The T was crowded and my men were either on patrol or asleep— they had little chance to get a haircut. They didn't look like fleet sailors steaming into San Diego for a hot weekend's liberty, but they didn't look all that bad either, considering the way they had to live. This was a way of life for them; they were here to fight on the rivers and, my God, they were good at it.

A month or so before, the chief staff officer, a commander on the Game Warden staff, decided that the appearance of the PBR sailors should meet recruiting-poster standards. He put a message out to all Game Warden forces to sharpen up. We considered it a bit of a joke but nonetheless tried to appease him around Tra Noc, where it didn't take much effort to be sharp. Since the chief staff officer never strayed far from headquarters, the rest of Game Warden appeared as they always had.

As luck would have it, while I was on patrol around Dung Island the chief staff officer was taking a helo ride and landed on the T. He became livid when he saw the appearance of the men. Never mind taking note of what caused it; all he saw was the results. He left immediately and sent a message to Lieutenant Henry.

```
R 140117Z                                          ROUTINE
FM: CTG 116.1
TO: OINC RIVSEC 511
INFO: COMRIVDIV 51
      COMRIVRON 5

BT
UNCLASS-EFTO
MILITARY SMARTNESS
A. MY 020837Z APR 67 NOTAL
1. YOUR BOATS AND THEIR BEARDED CREWS ARE UNACCEPT-
ABLE. THEIR SLOVENLY APPEARANCE IS PARALLELED BY THEIR
STAGGERINGLY UNSATISFACTORY SEAMANSHIP. YOU ARE DI-
RECTED TO COMPLY REFERENCE A AND REPORT BY MSG NLT
17 MAY WHEN ALL BEARDS ARE REMOVED AND HAIRCUTS ARE
IN LINE WITH NAVY, NOT BEATLE STANDARDS.
2. FOR COMRIVDIV 51: REPORT UPON RETURN TO TRA NOC
CORRECTIVE MEASURES INSTITUTED TO ENSURE LONG TERM
COMPLIANCE REF A. IF YOU CANNOT EXTRACT CONFOR-
MANCE MY STATED SMARTNESS STANDARDS FROM THE OINC
RIVSEC 511, I WILL ASSIST YOU IN OBTAINING A MORE DE-
PENDABLE REPLACEMENT.
BT
```

In one fell swoop he implied that I failed to control a situation by not taking authority and exercising leadership and control over one of my river sections. He got to Lieutenant Henry by alluding that he was incompetent to lead and could not even control his men's seamanship. And worst, stating that Lieutenant Henry was a candidate for relief from duty for cause was tantamount to ending any future promotion for him. By using his operational title, he tried to imply that he had muscle to carry out his threat. I returned to Tra Noc immediately to defend my men.

The effect the whole affair had on morale was devastating, not only on the Bassac but on the entire Game Warden operation over three other river areas equal to mine. How easy it was to lead from an air-conditioned officers' club.

After a week or so, things calmed down. I had won but was scathed and blooded. Then, the inspector general arrived from Saigon. After the obligatory questions about drugs and morale, he tested some of our operational procedures. One test was to see how fast our boats could get under way in an emergency. We failed. At the critique, Lieutenant Simon and I got our butts chewed. It'll never happen again, we reported. Assholes!

Action on the river was slow. It had been a week since I lifted the blockade, and we'd had only one small firefight since. Our help-the-people program started again and progressed nicely. We were helping them improve their villages. The supplies we begged or borrowed, and delivered as fast as we could.

The men made up small packets with the goodies they received from home. These they passed out to the sampans and junks that they stopped on the river. In some small measure this made up for the inconvenience we caused them, and was a lot more fun than giving out the many different leaflets we got from Saigon. The leaflets extolled the virtues of the government and how pleasant life would be without the VC. They said that everyone must cooperate with the government and all would live happily ever after. Most of the men were courteous and friendly. Those who weren't we weeded out.

We had Polaroid cameras on each boat and found that taking pictures and giving them to the people right away gave the Vietnamese immense joy. They would laugh and point at the magic. We expended a lot of film entertaining the boat people.

These stories, however, lacked excitement and were therefore rarely told or reported. One seldom read in the papers of the compassionate acts of the men. I was more guilty of this than all the others. I kept official score on how many fights a man had been in, how many Viet Cong he had killed, how many enemy hootches and sampans he had destroyed, how much contraband he had captured or sunk. No one counted the number of sick people he gave medicine to, or the number of small wounds and cuts he cleaned and dressed. No one took pictures of the boat engineers fixing sampan engines from the parts they purchased with their own money. No one counted the good things. No one, perhaps, save the Vietnamese people themselves.

As our program progressed, the people's fear of us turned to indifference and then to a slow, reluctant acceptance. The people who once scorned us would now smile and offer their hurts to our treatment, which if they were serious enough, we would rush to the hospital at Can Tho. Some boat crews ran fix-it shops and the Vietnamese brought small items to be repaired. The people were not hostile to us.

The Vietnamese policemen or one of Thanh's men who accompanied most patrols were gaining great status in the eyes of the river people. They were our primary language link; without them we could not have been one-tenth as effective. Officially they reported to the district police chief. Unofficially, they took their orders from Sergeant Thanh. This arrangement was okay with my police advisor acquaintance as long as I passed to him any "interesting" information.

The immediate and most dramatic payoff of our help-the-people program was the information. A few of the river people who were once taciturn and sullen now chatted with us and told us things. They told us where the tax collectors were, when there had been Viet Cong in their villages, what the Viet Cong's plans were, and, best of all, where they had seen an ambush being set up. Most of the information was old and useless; much was of no value, and some could be plants by the Viet Cong, but nonetheless it was refreshing to get it.

One incident reported from Saigon concerned a *hoi chanh* (returnee, a Viet Cong who returns to the government's side) who turned himself in somewhere north of Saigon. When asked why he'd returned, he said, "My relatives live on the Bassac and Americans treat them nicely."

We were leery of the Chieu Hoi program, the open-arms program under which the hoi chanhs returned. Ong Tam told us that the VC would use the program when captured to avoid the prison camps, or, worse, to catch us off guard and attack us as we helped them. The story was that every VC had one of the tens of thousands of Chieu Hoi passes that the air force dropped all over the delta. They were instructed to use them just before capture. My instructions were to treat anyone saying he was a hoi chanh as a prisoner until we delivered him to the Vietnamese officials.

Unfortunately, after a particularly bad firefight, especially after one where our men received heavy wounds or died, the men took it out on the river people. At best they used only verbal abuse; at worst, rough physical handling. These incidents were difficult to control and would set our program back for weeks. It was hard to blame the men.

It appeared natural that the blame be put on the Vietnamese. It was their fault we were here. It was their fault we were bored. It was their fault we were hot. It was their fault we were miserable. It was their fault we were getting hurt and killed.

Perhaps medical evacuations, medevacs, were our most important humane action. We were always on call to any Vietnamese who required medical attention. We averaged eight to ten a week. The villages or outposts would call us by a prearranged signal and we would go in and pick up the patient, then rush him to Can Tho. By radio we would arrange for an ambulance to be waiting. These trips included the sick or injured person and also some or all of his family.

The pitifully understaffed condition of the Vietnamese hospitals forced the patients to furnish their own help, including preparing the meals. Long-term patients even had small garden plots planted behind the hospitals. This self-help situation accounted for the deplorable overcrowding of the facilities. The families were exposed to all the diseases, and often, in the process, became patients themselves.

The largest amount of evacuations came from the city of Tra On. Here all injuries for miles around filtered in, and the American advisors could call us directly by radio. Fifty percent came from Tra On. The Viet Cong were active around the town and the outlying areas and, for protection or downright cussedness, placed booby traps everywhere. Kids play. Kids trigger wires. Kids die. Those who didn't were carried into Tra On to await the PBRs. But the PBRs might have been far off and by the time they arrived, the wounded were all but dead. Most of the wounded from Tra On died before we got them into Can Tho.

The VC knew well our procedures, and we were sure they staged attacks on civilians just to generate the medevac. Once we were off station they would cross. What could we do?

My first life-and-death decision came early on from a medevac out of Tra On. A patrol diverted to evacuate a wounded PF to Can Tho. Five minutes after the patrol left Tra On, the advisors radioed for assistance for an outpost under attack. The patrol officer called in, asking for instructions on contradicting requests. The decision passed to me. I agonized. The man was gut shot, the patrol officer reported. He'd probably die if we didn't get him to Can Tho immediately. The outpost was under heavy attack, he said, and no helos were available. The VC were too close to the outpost perimeter for artillery support.

What should I do? I agonized for what seemed like hours. I looked at the faces around the ops center for a hint of suggestion. Nothing. Shit! Support the outpost, I ordered. Netted out, maybe more lives would be saved that way. The PF died.

Medevacs are heartrending things and, though we did our best, how can you save the life of a child whose stomach has been blown apart? What do you do when they die in your arms? You weep, that's what you do. You curse the Viet

Cong for causing it, and you curse the oppressive heat that makes the wounds have a retched odor that permeates the boats, clogs your nostrils, and clings to your clothes. You can look away but you can't escape the smell and the cries. You try to save the others.

We helped one young mother limp aboard my patrol one sultry afternoon in Tra On clutching two small children. One—a young baby—dead, its mouth still clutching at the nursing breast where it died. There was no torso or legs below its chest. It was horribly white, all its blood gone. The other child she nestled in her right arm. It, too, was dead—it had no face. She wouldn't let go of either child and her arms couldn't be pried loose. She was in a state of deep emotional shock and was easily led about as she chanted a soft Vietnamese lullaby.

She was the wife of a PF soldier and was playing with her children when a Viet Cong walked up and tossed a grenade into their game. She had snatched up her wounded children and ran two miles into Tra On. We got there perhaps an hour after it happened.

Two PF soldiers put her in the stern of the boat. She sat there as we sped toward Can Tho. She rocked back and forth, muttering the children's song. I tried to talk to her but she just sat there covered with blood, eyes with a distant, incoherent stare. I reached for one of the bodies she held, but she screamed. I withdrew. It was too much for me; I vomited over the side of the boat. I sat with her again. With a wet towel I washed her face as best I could. I sang and rocked with her. She tried to smile. I wept and rocked.

As we pulled into the Can Tho Canal, she handed one child to me. I laid it gently on the engine cover. She handed me the other. I placed them together and covered them with my blouse. When I looked back, her eyes were closed. She was dead. I felt her pulse; she was dead.

I wondered if God, too, were dead.

"Sir, Binh Thuy's on Fire!"

———————•———————

It was Sunday. I decided to take a day off, the first since I had arrived. I slept till ten o'clock, got up, shaved, and strolled into the ops center. "Anything hot?" No, all quiet, was the answer. I read the message traffic but nothing required action. I had a cup of coffee and sauntered back to my room.

A few weeks earlier I had moved onto the barge so that I could be closer to the ops center. My room had the added advantage of being periodically air-conditioned by a 1940s fifteen-kilowatt Onan generator powering a dilapidated compressor that worked at best only intermittently, but it was working today.

I finished reading *Alice in Wonderland* and started on *Hawaii*. I read till noon, got up again, had lunch and four beers, chatted with a few of the boat crews getting ready to go out at 1300, then went back to bed. I slept till 1700, cleaned my .38, and for half an hour dry-fired it at the Viet Cong flies buzzing around my room.

Charcoal-broiled steaks were for supper. I washed two down with a full bottle of wine and walked slowly back to the barge, stopping several times on the causeway to talk to the guys fishing. I didn't know what they did with the fish they caught; perhaps they gave them to the maids.

I checked the day's traffic again: nothing. "I'll be in my room," I told the watch officer and added just for something to say: "Call me if anything comes up."

"Read the *Stars and Stripes* today?" he asked.

"Yeah."

"Wonder who the irresponsible commanding officer on the Bassac could be, sir."

"No one likes a wise ass jg," I answered. "Weren't you on watch when it happened?"

"Yes, sir. Great that Bradley's okay. Asshole should've kept his mouth shut, though. He'd have been in fat city by now."

We were talking about an incident that happened the week before. Petty Officer Bradley was the forward gunner on PBR 127 when his patrol was called into Tra On at dusk for a medevac. As they were tying up to the pier, someone in the crowd tossed a hand grenade into the boat. The report over the radio as they sped back to Can Tho was that Bradley threw himself on the grenade and took the full force of the explosion in his chest. Luckily, the patrol officer said, it was only a small-order detonation and Bradley had his flak jacket on, but he was in bad shape.

I was in the ops center talking to a reporter from the *Stars and Stripes* when the calls came in. "Wow! Wow! Wow!" he kept saying. "Whataya think of that? Whataya think of that? Wow! Wow! Whatta story. Whatta story. Whataya think, Commander? Whataya think of that?"

"Well," I replied, "that's the sorta thing Medal of Honor winners do." The reporter wrote and filed his story right there in the ops center without waiting to interview anyone. He was doing the Pulitzer Prize jig.

The story appeared the next day quite accurately from what he knew from the radio transmissions. He erroneously quoted me as saying that Petty Officer Bradley would be awarded the Medal of Honor. I got my ass chewed. No one except Captain Laske believed that I didn't say it. I received a censure for allowing the reporter to use our telephone to call his bureau in Saigon.

Hell, I wasn't going to stop a reporter from calling Saigon, especially one from the *Stars and Stripes.* Weren't they on our side? I could only imagine the additional trouble I'd be in for that. The staffies in Saigon were having a field day on me.

The *Stars and Stripes* and the wire services kept the story going with follow-up articles from interviews with the boat crews and gory photographs of the shrapnel-battered PBR 127. Each story got me deeper in trouble. Bradley was recovering in Japan—unconscious but progressing well. I had heard that the *Stars and Stripes* even flew his family to Japan to be there when he regained consciousness.

The *Stars and Stripes* today said that he regained consciousness and when questioned by the crowd around him on what he was thinking when he threw himself on the grenade, he replied: "What are you talking about? I heard 'GRENADE IN THE BOAT' and as I was running away I tripped and fell. Don't remember anything after that."

The story in the paper ended with: "It is regrettable that an irresponsible commanding officer on the Bassac could have initially made such misleading statements to the press."

"Well, anyway, call me if anything else comes up," I said again to the watch officer.

ERRRRrrr! ERRRrrr! ERRRRrr! The emergency siren blasted into my head. I jumped up, glancing at my watch as I frantically pulled on my trousers and boots. It was 2203. I was putting on my flak jacket and pistol belt as I rushed into the ops center.

"Binh Thuy's under attack, Commander! The boats are getting under way!" By Binh Thuy the watch officer meant the Vietnamese air force base across the main road leading into Can Tho.

"Okay! I'll be on the river," I said, rushing out. I ran to the dock, arriving just as the last boat disappeared around the far side of the barge. Damn! I guess they really took it to heart when they got their butts chewed about being too slow for the inspector general. They must have all rushed over from the club when they heard the siren.

I dashed back to the ops center. By the time I got there, the watch officer had everything under control and the boats were on the way to their base-under-attack blocking stations. There was nothing for me to do.

"Just Binh Thuy Air Base is gettin' it . . . nothing anywhere else," the watch officer reported. "They got some pretty bad fires going."

"Yeah? I'll be over by the club if you need me. Might as well enjoy the fireworks while I can. Let me know if the boats make contact."

The fires lit up the sky as I walked down the causeway from the barge. They must really be in trouble. A rocket went long, missed the air base, and landed in a field three hundred yards from me. There was a terrible explosion, noise and dirt everywhere, but no damage done. I felt detached, scared, but with that distant fear one feels in a good movie. It was there, but I was only a bystander.

Binh Thuy Air Base was our best insurance against an enemy attack. The airfield, with all its fighter planes and "Spooky" AC-47 gunships, was a much better target than just ten puny PBRs. Consequently, we never got it, but Binh Thuy did. Not so good for the air force, but better for the navy.

"Good evening, Cap'n Laske, sort of like the Fourth of July, eh?" Jesus! I thought. What a stupid thing to say.

"Miss your boat, Interdictor?" he asked.

"Yes, sir. They were too fast for me." I felt like a damn fool. "How many rounds have landed do you think?"

"I don't know."

A breathless messenger running up from the ops center interrupted our conversation. "Sir, Binh Thuy's on fire!"

"Yes, I know," Captain Laske replied stoically.

"They want some help from us if we can spare the men," the messenger shouted.

"Very well, put out a call for volunteers."

"Well, Cap'n, with your permission, I'll go man a hose. No excitement around here."

"Be careful" was his permission.

The sailors gathered and we jumped into a couple of trucks and barreled down the road; the ruts and holes almost tore us apart. We made the trip in three minutes, zooming into the approach road and screeching to a halt in front of the gate. Glaring at us were the startled eyes of the American and Vietnamese air police huddled in their bunkers. They jumped out, brandishing their machine guns. I was afraid they were going to shoot.

"STOP!" one of them ordered. "You can't go in there. The base is under attack."

I got out of the front seat of the truck and the air policeman pushed his M-16 into my chest. I tried not to notice. "We're here, soldier"—I knew they hated that—"from the navy base across the road to help fight the fire."

"You can't come in. The base is under attack."

"Yes, we know. Please call someone."

"The base is under attack," he turned and yelled at me as he walked back into the bunker.

Seconds later he came running out, ordering the razor-wire barricade moved, waving us through.

Our driver jammed on his brakes and came to a stop on the edge of the flight line, the other truck full of sailors almost smashing us from behind. Fifty sailors and I jumped off the trucks and ran in all directions. I stopped and stood there, staring, trying to comprehend what was going on.

"Jesus Christ! Jesus Christ!" I kept saying. The sight of the holocaust glued me to the spot. A huge, open hangar, about three hundred feet long, was engulfed in flames. The three Skyraider A-1 aircraft inside were burning a bright cherry red. The flames had reached the 20mm ammunition and started cooking it off. In one corner of the hangar was an ammo storage room. It was burning. The sharp crack of the exploding 20mm rounds sounded like rifle fire. Tracers from the loads split through the sky, making eerie, death-hinting patterns through the smoke.

On the flight line fighter planes and helicopters crackled with brilliant white magnesium flames. The bent and twisted aircraft in various stages of consumption were unreal, grotesque. A half-blinding, stinging smoke hung low over the ground, making breathing an agonizing, coughing chore. And the heat crushed my body. Rocket rounds still screamed in, landing on the other side of the field.

I looked around for someone to report to, but except for the sailors, who were now returning to the trucks yelling and milling about, no one was in sight.

Small groups were beginning to organize themselves, but we were no better than a confused, frightened mob, knowing something had to be done but not knowing what to do.

"QUIET! QUIET!" I yelled. "PAY ATTENTION. GODDAMNIT, QUIET!" The men looked for the source of the command. At a time like this people will follow the slightest amount of leadership.

"YOU! MISTER LANGE, take ten men and move those trucks and cranes away from the hangar." He grabbed the ten closest and whipped off. It surprised me that he had volunteered to come.

"CHIEF TANNER!" I singled out. "Take ten men and dig up some fire-fighting equipment. HURRY!"

"Aye, aye, sir!" he replied, running off with another group toward what appeared to be a firehouse.

I pointed to two first class petty officers: "YOU TWO! On the double, split up the rest of the men and start moving those undamaged airplanes out of danger. Get with it!"

The trucks and I were suddenly alone. What to do next? I'd done as much as I could for right now.

"YAHooo!" I heard, turning to see Chief Tanner riding the running board of a small fire truck. They lurched to a stop only inches from me. There were two air force men in the cab.

"Move it!" Chief Tanner commanded, pointing to three

sailors. "String out those hoses. Get the pumps started!" he yelled at the airmen as they jumped out of the cab. Four other men came running up with four huge-wheeled CO_2 fire extinguishers.

"Hit that first helo there. Never mind those in the center," I ordered. It was too late to save any of the burning planes. All I could hope for was to keep the others from catching fire. Within seconds the men were spraying the chemicals on the burning planes near the ones that had not yet ignited.

The pump on the fire truck wouldn't start. "Never mind," said a sailor holding up a riddled hose. "These are useless."

"Go get more hoses!" Chief Tanner said in disgust to the frightened airmen. They scurried off. "And snap it up," he screamed. Chief Tanner was from the old school.

I ran over to the aircraft-moving detail and lent them a hand. We couldn't budge one helo on its flat tires. One sailor ran to get the truck. They hurriedly hooked it up to the helo with a length of damaged fire hose and took a slow strain. The helo groaned its reluctance to move, turning the fire hose into a violin string ready to be plucked. The heat of another burning helo next to us allowed only a few moments of work at a time. The damaged helo started to move. Slowly. Slowly.

"Watch out!" someone yelled. "Clear out, it's falling!" The starboard landing gear, riddled with shrapnel, collapsed under the strain.

"Run! Run!" I screamed. The men leapt for safety. One tripped. I whirled to grab him. He rolled away just as the huge rotor blade came smashing down on my right hand and arm. Christ! Not my right hand again.

Three men rushed over and pulled the rotor blade off me. My whole arm throbbed. They dragged me away just as the burning helo crumpled over the same spot.

"Pull this fuckin' helo outta here!" I barked. The truck strained and the helo slowly, grindingly, scraped to safety.

They worked fast. Someone wrapped my bleeding hand and arm with a T-shirt while the truck pulled all the other birds to safety.

I turned my full attention to the burning helos. We abandoned the useless fire truck. Chief Tanner's men kept the fire bottles coming, but we couldn't control the incredibly hot magnesium fires. I continually cautioned the men to move in slowly, to use short blasts. If the fire flared up any worse, we'd need all the extinguishers we had. I didn't want to be caught with empty bottles.

The plane-moving detail split up, rushing around to find more equipment and to help move the trucks and cranes by the hangars. They were having difficulty. I couldn't worry about that right now.

High-octane aviation gasoline leaked from the damaged airplanes. I dispatched two extra bottles to hit it if it looked as though it was going to flame. With a shattering blast a helo exploded fifty feet away, throwing burning hot metal down on us. The gasoline ignited in a blinding flash. The positioned CO_2 hit it instantly and kept it back.

"More bottles! More bottles!" I screamed, but the men were already rounding up as many as they could. I had the horrible feeling of giving orders that were already being carried out, a stupid result of my fear and excitement.

We were losing the battle. Where were those damn bottles? Where were the hoses? Where were the air force people who were supposed to fight these fires? In a few moments the whole flight line was going to blow. We had about twenty CO_2 bottles in play. I kept getting the report, "There are no more bottles, Commander." I screamed back at them, "Get 'em anyway—move it!" They always returned with more bottles, more breathless, more exhausted.

I was about to order my men to clear out. We were pushing our luck even now. If those planes went up, we'd go with them. On the other hand, if we let those planes blow, many soldiers would die for the lack of air support. The planes couldn't be replaced easily.

One man threw down his nozzle and ran, screaming, "We gotta get out. We gotta get out!"

I was ashamed but didn't have the time to stop him, nor did I know who he was. But he did.

I kept circulating, encouraging the men. Their faces and arms were turning beet red from the intense flames. "Keep it up . . . we're licking it," I lied. They knew, but remained at their futile task. We couldn't stay much longer.

From behind, I heard: "Gangway for the hoses!" As I turned, two hoses started spraying the gasoline flames. Rainbows formed in the water fog from the nozzles. Two more hoses arrived and Chief Tanner came dragging another. We had a chance. We were hitting the fury from three sides now and slowly beating back the flames. I stationed myself between two hoses, grabbed the nozzle men by their shoulders, and moved into the hottest part of the blaze.

I was actually enjoying it. I was having fun. I mentally berated myself for these childish thoughts but couldn't deny my pleasure. As a fleet officer I had practiced fire-fighting too many times under simulated conditions to be afraid now. Now that we had CO_2 and the hoses, we could do the job.

I had fought worse at the fire-fighting schools, but this one was for real. We moved closer. The flames recoiled; we were winning. One hose went limp and a searing wall of heat smashed out at us. "Back down!" I ordered. We slowly pulled away under the protection of the remaining fog nozzles.

In a few moments the languid hose shuddered, squirming like a writhing snake, and with a violent swish jumped back to life. The men strained to hold it. The flames fought back, but with an agonizing slowness died down. Gradually, we beat back the threat to the planes.

As the area darkened, the heat became bearable. We were really winning. I almost danced a jig. The sweet taste of victory filled every man. Burns and injuries were forgotten as the remaining flames withered under our vigorous attack. The last fire was drowned out. Twenty or so planes had been saved from destruction.

I left men with CO_2 bottles on a flashback watch and ordered the rest to follow me. They dragged the hoses behind them.

Damn! Most of the trucks and airfield crash equipment hadn't been moved. The job must have been too much for the men I assigned. Twenty more of us jumped to the task. I started to chew on Mr. Lange, whom I had put in charge, but a 20mm tracer ripping through the smoke just above my head and the unmistakable pop of more 20mm ammo cooking off told me why the delay.

"Anybody been hit?"

"No, sir!"

"They're all going high, then," I shouted, biting my tongue for such stupid reasoning. "C'mon! Get everyone to put their backs into it. This equipment's gotta be moved . . . it's valuable. C'mon!"

Orders passed down the line and in minutes we were shoving, pulling, straining to move the monolithic steel monsters. There was no chain or rope, so we couldn't use our trucks; they were even too close together for our trucks to get behind and push. We mule-hauled them out. How any man escaped a hernia was beyond me.

Our hose men were playing their hoses on the end of the hangar but were too far away to do anything about the exploding ammo. Inconceivable as it seemed, except for the two airmen who had driven up in their useless fire truck when we arrived—what seemed like hours ago—I had seen no one but the sailors who came with me. I wondered if the air force had been killed, but I rejected the thought as foolish. I sent a man to check the back of the hangar.

As we groaned the last piece of equipment to safety, a group of sailors began fighting the blaze in front of the hangar. I gathered my two leaders, Mr. Lange and Chief Tanner, as the man returned from behind the hangar.

"COMMANDER, THEY'VE GOT—" he yelled.

"Not so loud, I can hear you."

"Commander, in back there's a lotta small shops, but the fire ain't reached them yet. Lotta shops, lotta men . . . I mean Vietnamese who ain't doin' nothin. Just standing there."

"Okay . . . you think we can save the shops?"

"Yes, sir!"

I sent Chief Tanner and his men off again to find more hoses. Mister Lange and the other groups I sent to get the shops cleaned out. "Divide up your men, so many to a room," I managed to yell as they scurried away. My right hand and arm started to throb again.

By the time I reached the back of the hangar, a matter of minutes, daisy chains had formed and the invaluable guns, instruments, tools, records, and what have you were flowing smoothly into huge piles on the other side of the road that paralleled the shops.

The Vietnamese were sure enough just standing there watching. Damn them! This was their base we were trying to save. I went up to one wearing a flight suit who appeared to be an officer. "Have your men start working, goddamnit! Get your men moving," I shouted, pushing him toward the flames.

"Yes, yes, Thieu Ta."

He yelled something to the other Vietnamese but they didn't move. I grabbed another one and pushed him gently toward the shops. At the proper distance I kicked him square in the ass. He moved. I grabbed for another but he dashed away for the daisy chain. They got the message. The others all sprang to action as I walked toward them.

The equipment moved faster now that we had thirty extra men. Good thing for me they moved. I was so angry I would have shot every one of them.

The flames were licking closer to the shops. The backs of a few were already on fire. Men came choking and coughing out of the rooms. They couldn't bear the smoke and heat.

The 20mm ammo was silent but the flames shoshed and crackled. Two hoses arrived and started spraying cooling water on the end of the hangar. A siren sounded and a beautiful red fire engine, with Chief Tanner on the running board, pulled to a jolting halt.

"Get this mother going, Ace!" he yelled to the driver. "NOW!"

"They ain't gonna like—" the airman blurted as he rolled out of the cab.

"Just shut up and start the pumps!"

"Where'd you get this thing, Chief?"

"I'd rather you didn't know, sir."

I didn't ask again.

In seconds the sailors had two hoses run out. The engine whirred to life, and the hoses shimmied, jerked, and quivered, finally spewing out water in a violent stream.

Two sailors ran up to a fire hydrant, attached a two-and-a-half-inch coupling, and while seven men clutched the hose, a sailor put on a wrench and pulled. The hydrant valve didn't budge. Another man helped. It didn't budge. Another man joined. "Once more!" the sailor yelled. They groaned. The valve screeched, moved, screeched, then SNAP! The three men flipped twice in the air, then tumbled to the ground.

"The valve's rusted out!" another sailor said between his raucous laughter. "The sonovabitch is rusted out. This place is unfuckingbelievable."

Three other men came running up, dragging an inch-and-a-half hose. "Where d'ya want it, Commander?" I pointed to the back of the shops. Two of them ran over to the spot and a third ran off into the darkness. In seconds he came rushing back. "I'm winning, I'm winning," he yelled.

I thought he'd flipped out until I noticed a bulge of water racing down the hose. Behind it the hose was stiff but in front, still limp. "Hurry! Hurry!" I spurred him on, but he lost and only barely got to his two buddies before the hose nearly jerked out of their hands. The three of them got down to the more serious business of putting out the fires at the backs of the shops.

Another pumper arrived just as the first one ran out of water. The sailors quickly shifted hoses. The airman driver told another air force man something I couldn't hear, but it must have been effective for in minutes a hose showed up from somewhere and they started filling the empty pumper. My! but those fire engines looked pretty and shiny there in the red yellowish glare of the hangar flames.

We now had seven hoses in play but the fire didn't seem to care. Its fury roared unabated, seeming to laugh at our puny efforts. I could sense its fury like an evil genie released from its captive bottle. We could communicate.

A Vietnamese fire truck drove onto the scene, the men inside gaping at the flames.

"WATCH OUT!" a sailor yelled uselessly as the truck slid into a muddy drainage ditch. Four Vietnamese jumped out, screeching curses at one another, running, waving their arms over their heads, round and round the truck. We laughed like hell.

"Hey, Brown," I yelled to a Seabee standing next to me. "Get that sonovabitch outta there!"

"Aye, aye, sir! Already under way." Another useless order. Those Seabees were already hot on the job.

"How many Seabees you got over here, Brown?"

"Four of us, Commander."

From God knows where, one of them came driving a giant forklift and, by judicious lifting, pushing, and hauling, pulled the fire truck free. It was a beautiful thing to see those Seabees playing that forklift like a fine instrument right under the hazard of a burning wall. To top it off, they put the freed truck in operation and it was pumping water in minutes. Hose number eight! "How do you like that, Mister Fire? You bastard!" I yelled.

I stationed myself midway between the two sets of hoses and, by watching the entire picture, I could adjust them to the greatest threat areas. I kept two messengers constantly running to the nozzle men with orders: "Get this area; concentrate on that; move here; move there." By this method the fire was coming under control rapidly.

"Sir!" a messenger reported, "some air force guy—nozzle man on number three hose—says he ain't taking no more orders from any navy puke."

"He does, eh? You tell him that if he doesn't, I'm going to come over there and put a size twelve combat boot up his ass, and if I can't do it myself I've got fifty sailors to help me.

Oh yeah, give him my name so he can complain to his colonel tomorrow."

An ambulance drove up, and I motioned it over. The messenger returned: "The guy said he was sorry and he would put his hose wherever you wanted it." I thought of a good place but it would have been uncomfortable for him. The air force corpsman dressed my arm and hand, telling me very autocratically that he was taking me to the dispensary. I told him thanks but no.

He insisted. I barked at him. He then allowed I could do anything I wanted, but the harsh way he yanked the T-shirt off my wound, tearing away the coagulated blood, reminded me that you should not argue with a corpsman when you have a wound.

"Where you been all night?" I asked.

"Over on the other side of the hangar. Bunch of our guys are fighting the fire from that end," he replied.

"How they doing?"

"Okay, I guess. Not much they can do but maybe keep the other buildings from burning."

"Anyone hurt?"

"No . . . really, Major—"

"Lieutenant commander."

"Yes, sir, you really should go to the dispensary with that arm."

"Yeah, I know, but I'm just too busy now. I appreciate your concern but—" My words were cut off by an uproar. "WATER! WATER!"

Under the yellowish haze of the flame I saw five of the seven hoses go limp. Men were running into the darkness along the flaccid, wormlike canvas.

"What happened, Mister Lange?"

"Don't know, sir, the water just quit."

"Get a hose hooked up to that pumper you were filling."

"Almost done . . . there, it's going." At least we had two live hoses. "Can't last too long. Just shifted pumpers . . . this one isn't half full yet."

Sensing that the pressure was off, the fire, like a horrible giant flexing its muscles, roared with new life. It vented its fury, shooting brilliant flames high into the air.

"Commander! We'd better secure one of those pumpers before we're all out of water."

"Very well, secure it. How much water we got left?"

"About half full in this one; maybe a fourth in the other. The Vietnamese pumper crapped out."

The heat built up again. The sizzling from the water hitting the backs of the shops gave an ominous warning of what was going to happen if we didn't get more water. Higher and higher the flames grew, forcing one hose team to retreat from the blistering heat. The fire was on the go again.

Petty Officer Brown ran up to a pumper. "You guys got a two-and-a-half-inch spanner and a big pipe wrench?" he yelled breathlessly to the airman standing there.

"Yeah! Somewhere here . . ."

"What did you find, Brown?" I asked.

"Main busted down the road a bit. Almost got it by-passed. Found some more hose in a warehouse down there. Gotta go. See ya, Commander," he shouted, running off.

We moved farther back from the heat. I sent the pumper with the airman to the other fire party down the field to see if they'd give us some water.

The helplessness we all felt showed in the bitching of the sailors. There was nothing we could do. "Screw it," one said in disgust. "We should let this goddamned place burn to the ground."

"Yeah, I ain't seen none of them air force bastards riskin' their ass."

"Them Seabees are probably havin' a beer down there."

"Where's that mother-humpin' water?"

"Look at the place burn . . . ya got any marshmallows?"

"Go piss on the fire if you're in such a goddamn hurry."

"Be more'n we get out of those hoses."

"Where's the water?"

"I wonder if there's any more twenty mike mike ammo in there."

I don't think I ever felt more helpless in my life. Here a building was burning and in seconds all the shops would go. There was nothing I could do. I wanted to rush over and help Brown and his Seabees but I knew I'd just be a hindrance. They were doing the best they could. I was pissed that the airmen in the pumper never came back.

My early fear had disappeared. We could never have saved the hangar anyway. There was no danger to my men as there had been on the flight line and when we were pulling the heavy equipment out of danger. All that we could lose now was the shops and offices. Buildings, just buildings.

We had saved everything of value out of them. I would not risk any of my men's lives to save wooden buildings. If the water got here in time, great; if not, too bad. The Vietnamese would blame us anyway, and we'd have to rebuild them, but how much could that cost? Surely not as much as one of those useless B-52 bombing raids on rice paddies and footbridges in North Vietnam. "Damn you, Brown, where's that water?"

The fire in full fury reached out, grabbed the shops, each time pushing a little farther, getting a little closer. An evil god of winds blew out of the north. The fire seemed to scream its thanks and grew for it. They're mine, they're mine, you could almost hear it sing.

But in answer Brown came running up. "Man your hoses, assholes, water coming, water coming," he shouted, and thirty sailors scampered.

The water grabbed the fire and beat it back. The clubs of water hit it blow after blow. "Take that, asshole. You can't have the shops. Die, die!" I chanted gleefully under my breath.

"You okay, Commander?" Brown asked.

"Yes, yes, it's just something about me and fires. I've practiced for ten years. This is my first chance to fight one. I guess I got carried away."

"I know what you mean, sir. I feel the same way about girls."

"Smart ass, it's not quite the same. Good work on that fire

main down there. Now get your ass outta here so I can orgas' in private."

"Aye, aye, sir. But one thing . . . some of the guys are really wondering . . . of course I don't care, what with being a Seabee and above all earthly desires . . . but some of the guys were just wondering . . . just asking you know . . . not that they really care, but just wondering—"

"Wondering what for Christ's sake, Brown! Wondering what?"

"Well, they're wondering, sir, if you're humping that young, good-lookin' schoolteacher down at Golf."

I was a bit startled by the question. "Why, Seabee Petty Officer Brown, if I did that I could be arrested for violation of the Pure Foods Act. Besides, I am an officer and a gentleman."

He laughed. "Yes, sir, and a mustang first." I slapped him on the back as he walked toward the pumper.

The fire stopped growing. Ten minutes without water had given it a good foothold, but we were very slowly beating it back. In any case, the hangar would be completely lost. There was no hurry now to put it out. Actually, the more we let it burn, the less debris to be carted away. I went from hose to hose; the men were in good spirits. They again had something to fight with. The hoses were winning. The blaze shrank more—just a little at first, then more and more. Now rapidly. Not much excitement left here.

I strolled toward the front of the hangar, joining Chief Tanner heading the same way. The building was devastated. The powerful streams of water shooting from the back made pleasing transparent arcs in contrast to the twisted metal of the structural steel and the grotesque skeletons of airplanes we couldn't save. Depressing. Maybe fire fighting wasn't as much fun as I had thought.

The air force fire party at the other end of the field seemed to have their share under control. In the dim light from their fire I could see that they had a helluva lot more equipment than we did. I couldn't really tell, but it seemed that the fire had started in the center of the large hangar complex, burning toward both ends.

A Spooky gunship was working over the area to the south of the airfield. The attack had probably come from that direction.

"Jesus! Look at that, Commander!" Chief Tanner said. "God, how much ammo they carry?"

"I think about twenty-four thousand rounds. They don't last long unless they take it easy." The firing detonation of the rounds was so fast that only a steady roar could be heard. "Their firing pattern covers a football field–sized area, with each five square inches receiving one bullet per minute," I added.

"How come we can't get support on the river from those babies?"

"I understand that only Seventh Air Force in Saigon can release them for a fire mission after it's been cleared somehow through the U.S. Army, plus permission of the ARVN commander and the province chief of the area."

"So, why not get permission when we get in the shit?"

"Not that easy, Chief. I've tried to grease the path, but the air force contends that we are a mobile unit; therefore, we could pull away from any fight, ergo, you don't need support—logical from their point of view, I guess."

"Fuck 'em. Let's let this place burn."

"Now, Chief Petty Officer Tanner, you know better than that, and anyway I'm not too convinced that they're all that accurate. We don't have that much maneuvering room when their shit rains down."

A big shiny, chauffeur-driven black staff car drove up and parked thirty feet from us. An air force colonel and another man stepped out. The colonel looked important. I walked over to report. His clean, impeccably tailored gray flight suit and impressive garrison cap with its silver-billed clouds and lightning bolts (farts and darts, we called them) was in sharp contrast to my wet, bedraggled, burned, and soot-covered greens. It made me extremely self-conscious.

I saluted. "Lieutenant Commander Sheppard, sir, with

fifty sailors from the PBR base. I think we have this end under control. The flight line fire—"

"Harumph!" he gurgled, cutting me off and returning my salute with a casual movement toward the bill of his beautiful cap. He looked me up and down as if I had offended him. I stood there awkwardly, waiting for him to speak.

In a few minutes the other man who had gotten out of the car, a lieutenant colonel I could now see, strolled over. His dress equaled the elegance of the colonel's. He came to attention, saluting smartly. "Looks like rockets, Colonel," he reported, handing over a piece of jagged metal. The colonel drew his hand back as if not to touch the dirty thing. The lieutenant colonel stared at me.

"Sheppard, from the navy base," I volunteered.

"What happened to your hand?" he asked.

"He hurt it," Chief Tanner interrupted.

"Harumph," the colonel grunted again. "Come on," he said, and they got back in the car and drove away.

Chief Tanner spoke first: "Well, I'll be goddamned . . . that sonuva—"

"That's enough, Chief," I cut him off. "He's got a lot on his mind."

"Yeah, like getting ashes on his shiny black car."

"Shut up, Chief."

We went back to the fire parties. They had the fire down to isolated pockets, and even those were being rapidly extinguished. Again, though it wasn't needed, I went from hose to hose, pointing out hot spots and timbers, which for safety's sake had to be knocked down with a solid stream.

And then it was out. It was dark. We used the headlights from the vehicles to see. The Vietnamese air force people started returning. The ones I had put into action had disappeared hours ago. Now they were all over the place, shouting, giving orders to each other, and generally getting in the way. For another twenty minutes we hosed down the area to cool off any places we might have missed. No sparks or embers remained; no metal hissed when water touched it. I released the pumpers and they drove off. I sent a messenger to secure the flashback watch on the flight-line aircraft. The fire was out.

"Let's wrap it up!" I ordered, and as the command passed down the line a hearty cheer arose. The petty officers took charge and soon the coiled hose and policed-up area showed that fleet sailors had been there. The Vietnamese graciously consented to help.

"Jones!" I yelled to a messenger. "Go tell those air force guys that we're securing here and if they want a flashback watch, they'll have to set it themselves. Make damn sure you tell the man in charge, and get his name," I yelled after him.

The first truckload of sailors pulled out. I was on my way to the front of the hangar when two trucks arrived manned by Vietnamese sailors from the RAG base at Can Tho. One of the junior American advisors jumped out.

"You guys are just too late. Your friendly PBR sailors have put it out already."

"Had a hell of a time getting here. The bridge was down and we had two flats. Sorry we missed the party," he replied.

"You could set a flashback watch. Doesn't look like anyone else is going to. I'm taking my boys home."

The Vietnamese sailors were stringing out hoses. I think. I had lost interest. My arm throbbed all the way to my spine.

The lieutenant colonel's chauffeured car drove up again. "Well, it looks like we got 'er licked, eh?" I almost threw up.

"Hey, we better take care of that arm . . . ah? . . ."

"Sheppard."

"Oh, yes. Come on, I'll take you to the dispensary."

"Thanks, but I'd mess up your seats. I'll just walk over."

"No . . . no, that's okay. There's a war on, you know," he chuckled.

"Yes . . . I know."

After the messenger came back, I sent the truck by the dispensary to pick up any injured sailors who might still be there and told the driver to send a jeep back for me.

Don Sheppard

Streaks of light from the dawn penetrated the darkness as I stepped out of the electrified shower and dropped into bed, numbed by pain-killing drugs on my quiet Sunday day off.

The Viet Cong had won today, but not so much for our being there.

Decoy

———•———

The winds were shifting. A steady breeze blew from the southwest, and the rains, the blessed cooling rains, would soon come. There are no real seasons in the delta—it's summer all the time. The closest thing to a change is the monsoons. The northeast monsoon blows from November to about mid-April, bringing hot, dry weather. Dry only comparatively—the humidity is still eighty percent. During May the winds slowly shift to the southwest, and little air stirs. It is the hottest time of all. Only from late June to early October, when the rains inundate the land, is the temperature low enough—high seventies at the coolest—to live with minimal comfort, if you are inside. During the rainy season most of the annual rainfall of eighty inches falls.

During the time between monsoons men moved slowly; work was held to a minimum. Just the effort of sitting caused great beads of sweat to form. The boats, which normally drifted during the greater part of their thirteen-hour patrol, now kept moving just for the breeze. We did not carry enough fuel for this, only for about eight hours; consequently, they had to come off station to refuel at Can Tho or down south to the T. This took the boats off the river and gave the Viet Cong even greater chances to cross. It was the best we could do.

I often discussed Tanh Dinh with Captain Laske, but even he was unable to secure decent troops—that is, American troops—for an operation. "We'll use our own resources," he said one day. "I've got the SEALs and their battleship." The battleship was a modified, heavily armored mike boat officially designated a heavy SEAL support craft (HSSC). It was the same basic hull design as the mike boat we used to ferry supplies to the outposts and for our underway replenishment during Linebacker II.

"You know, Captain Laske, we're going to get in trouble with those SEALs pretty soon. They're operating independently for the most part and we don't know where they're at half the time. We're going to have a real shoot-out if we don't get better coordination."

"Whataya mean? I thought all operations were cleared with you beforehand."

"No, sir. Those fast little boats, their STABs, go tearing around when they're making an insertion, looking just like a sampan on our radarscopes, and you know who uses them and what we do to fast-moving sampans. We gotta pull this operation together. The other night a PBR was in ambush position, their fifties already double-cocked, when a STAB (strike assault boat) came right in front of them, landing its SEALs about fifty yards away. Shit! One night the Seawolves put in an on-call strike for the SEALs just a klick away from a patrol. Too many players, Captain.

"You've heard the story about the Coast Guard cutter and the two PBRs shooting each other up because each of them thought the other one was the enemy?"

He looked at me. Of course he'd heard the story. I was prodding him and he didn't like it.

"I'll take care of it," he answered in disgust.

Several days later, Captain Laske called a meeting with Lieutenant Baker, the SEAL OinC, Lieutenant Simon, and me. Captain Laske asked Lieutenant Simon if his troops and boats were okay this long after the blockade. Simon told him okay but with a hint of reservation in his voice. Laske asked Lieutenant Baker how his SEALs were doing. Okay was the answer. He asked me how my arm was. I, like Lieutenant Simon, lied and said okay. Captain Laske said he wanted an operation behind Tanh Dinh. In an hour the framework took shape. The operation would kick off day after tomorrow.

"Good afternoon, gentlemen," I started the briefing. I felt lousy: I had eaten too much lunch—two hamburgers, potato salad, and a beer. It lay like a lump in my stomach. My right hand after three weeks was just starting to have full use again but it still hurt. I refused to take pain pills because of the adverse effect on my judgment.

"We've got a little operation planned for tomorrow that each of you will be involved in." I searched the room, my eyes contacting each man—two patrol officers and four boat captains from RIVSEC 512, the SEAL squad leaders, and the OinC and coxswain from the battleship. The Seawolf pilots sat in the back of the room. Captain Laske sat at a table in front. They looked at me in anticipation, in fear perhaps. I had taken the PBR sailors to the margin of endurance with the blockade. Maybe they didn't have confidence in me anymore.

"It's a simple operation but timing is important. What it amounts to is taking PBRs through Titi and marking the places where we draw fire. The battleship will follow at a respectable distance behind the PBRs and with their fifty-seven mike mike recoilless rifles wipe out those areas that fire on us.

"The SEALs will be involved; they will establish an ambush on the northern end of Tanh Dinh and hopefully we can drive the VC into them." The PBR sailors had a dumbfounded look; the battleship crewmen were devoid of expression.

"Four PBRs will make the initial incursion starting at first light. Ten minutes after we enter, the big stuff'll follow. Seawolves'll be standing by at Can Tho in case we get into the big shit. The PBRs will continue through Titi, exiting the southern end. We'll then come north again outside and make shorter and shorter incursions back in from the top. Lieutenant Baker will brief on the SEAL portion."

"Rather standard operation for the SEALs . . ." Lieutenant Baker was a big man, dark with a mean look. He was completely bald, had long, delicate fingers, and like all SEALs was in outstanding physical condition. The SEALs were overtrained for the job they were doing here on the Bassac, but they were all we had. It was like using a semi when a pickup truck was good enough. They were hard men and excellent fighters, but trained for a clandestine war, an ambush war, whereas the PBRs and Seawolves stood up and slugged it out. On the Bassac it would be a while before the SEALs could be successfully integrated into the Game Warden mission.

"We'll land on the northern tip of Tanh Dinh at 0300 and wait. When the PBRs come in the second time they'll continue in until they draw fire, then turn around and haul ass out. They'll continue doing this, each time going in a shorter distance. Hopefully, this'll suck the VC toward the tip of the island and we'll be there waiting for them. We'll extract on my order. Any questions?"

Silence.

I got up again. "Okay, on command and control, I'll be in charge of the PBR element and in the lead boat. Lieutenant Baker will be in charge of the SEALs and Captain Laske will be in command of the heavy element and in overall command of the operation. As you know, we now have another helo fire team on the Bassac. They're stationed at Can Tho until the new base is completed. Lieutenant Commander Roberts will be the Seawolf flight commander standing by for a call mission. Although it's a lot easier flying out of Can Tho compared to the T, we'll still use the scramble codes.

"Each unit adjust underway time as required and we'll

use standard, tactical 511 common, with the other radio tuned to Bassac common, just like every day.

"Call signs: Captain Laske will use Betray; Lieutenant Baker will be Cycle One; Lieutenant Commander Roberts, Seawolf Three Six; I'll use Handlash; and the boats will use their normal call signs." I turned toward the captain. "Captain Laske?"

He stood and told of the danger of the strike and that this would be the first of many combined operations to carry the war to the enemy. He turned the floor over to me. I dismissed the briefing, telling Lieutenant Simon and his men to meet me in my office.

"Well, Interdictor," Captain Laske said as we left the room, "we'll get 'em tomorrow." It embarrassed me when he called me Interdictor. The name for all of RIVDIV 51 was the Bassac Interdictors, not just me. It got twisted around somehow and quite undeservingly applied only to me.

"Yes, sir, I hope so."

"Sit down, gentlemen. You may wonder why you were picked for this operation. Well, you weren't, you were just scheduled for the normal patrol tomorrow. We'll leave the Juliet side uncovered."

"The way I see it, Commander, we're just going to be decoys for the battleship," spoke up Lieutenant (jg) Lange, the patrol officer for Golf Patrol tomorrow.

I'd be taking Echo. I could do without Lange's bullshit on this operation. "That's the way I see it," I said.

Santez, one of the boat captains, shuffled his feet and didn't look me in the eye as he spoke. "Seems dangerous to me. Hell, the battleship's got all kind of steel around it. We ain't got nothin' except around the coxswain's flat and that shit on the engine covers." He seemed ashamed to speak.

"It'll be dangerous no doubt and something new for us. Anyone wants out, it's okay with me. Also, brief your crews in secrecy and if they want out, that's okay, too. I don't want word of this operation getting out, and I've never been convinced that all the Co's around here aren't spies. I'm sure Mister Simon can get replacement troops."

"Hell, Commander, we ain't scared," boasted First Class Boatswain's Mate Kramer, the young senior boat captain of Echo Patrol.

"Bullshit, Kramer, it frightens me. If you're not scared you're crazy, and I'm not riding with you and I'll pull your ass off the river," I barked.

"Well, I'm scared," Santez chimed in.

Looking out the barge window, then down to his feet, Kramer admitted in a barely audible whisper: "I'm scared."

"For Christ's sake," I yelled. "I'm not taking an I'm-scared, not-scared poll. Knock it off."

I sat leaning back while lighting a cigar, trying to give an air of nonchalance after my outburst. I plopped my feet on my desk. The others relaxed, lighting up pipes and cigarettes. With a long pointer I casually traced our route through Titi while I ran through the operation again.

"Finally, gentlemen, I have no idea what's behind Tanh Dinh. For all I know the whole Viet Cong 306th Battalion could be there . . . that's what I hear. Mister Jenkins and three boats tore through during Linebacker II but were too busy to sightsee, and no government troops have been back there for maybe twelve, thirteen years. Every agent they send in ends up with his head on a spike stuck in some rice paddy.

"We've dropped thousands and thousands of leaflets in the area but are yet to get a hoi chanh to come out. After that little sampan shoot during Linebacker II, I doubt if the PBRs are that popular with them."

Lieutenant (jg) Lange spoke up again: "We sure didn't get much notice on this operation, Commander. Hell! We'll be getting under way," he looked at his watch, "in ten hours."

"Plenty of time. The more you think about this sorta thing, the bigger it builds. Whataya need more time for? It's a mighty simple operation. Hell, man, we're just going to rush through, come back around, and zip in and out a couple of times. Whole thing, what? a couple of hours."

"I've been with you before, Commander. It never seems to work out that way," Kramer said jokingly.

"C'mon, Kramer, we country boys have gotta stick together." Kramer and I were from the same small rural county in southern Illinois.

"I reckon you're right, but it always seems ya gotta plan these things," Lange said.

"Maybe it's your academy background," I dug at him. I didn't relish all this questioning from an officer; they were to accept orders on faith. Though Lange had done well at the fire, I just didn't think he was cutting it on the boats. I should take him off the river, I thought, but it would mean the end of his navy career. I'd consider it after this operation. "Nothing to plan. We have zero intelligence, same communications frequencies. We'll call firing coordinates to the battleship as we whip by. The only screwup I can see is if we don't know where the SEALs are."

"How'll we know that?"

"I was coming to that. On our way in, Lieutenant Baker will click his microphone twice as the lead boat passes his most southern position. Each time in he'll do the same. In any case they won't be more than five hundred yards from the northern tip of the island. So don't fire into them; it costs a lot of money to train a SEAL."

Halfhearted laughter.

"Okay, gentlemen, if there are no questions, that's it. First light's about 0530. What time you figure under way?"

"About quarter after four," volunteered Santez, the boat captain of Echo Two.

"Okay, make it so. I'll brief again at 0345. Put a double ammo load on. It might get sporty tomorrow."

The men shuffled out of the room. Kramer reached the door, paused, and turned around. "Commander . . . I . . . ah . . . I . . ."

"Oh yeah, Kramer, better bring some extra toilet paper

tomorrow. We'll all be shittin' our pants before this one's over," I said before he had a chance to be ashamed of himself.

"Yes, sir! I'll bring two extra rolls." He turned and disappeared out the door.

At supper I ate too much, drank too much, and joked a little too hard. I tried to go to sleep early but couldn't. I just lay there thinking of tomorrow and thinking of the bullets that could kill my men. I never thought of myself being killed, only my men.

They were my responsibility; their lives rested on my decisions and I wasn't convinced that this was a good operation. The canal was narrow, I didn't know the strength of the enemy, I didn't know the depth of the water, and I didn't know the locations of the sandbars or the fish stakes. If we got into trouble, deep-shit trouble, could that floating tank save our ass in time? Lieutenant (jg) Jenkins had a pretty hairy ride back there. A church firing at him, he had reported. Hell! What does anyone really know anyway?

I fell asleep about two and awoke at three. My head ached and my right arm throbbed. My muscles rebelled at getting up, and a cigarette tasted like cotton. The coffee tasted like axle grease, I cut myself shaving, and I wished to hell I were home. What a panacea that first round of enemy fire would be.

The low, rhythmic melody of the eight idling engines was reassuring. The smooth, orange circling sweep of the radarscopes painted bizarre reflections on the taut faces of the men and finely oiled surface of the guns. The soft voices conducting radio checks were reassuring: "Echo, Echo Two loud and clear. Handlash One loud and clear. Golf Two, Echo One . . ."

As I stepped aboard PBR 127, Bayer, the coxswain, snapped my burgee pennant up. I pointed downriver and the four boats slipped their lines, easing out from the pier. Within minutes we were at speed, four in a line.

The radarscope continuously etched out an orange short-range map of the Bassac. Its turning sweep mesmerized me to its view. They were direct, off-the-shelf, civilian, high-definition navigational radars costing only $1,900. I sat on the fold-down stool in the coxswain's flat, slowly smoking my pipe.

"Hear ya got the clap, Kramer," I said.

"Yes, sir, afraid so."

"Hurt?"

"Only when I pee."

"Sorry."

Can Tho passed silently down our starboard side. Cu Lao May came in view. We turned into the northeastern fork of the river, taking five point five to the right. Tra On, a bit ahead, was just waking; a few lights flickered in the marketplace as we left it to port.

"Kramer, you bring the Tabasco sauce for the C rats?" I asked.

"No, sir, I forgot."

"Shit, Kramer. I love hot sauce on C rats."

"We'll borrow some from another boat, Commander."

"Okay."

The mammoth outline of the battleship, which had gotten under way an hour ahead of us, loomed off the starboard bow, their churning, twelve-knot wake shining white in the predawn haze. We roared past at twenty feet just to show off. It rocked gently from our wakes.

Tanh Dinh, silhouetted dead ahead, came up fast. The tide was coming up full. I looked at my watch—0517—slack water in thirteen minutes.

"You ever jump a sandbar with one of these, Bayer?" I asked.

"No, tried once when we were chasing a sampan. Got stuck, though. Got off right away . . . I know that on step we only draw nine inches of water. Sometimes it just looks like they're jumping sandbars. Love those Jacuzzi pumps . . . wish they wouldn't clog up with weeds so much . . . pain in the ass to clear the pumps. Sometimes you have to go over the side. Don't like that. Don't like that. Saw a little alligator or crocodile the other day, don't know which. Look the same to me. Snakes in the water, too . . . don't like that . . . hate to get the pumps clogged. Saw a dead man float by the other day . . . don't like to go over the side." Bayer chanted on. I could see his hands stark white from clutching the wheel.

The east was a dirty, dull gray, with only a few stars remaining. White mist rose from the river as we tore through its small clouds, racing into Titi. My pipe was out. I sucked on it, clamped unconsciously in my mouth. I eased my helmet on. A huge white bird rose from the island, swooped toward us, and disappeared into the darkness of the west.

My forward gunner pulled back his cocking levers, once to feed up a shell and again to seat the half-inch round into the chamber. With two authoritative clangs he was ready.

My eyes strained through the binoculars to catch a glimpse of anything down the canal or any activity on the shore. It was useless; even in full sunlight, penetrating very far into the jungle tree line was impossible. But it was something to do; I had to do something.

"Your pipe's out, Commander."

"Yeah, I know. Gotta light?"

"No, sir."

I put down the glasses and picked up the mike. Our bow swept over the threshold of Titi. "Betray, Betray, this is Handlash. COMEX, COMEX. Out." COMEX meant commence exercise; it didn't really fit—this was hardly an exercise—but we used it anyway.

I waited for Lieutenant Baker to key his PRC-25 portable FM radio, indicating his southernmost position. The fourth boat crossed the sill. I bent forward to the radios. I mustn't miss the signal.

Click! Click! The receiver light blinked twice.

"Mark!" I said aloud. "Echo Two, Golf acknowledge. Over."

"This is Echo Two. Roger. Out."

"This is Golf One. Roger. Out."

"This is Golf Two. Roger. Out."

Five minutes passed. Cook fires flickered on the mainland to our left. Eight minutes passed. It was nearly light now. Nothing moved on the shore. A sampan pushed into the canal three hundred yards ahead, then frantically back-paddled out of sight.

"He saw us!" Kramer said.

A shot echoed in the distance. In a few seconds another. Still farther away, another. The morning newspaper. The early edition.

"That's it," I murmured. The overhanging mangroves zipped by us. Each man stood hyperalert. I wanted to blast away into the unknown morass. Why didn't I? I wanted to burn the whole goddamned place.

We came to a small island in the center of the canal. I pointed to the left. "Gotta light, Kramer?"

"No, sir."

"Wish you'd brought that hot sauce."

"So do I. We can borrow some from another boat."

A little village loomed to port. A beautiful white church sat in its center. Huge fishnet drying racks drooped under their load. A few pigs and chickens sauntered about but no people. This is what Jenkins had described.

"Catholic?" Kramer asked.

"I don't know . . . looks like it."

We passed the island and the village. Titi widened. I kept checking to see that my M-79 was still loaded.

"Handlash, Handlash, this is Betray. COMEX. Out!" The battleship had entered; I wondered if they were scared.

Another island: this time I pointed to the right, another narrow passage. We were coming up fast to the farthest ingress point of Linebacker II. My boat rounded the island, followed by Echo Two, Golf One, Golf Two.

"Looks like a milk ru—" BRACK! ZING! CRACK! ZING! BURRAT! BURRAT! punctuated my words. The trees on the mainland spit steel at us. Our twelve .50s lashed back.

The pain in my right arm vanished, my head cleared, my body strengthened, my muscles vibrated. Four M-60s joined the party. A huge splash erupted off our port bow—a rocket!

"Betray, Betray, this is Handlash. Under fire south of last island. Interrogative your position. Over."

"This is Betray. Coming up to the first island. Over."

"Roger, Betray, we'll maintain contact. Do hurry! Break, break . . . Seawolf Three Six, Seawolf Three Six, this is Handlash. Scramble two! Scramble two. Over."

Nothing!

"Betray, this is Handlash. Get Three Six for me, please. Over!"

The battleship was closer; maybe he could reach him. Serious flaw in the plan. Propagation was shit today. Should have figured that. Too late now. "Come about," I ordered. "We'll play tag awhile."

The trees kept up their fire; the red-orange muzzle flashes looked like dainty flowers. Hell, they weren't even coming close. We were only three hundred yards away and their shots were going wild. Except for the first few rounds I couldn't even hear any zings of close shots. Farmers, just farmers. We'll wax their ass.

We headed directly for the ambush site. Only the forward gunner on my boat could bring his .50s to bear. The shooting stopped. Fifty . . . sixty seconds. We roared in. Then from the tip of the little island a light machine gun opened up. It sounded like an AK-47. My forward gunner shifted his fire in answer. The mainland position started again—three AK-47s. Now, flashes from Tanh Dinh across the canal.

A three-point ambush. I'll be a sonuvabitch. Three points —farmers? I didn't believe they could do it. My forward gunner quit firing and quickly reloaded. The mainland position was finding our range. The zings and splashes danced around us. Another rocket exploded next to the third boat. I fired my M-79 over the bow as we closed in on the small island.

"Stand by for a starboard turn, stand by," I yelled to

Bayer. The trees on the little island raced toward us . . . seventy-five . . . sixty . . . fifty . . . thirty. "TURN! TURN!" I screamed, punctuating it with a slap on the back. We banked hard, sliding around, echoing a broadside with our .50s, Kramer and I punching grenades into the muzzle flashes. We came about and headed for the tip of the small island. They were good; their slugs were tearing into my cover boat behind me.

We gave the small island our full treatment as it and the mainland position blasted away at us. Tanh Dinh's guns started again. I saw gun flashes but no hits on our boats. I laid my grenades into them with no stopping effect. On my order Golf Patrol had broken off from us after the initial turn back. He blasted away at the mainland. Lange seemed good at it.

We headed straight for Tanh Dinh to a point just upstream from the deadly, angry, spitting jungle. "Turn at about fifty yards from the beach," I yelled over the terrible noise. I continued my barrage into the flashes but they wouldn't stop. Echo Two was just passing the tip of the little island, working it over with grenades and .50 caliber.

Tanh Dinh jumped at us like a monstrous locomotive. "TURN! TURN! TURN! BAYER! TURN! TURN!" I screamed.

But Bayer was in a trance, mesmerized by the gun flashes. I dove into the coxswain's flat, frantically spinning the wheel to the left, smashing it hard into the stops. We were no more then ten yards from the beach when she answered, the helm coming slowly to the left. The ground effect from the shallow water lifted us like a toy, tossing the boat at a crazy angle to port, over so far that we had to cling savagely to anything to keep from being thrown out.

The .50s swung wildly, spewing their slugs in all directions, cooking off their rounds from the cherry-hot gun barrels. Ammo boxes clattered over the deck; 40mm grenade boxes tipped, spilling rolling grenades throughout the boat. The starboard whip antenna slashed the overhanging branches, crashing them down on us.

We slowed with a grinding, abrasive shudder as the boat ran over the narrow beach. I spun the wheel into the starboard stops. We righted, gained speed. I shifted the wheel to port. We paralleled the beach for seconds, then eased away and headed downstream.

"BAYER, YOU STUPID ASSHOLE!" Kramer screamed, picking himself up.

I reached down, lifting Bayer's limp body from his crumpled position on the deck, where my flying dive knocked him. "You okay?"

"Yes . . . yes . . . I'm—"

"Here, take the wheel, Bayer. You okay?" I tried to appear calm, my shaking hands attempting to find my head to place a helmet on. The other three boats were still firing. All three positions were letting us have it again, as if they had ever stopped.

"Echo Two, Golf, this is Handlash. Break it off . . . join me. Over."

Golf Patrol turned toward us immediately. Echo Two continued heading for the small island, all his guns blazing. I called again. Nothing. I called again as he came about momentarily, not firing. He acknowledged. "Keep your guns in the air . . . keep your guns in the air!" I ordered over the radio. We had been firing so much that the overheated breeches of the machine guns would automatically ignite the gunpowder in the round in the chamber firing it off, feeding in another round, firing it off in a cycle ending only when the last round cooked off. We pointed the barrels skyward and yanked apart the ammo belts to stop the hot firing as fast as possible. We had to wait anxiously, uncomfortably, for them to cool before reloading.

We ruined a lot of gun barrels by getting them so hot. Pointing them skyward was the least dangerous thing we could do, but we had to be especially careful of helos in the air. The inability to stop a gun from firing was frightening and could panic the most experienced gunners.

When the three other boats joined up, we kicked ass out of there. "Betray, Betray, this is Handlash. We are breaking contact . . . too hot . . . three positions. I say again, three positions: one on south tip of last island, one on mainland across, and one on Tanh Dinh across. Be advised they have rockets. Say again, rockets, and the boys on the island are damn good. Break, break . . . interrogative Three Six. Over."

"This is Betray. Roger, copy your last . . . no joy Three Six . . . interrogative casualties. Over."

"This is Handlash. Negative here. Stand by. Break, break. Echo Two, Golf . . . sitrep. Over."

"This is Echo Two. Minor. Out."

"This is Golf One. Minor. Out."

"This is Golf Two. Two for Can Tho."

It was almost axiomatic that the lead boats suffered fewer hits than the others.

"Cry Havoc"

———————•———————

Golf Two's after gunner, a man named Brewer, took bad wounds in his leg and chest. Walker, the coxswain, had a torn-up left shoulder. Our other wounds were just minor burns and small shrapnel cuts.

We tied up together in a wide spot midriver, just upstream from Tanh Dinh, transferring almost all of Golf Two's ammo to our other three boats. This lightened weight would gain him fifteen to twenty minutes on his trip to Can Tho. He was under way again in three minutes. Only the after gunner's chest wound was life threatening. He was new and I didn't even know his name.

We sat in silence for several minutes, regaining our composure. The sight of our own wounded always unnerved us, bringing our own mortality to mind. Bayer was the first to speak: "Mister Lange, know what?"

"No."

"Commander's pissed at Kramer for forgetting the hot sauce," he said in the tone of a little sister telling on her big brother.

Kramer stared at him. "Bayer, you're such an asshole."

"Are you pissed at him, Commander?" Lieutenant (jg) Lange asked in a childish voice.

"You guys got any hot sauce?" Kramer asked.

Santez answered, "Yes, but if we give it to you we'll come under fire and have to split up and we'll never get it back. Happens all the time."

"I can't believe you guys," I joined in. "I give you an exciting morning with fresh air and you won't even share your hot sauce with an old man." I had established early on that we didn't need all that saluting and verbal kowtowing we used in the fleet, especially while on the river. We shared the common bond of combat, and life being as hassle free as possible. I enjoyed the easy camaraderie of these sailors. They were professional enough not to take advantage of it.

"You know, Commander, we should have had my cover boat bring you back a towrope in case you wanna run up on the beach again," Thomas said, grinning.

"Hell, Thomas, that's the way he clears the barnacles off the bottom, don't you know?" Lieutenant (jg) Lange answered.

"Hey, Commander, I thought you always took Thanh with you when you went ashore." Santez, the junior boat captain of Echo Patrol, entered the ribbing.

"If you Girl Scouts could shoot straighter we wouldn't have had to get in so close."

"What's our motto again, 'close and crash' or something like that?"

The radio blurted out: "Handlash, this is Betray. Negative fire, am exiting now. Over."

"This is Handlash. Roger. Out."

"Look at this boat, Commander, don't it look like a shithole? Can't those guys do any better repairing them?" Kramer asked.

"Well, Kramer, this boat had a low-order grenade go off in it a little while back. You guys fuck these boats up faster than they can fix them."

"Ain't our fault, Commander, the fuckin' sampans bang into us when we call 'em alongside. Always tearing up the fiberglass. Shit, ain't their fault either. We're the ones who make 'em come alongside," Santez rebutted angrily.

"Whoa! Whoa! you guys, I'm just shitting you." I knew how touchy they were on boat conditions. I looked around. "C'mon, let's go in again. We'll see if we can get the SEALs some action."

Kramer was putting C-ration meat cans on the manifold to heat. He closed the engine covers. Bayer touched the starter buttons and the engines came to life. Thomas's boat followed. From Santez's boat came only the grinding of the starters. One GM 220 started, died. A stream of cuss words didn't start the engine. The boat engineer was all elbows and ass in the engine compartment. "Wires shot up. Twenty . . . thirty minutes to fix," he yelled up.

"ASSHOLE! Goddamnit! Why didn't you check it before? Stupid shit," Santez growled.

"Sorry, Boats."

"Knock it off, Santez, we'll go without you," Lieutenant (jg) Lange said, looking at me. I nodded yes.

"Betray, this is Handlash. Commencing phase two. Over."

"Roger. Out."

Our two boats headed in. "Pssst," I heard from Bayer. I looked. He smiled, showing me a bottle of hot sauce.

"Why do you still have that M-14, Kramer?" I asked.

"He thinks he's Daniel Boone, Commander," Bayer answered.

"Christ, Bayer, but you've got a big mouth. It's a sweet weapon, Commander, much better than that M-16 toy. I used to hunt rabbits with a twenty-two about the same size."

"Not with a muzzle velocity of more than three thousand feet per second, you didn't," I rebutted.

"I know, but this here M-14 is accuratized and fires a thirty-caliber slug. I can put a bullet in the eye at three hundred yards. Great for warning shots ahead of the bow. They can't even hear that Mattel toy sixteen. That's what the M stands for, you know."

We entered at full speed. Within a minute Lieutenant Baker's two clicks welcomed us. We continued in until we were just abeam of the church. An AK-47 opened up, splashing water around us. Two rounds cut straight through our boat just forward of the engines. The muzzle flashes came from a window in the church. "Hold your fire," I ordered, radioing the same to Golf One and telling him to come about. "Don't fire on the church . . . don't fire."

On the way out a rifle joined the machine-gun bullets coming mighty close. My Judaic-Christian background rebelled. A church firing at us? I stared at the big white building in disbelief. Those dirty bastards were using the church as cover. They knew we wouldn't fire back. What's the matter with me? Why not fire back? You're stupid, Sheppard.

Baker's two clicks signaled his position just before we exited. Santez still didn't have his engines fixed. We made a wide, sweeping turn and reentered. It was mighty quiet.

Click. Click.

We passed the fish stakes again. On the mainland side we could see several small hootches. It was no different from most areas on the Bassac except that the jungle was more dense. The bank was well used: On the clotheslines hung dull, dirty wash; little garden plots nestled up to each hootch; big, clay water urns stood by each front door; and small sampans were beached well clear of the water. A few VC dogs and a couple of fat VC pigs snorting around in the mud and a score of indifferent VC chickens were the only life watching our foolish incursion.

The church popped into sight. A crack of a rifle and a zing over our heads signaled the coxswain to come about. Maybe it was working—the shot had come from closer to the entrance of the canal.

From near a big hootch a short burst of light machine gun fire waved us by. We waved back with a blast of our own. Three shots from Tanh Dinh hit Golf One ahead of me. We swung our guns around and gave them a broadside.

Two clicks and safety.

Another sweeping turn and in again. Just as we crossed the entrance, another machine-gun burst winked at us from a bunker on the mainland.

"Handlash, Handlash. Golf One. Lost port engine. Over."

Golf One had dropped off step and was wallowing forward like a flat-fronted barge fighting the tide. We came about, my forward gunner blasting the bunker. "Golf, Golf. Handlash. EXIT! EXIT! Out."

We pulled up close behind Golf One, matching his snaillike speed as we pumped every round we could into the mainland.

Click, click.

Once clear I pulled ahead toward Santez's boat. "What's the story, Santez?"

"About twenty more minutes, Commander," Santez's grease-blackened engineer answered.

"What's with Thomas?"

"Lost an engine, Santez, I don't know. He'll be here in a few minutes."

Golf One pulled alongside. Only the butts of the engineer and Thomas could be seen as they frantically worked on their starboard engine. Lieutenant (jg) Lange kept looking down at the engine, then back to Tanh Dinh, his face drawn in disgust. "Rotten luck, Commander. Took a hit in the oil line. Mighta ruined that engine."

"Anybody hurt?"

"Commander," Kramer shouted, "look at this." He pointed into the engine compartment that the engineer was inspecting. It was torn by bullets and shrapnel. Grimy, burned food from shattered C-ration tins covered the engine and sides of the well. Several wires dangled loose, frayed and broken. Oil dripped from a punctured filter. Water ran out of a severed cooling line.

"Fix it," I ordered, as if my words were magic. Adrenaline surged through my body more powerful than any narcotic. I was ready to fight. I had been kissed by combat and must respond. No more, though, than any of the others. "Fix it!"

They bent to the task. In eight minutes, current flowed through the taped and replaced wires and the jury-rigged cooling line held pressure.

"There—" Kramer was interrupted by the shout: "COM-

MANDER, COMMANDER, look at that! LOOK! Hundreds of 'em. Where'd they come from?"

I focused my binoculars on the canal. What seemed like hundreds of sampans full of women, kids, and old men were pouring out of the entrance. What the hell was going on? The battleship must have scared the hell out of them. The women were evacuating. We'd caught them by surprise; no spies this time told them of our operation.

I looked at Kramer; his face was noncommittal. "Start the engines, Bayer," he said, putting on his helmet. Inwardly, I thanked him. It was always nice to have company when one was about to be a damn fool.

"Mister Lange, scramble two the Seawolves. Call Betray and brief him . . . tell him to haul ass." I stepped down into the coxswain's flat. "Kick 'er in the ass, Bayer."

The other two boats rocked violently from our wake as we leapt away from the nest. The bolts flew home on the .50s. Kramer filled the ready ammo box with 40mm grenades. Bayer's jaw set as to meet some unexpected blow. The after gunner opened extra cans of .50s, stacking them around him. The forward gunner swung his mount from side to side.

"Use the seventy-nine, Kramer."

"Naturally," he answered, picking up the short shotgunlike weapon. He handed it to me while picking up another, then breaking the breech and inserting a round.

Don Quixote and his Sanchos leapt to the attack. We entered the canal; sampans were everywhere, making for the exit, just like in Linebacker II. I wondered what they were thinking. Click! Click! We were on step with very little wake but stayed on the Tanh Dinh side so as not to take a chance of swamping the sampans. I heard Three Six acknowledge the scramble. I heard Betray ask for more information.

A hushed radio call from his ambush position: "Handlash, this is Cycle One. What's up? Over."

Before I could answer, a chattering blast of steel tore at us over the heads of the near-solid mass of sampans. "HOLD YOUR FIRE!" I bellowed. "Kramer, fire back into the jungle with your seventy-nine." We fired high and far back. The grenades, armed after a fifteen-foot travel, were exploding in the treetops when their contact fuses hit a tree branch or anything slightly solid at all. We weren't doing any damage. I lowered my aim to just over the heads of the panicked small boats churning out away from us.

The fusillade continued. The VC seemed unconcerned about the women and the kids and the old men. We were getting deeper into the canal, deeper into enemy territory. Their bullets were tearing up my boat. No wild shots now; they seemed to know that I wouldn't fire back, I wouldn't take a chance of hitting innocent civilians. Innocent civilians back here? Oxymoron? What did I say at the briefing? They're all Viet Cong back here—every man, woman, and child. But they weren't soldiers. They weren't shooting at me. The men there in the bunkers, they're the ones shooting.

The after gunner crumpled to the deck, blood spurting from his leg. He hesitated, reached out, found the support for his after gun, and with a grimace pulled himself up, clutching his gun for support. He was ready again.

A bullet ripped through the awning three inches from my head. The forward gunner sat in a trance. Two bullets hit his gun shield. He flinched. Deeper we went, each foot drawing increased fire. Curse those sampans; curse those women and children and old men for being here. Curse my stupidity for coming in here. A bullet ripped into the first-aid box, throwing its contents violently asunder.

Did we worry about the women, the kids, and the old men in Dresden? I threw the forward gunner an M-16. "Shoot high!"

The after gunner sitting on the engine covers attempted to put a battle dressing on his leg. He wasn't doing a very good job—it kept slipping out of his hand.

What about the women, the kids, and the old men in Hamburg, Berlin, Tokyo?

I couldn't help the after gunner. Kramer and I had to keep up our useless barrage. A bullet creased Kramer. He screamed but kept firing. The forward gunner kept his M-16 hot. The coxswain zigzagged the boat. I wanted to crawl back into my mother's womb. The vile aura of death consumed me. I was desperate. "May God forgive me," I whispered, then yelled: "COMMENCE FIRE! COMMENCE FIRE!" Each man would have to live with my decision.

The after gunner pulled himself up and squeezed his trigger. A slight hesitation and the .50 blasted out. The people in the sampans ducked even lower. The forward guns joined; mud and dirt splattered as the slugs smashed into bunkers. Branches and trees fell, the tracers driving a deadly bridge of light between us and the jungle over the heads of the terrified sampans.

We came about. I ran midcanal. The .50s never stopped while Kramer and I salvoed our grenades ashore. The sampans scurried wildly. The Viet Cong never thought we'd fire. Take a lesson, Ho Chi Minh. The coxswain maneuvered violently through the turbulent, bullet-boiled water in our mad dash for the river.

A burst of fire cut diagonal holes across our battle ensign. Two sampans turned over behind us. A burst of ill-placed Communist fire cut across them—I heard no screams. Our exploding grenades painted ugly black smoke pictures above the bunkers.

Three bullets hit the engine cover armor plating, splattering all over the boat. Bayer screamed.

The after gunner's left sleeve was a mass of blood. His hands were shredded like a grisly coleslaw from handling the razor-sharp edges of the ammo cans. Bayer seemed okay. He swerved to miss a sampan running right over the full length of another. And another, and another. The crunching wood of the sampans and the drowning screams of the helpless women and children and old men crescendoed louder than our guns.

The port engine shuddered. Ran. Quit. We fell off step, the bow, digging into the water, jarring us to a near stop. The .50s went wild, the gunners losing control, bullets slicing into the air, down into the water, across the sampans, into the sky. Ten feet in front of us a frightful rocket explosion erupted a huge geyser of thick black smoke and muddy, frothing water, drenching us as we passed under. The port engine failure had saved our lives.

The fearsome BURAAT of multiple machine guns sounded over my head from Tanh Dinh. My heart sank. How much more could we take? I whipped around just in time to see a helicopter firing its flex guns as it launched four of its rockets from across the canal into the bunkers.

"Seawolves! Seawolves! Seawolves! How I love you, Seawolves!"

The rockets hit. The mainland shore disappeared in white, flaming smoke. White phosphorus—willie peter, beautiful willie peter. The lone helo pulled up the door gunners raking the beach. The enemy firing stopped, but we kept up our own guns as the helo covered our exit. We limped out of range.

"Seawolves, Handlash. Thanks. Where's your other bird? Over."

"This is Three Six. He aborted at takeoff. Should be ready in four five. Over."

"Roger, Three Six. Be advised that Cycle One still on station. Request you call for dustoff medevac at Tra On. Have one hurtin' bad. He'll be there in one five. Request you hose down area, then rearm. Inform me ETA soonest. I have one bad engine, investigating now, will keep you informed. Over."

"Roger all, Handlash. Wilco. Out." I could hear him putting in his strikes over his radio before it went silent.

We tied up again to the nest of two boats. They had their anchors out. "We'll have Santez's boat ready in a minute," Lieutenant (jg) Lange said. The after gunner's leg and hands, properly dressed now, were obviously painful. We carried no morphine on the boats because of the drug problems up north.

Santez's boat started up. Two good engines. We transferred the after gunner to him and he sped off for Tra On.

They had a helo pad, and the dustoff helo would probably be there before they arrived.

"What happened back there, Commander?" Lieutenant (jg) Lange asked.

"Only some wood in the pump, Commander." Kramer reported before I could answer the question. "Just a few minutes it'll be okay."

"They sucked us in . . . I was stupid. The VC shot our ass off. I don't understand this. I don't really know what happened . . . shouldn't have gone back in . . . had to shoot over the heads of the sampans . . . rotten show. Maybe they thought that the battleship was landing and they were getting their noncombatants out. I just don't know, Mister Lange, but it was the shits. Pisses me off so much I can't even think straight. God! we just ran right over some of those sampans and we shot over their heads, or I hope we did. Don't know if we hit any. Where's that fuckin' battleship?"

"Let's hit 'em again," he answered. I looked at him. He was serious. He had just grown three feet in my mind.

Kramer came out of the pump well, walked forward, and pressed the starter button for the port engine. It fired, throwing a jet of water out of the pump exhaust, straining against the nest. He cut the engine. "Ready, sir."

"You'll need an after gunner, Commander."

I looked at Lieutenant (jg) Lange in admiration. "Sorry about that academy crack. Who would you suggest?"

"I'm the only academy puke around."

"You got it, mister," I winked, turning to Kramer and his crew. Kramer had a bandage over the bullet crease on his head. "We're going in again. You guys up to it?"

Kramer looked at each of his crewmen. They looked back, not saying a word. They nodded. "We're with you, boss."

Thomas looked around his disabled, anchored boat, then at me. "Commander, you might need an extra gun hand."

"Welcome aboard."

We had requested a backup patrol from Tra Noc about ten

minutes ago. They were on the way. I could see the dustoff helo approaching the Tra On landing pad.

"Betray, Handlash. Interrogative ETA. Over."

"Zero ten, Handlash."

"Handlash, Three Six. Solo overhead in zero five. Out."

In we went. "Cry havoc," I muttered to myself. The waiting was over.

"And let slip the dogs of war." Lange completed the quote.

Thomas stared grimly ahead with a look of hate spurred on by a four-inch scar a Viet Cong bullet had etched across his stomach six months before. The wind rapidly consumed a cigarette clutched in his mouth. As it burned the tobacco blazingly hot, it left behind a grotesque jagged pattern of scorched paper.

He continuously flipped his weapon's safety catch on and off. Four beads of sweat rolled lazily down the back of his hand. His eyes, narrow slits, showed only deep, ferocious black pupils. Thomas was ready, the stock and barrel of his M-79 wet from his tightly clenched, blood-drained hands.

"Cycle One, Handlash. Out."

Click.

I pointed out the first position to Lange and Thomas. It was actually three bunkers, two on one side and one on the other side of a small canal that eventually led up to Saigon. Even as I pointed, the unmistakable red brilliance of muzzle flashes winked their bullets at us from the narrow slits at their bases.

The forward .50s answered back. A slow, high, gracefully arcing rifle grenade flew at us, exploding thirty yards off our stern. All three of our M-79s returned the fire, their black ball-shaped explosions demolishing any human within fifteen feet. The Viet Cong kept firing. Were we such poor shots? Kramer, now on the after gun, kept up a steady stream of probably useless fire from the .50s. I pushed the cease-fire alarm.

"Three Six, this is Handlash. Where the hell are you? Over."

"Look up, Handlash" came a clipped reply as his Huey burst over Tanh Dinh's treetops. Four streaming smoke lines trailed their rockets to the bunkers as the helo swooped in low and fast, the door gunners raining 7.62mm death on top of the bunkers.

The sound of angry hornets buzzed around us; an awning rail split; jagged holes appeared magically in the fiberglass; the compass disintegrated, splattering its fluid over the coxswain; Lieutenant (jg) Lange sank to the deck; the radar tube exploded; the lights on the lower radio blinked out with a hint of static; Thomas's arm turned crimson; my M-79 tore from my grip; a crease laid across the engineer's helmet; a full box of C rats jumped around the deck, with jagged dripping holes in its sides; the port engine sputtered; and only the forward .50 fought back.

The M-60 and the after .50 jammed. We had abused them mercilessly. The gunners tore open the breeches in a mad frenzy, trying to heal their battered guns.

Lange pulled himself to his knees. "In the leg . . . hurts." He picked up his grenade launcher, crawled to a gunwale, and started firing again. I looked at the shattered stock of my M-79. My stomach felt jammed into a blender; my hands tingled from the impact of the bullet.

Three Six flashed in again, hitting the bunkers with three rockets. A fire started, and smoke hung lazily in the treetops. The port engine sputtered again, coughed, coughed again, and roared up to full speed. Kramer ripped open Lieutenant (jg) Lange's trouser leg and applied a battle dressing. Bayer moved into midcanal, for what protection that was, while I dressed Thomas's arm.

Three Six swung around for another attack, this time lacing the bunkers only with guns. I guessed he was saving his rockets for a more defined target. He was keeping their fire off of us but taking it himself. I'd had enough; this was a job for the battleship.

"Three Six, this is Handlash. Getting too hot; we're pulling out. Over."

"Roger, Handlash. We'll cover ya. Out."

"Betray, this is Handlash. You copy my last? Over."

"Roger, Handlash. Turning into canal now. Out."

"Okay you guys, we're buggin' ass outta here. We'll hit 'em with everything we got." I looked at Lange and Thomas. "Sorry! I think we bit off more than we could chew."

They looked at me with forced smiles. "You saying never volunteer? I've learned the lesson again, I guess," Thomas said, adding: "Hell, Commander, I love this shit." His face belied his words. His expression had changed from grimly determined to that of a tired, old man. His jaw was no longer set in anger, and the fire in his eyes was now cold ashes.

A few men were running from the bunkers, but we weren't in position yet. The battleship came into sight as it was turning into the canal. The helo gunship circled behind us. "Handlash, Three Six. We received a few rounds from that church. Want us to hit it? Over."

"Negative, negative, Three Six. At the bunker . . . men running. Get 'em, get 'em."

I tapped Bayer on the shoulder, pointing to the bunkers. He eased his wheel to starboard; the shot-up PBR 127 leaned to the right as we started our run in. I adjusted my helmet again. It didn't need adjusting. I undid my flak jacket and tightened it up. It didn't need tightening. I put a cigar in my mouth. "Gotta light, Kramer?"

"No, sir."

The battleship turned into the canal. I checked again to see that my M-79 was loaded. It was. The forward gunner slinked down in his mount and ran his guns up and down, synchronizing them with the boat's speed so that they continuously laid on the bunkers. Lieutenant (jg) Lange and Kramer painfully uncrated more 40mm grenades. Thomas, for support of his bad arm, steadied his M-79 on the engine-cover armor plating. He looked somewhat rejuvenated. The crack of a rifle caused a small splash ten yards off the starboard quarter. Kramer, on the after gun, replied with a short burst into the tree line.

Sheppard, you asshole, what do you think you're doing?

You don't really think you're going to hurt that bunker, do you? Those walls are at least three feet thick. What are you trying to prove? Who do you think you are, committing these six men to a stupid fight? What about that lone helo up there just to support you. His ass is ten feet out on a broken limb. Face it, Sheppard, you're scared—bone-ass scared.

What about those guys crouched in those bunkers? I could only imagine their feelings as they sat poised behind the clay walls, watching the green boat getting bigger and bigger. Who was that running? The smart ones? They probably couldn't see the helo, but they know he's up there. They were probably scared. Why hadn't they bugged out? That's what they usually do. Stupid asses! Maybe the women and children and old men were their families. Maybe that's why they're staying. Why did they let them get in the sampans in the first place? Did they think we were white-hatted candy asses?

If they had run away I wouldn't have to be here. Why'd they have to shoot up our flag? Hell, what difference does that make? A boat never really got hit bad on the attack—the ambushes are what really kicked our ass. This wasn't too dangerous. Just think, I'll get another firefight on the tote board in the office. Now, isn't that important? You're brave, Sheppard—cool-ass courageous. Look at your hands—steady, aren't they? Feel that fine flow of energy through your muscles. Look how clear everything is. Look at the sun, it doesn't even blind you. You're ten feet tall, Sheppard. You can fly. Go ahead, flap your arms; you can fly.

See the blood oozing from the bandage on Lange's leg? I wonder if he can fly. Why does Thomas's arm keep falling away from his 79? How many holes you count in the boat? How much punishment can old PBR 127 take? Bayer, the coxswain, has an ass full of shrapnel. It looks as though he shit his pants. He's not sitting down, is he? How many women and children and old men did you drown and shoot—kill—today? Funsies, eh? Look at the blood all over. How come there's none of yours? Look at the shattered, twisted equipment. You've all but destroyed poor, old

127. Will she even get you home? Home, if you live, of course. "COMMENCE FIRE! COMMENCE FIRE! COMMENCE FIRE!" I screamed in rebellion against the accusing images.

The refreshing crescendo of the savage noise cleared my brain. This was the attack. This is why I'm here. Give me a fast ship, for I intend to go in harm's way. God bless America—my country 'tis of thee—Kate Smith—amber waves of grain—Mom's apple pie. "FIRE! FIRE! FIRE!"

Three Six came in low behind us, unloading six rockets.

We flashed by the bunker. Nothing. The battleship was getting closer. "Again, Bayer! COME ABOUT! Again, Bayer!" I shouted, all reason having left me.

We turned. The forward .50s churned up the dirt around the bunkers. Three Six circled for position. Lange no longer held his weapon. He lay on the deck, blood pumping out of his leg. Thomas looked at me, pleading: "I can't shoot fast anymore, Commander, my arm is like a rubber band."

"Use one hand, then. You can do it, Thomas, you can do it. Shit, man, Kramer's clap hurts more than that scratch on your arm. Fight the pain . . . fight the pain . . . few more minutes . . . few more minutes you'll be on a helo to Saigon."

He picked up his M-79 with one hand. "I'm . . . ready." His round flashed out to the beach. He fell. Got up.

The forward .50s clanked dry. "SHIT SHIT SHIT." The forward gunner ducked down to get more ammo. Kramer dove into the lower compartment to help pass it up.

Suddenly three Viet Cong bolted out of the bunkers. Thomas's shot—going high—exploded; one man fell. I fired simultaneously, hitting close but not before the two men threw themselves behind a fallen tree. I waited. We were rapidly pulling away. One man made his break no more than sixty yards from me. I aimed. Fired. "HIT! HIT!" I commanded.

I followed the black tearing dot of the grenade over the water, over the bunker, over the small canal leading into Saigon, and into the left shoulder of one of the fleeing men.

Black smoke obliterated him. But out of the smoke he came, running, twisting, heading madly toward the fallen log. Impossible! His left arm and shoulder flew off, but he kept running. His upper body grew in size, expanding, expanding, bursting in a bloody red eruption. His severed head kept running, running, arcing in a lazy path for twenty feet, dropping behind the fallen tree where the other man was waiting.

Three Six's rockets savaged the bunkers as we reached the sweet haven of the river.

Click. Click.

"Thanks, Captain"

———•———

I was sitting in my office when Captain Laske returned late in the afternoon. I hadn't done anything, just sat there vaguely recalling that I'd signed a few papers my yeoman had put before me. I was convinced that I was a psychopathic killer—insane—unfit for command. I must resign. I was a butcher, a murderer, all for what purpose?

"Good evening, Interdictor," Captain Laske said, coming into my office and throwing his combat bag into a corner. He took a seat next to my desk.

"My wounded are in Saigon."

"How many?"

"Three boats. They'll be back up sometime tomorrow."

"No . . . how many wounded?"

"Lange got it in the leg. Thomas's arm is pretty bad. A new kid, Walker . . . hip in bad shape. Bayer's ass is full of shrapnel and a new engineer from Golf Patrol took one in the chest. Shit! I don't even remember his name."

"What's that blood on your shoulder?"

"Nothing, it's okay."

"How are you, Don?" He'd never called me Don before.

"It's nothing, Captain, just a few scratches. My right arm hurts a little. I'm okay."

"I don't mean that, Don. How do you feel inside?" he asked, leaning over my desk.

He seemed so very close yet not quite there, only some filmy connection like railroad tracks coming over my shoulders from behind, disappearing in front of me to a perspective point on the horizon. In the distance a train was coming—just a speck, but coming—there was no time attached.

"Don . . . Don! How do you feel inside?" the speck—the train—asked.

"I . . . I never felt better."

"Why are you still wearing your flak jacket?"

I felt my chest for the first time and saw the dried blood on my hands. I stood. Captain Laske helped me off with my flak jacket.

"Silly, huh?"

"Not so much. Once in Korea I stayed in my flight suit for two days before I realized it."

"Silly, huh?" We sat there not saying a word, both of us staring at the large map of the Bassac. Five minutes passed.

"How was it, Captain, I mean after we left?"

"We destroyed those three bunkers and the SEALs went in for a body count. Seven."

I continued staring at the map. "Heard you've been shot down five times, Captain. That true?"

"No."

"How many?"

"Four."

"You really got the Navy Cross?" Five more minutes passed.

"Why, do you want one?"

"I was too young for World War II."

"It doesn't help, you know."

Someone turned on the lights. The black bugs started banging against the windows. "Lieutenant Baker do any good?"

"One Viet Cong stumbled in."

"How were things after we left?"

"Bad."

"Bad?"

"Bad."

"Figured so."

"You blaming yourself, Don?"

"Who would you blame?"

"Not you."

"I pulled the triggers. I kept going in. I ran over them."

"Feeling sorry for yourself, or for them?"

"Myself, mostly, I guess."

"Feel sorry for yourself, but don't blame yourself. Blame me; I ordered the operation."

I stared at him. "Hell, Captain, with that I could blame COMNAVFORV or CINCPAC or SECDEF or the president. That shit went out at Nuremberg."

My phone rang. Captain Laske picked it up. "Who? Eh? Yes, thank you, yes . . . yes . . . yes. Well, thank you, we're sorry, too." He replaced the phone and looked at me.

"I know, Captain. The kid whose name I can't fuckin' well even remember died."

"Name was Brewer. I'm sorry."

"Don't be, Captain. I've killed lots of 'em."

He ignored my self-pity. "Lange, Thomas, and Walker are in poor shape—on their way to Japan. They'll be okay. Bayer'll be back in a few days."

Sergeant Thanh came in carrying a bottle of whiskey. He stopped when he saw Captain Laske. "Thieu Ta, I . . ." He hesitated, looking at Captain Laske again.

"It's okay, Sergeant, come on in," I said.

"Yes, Sergeant, I was just leaving," Captain Laske said, starting to rise.

"Why everyone so sad?" Thanh asked, setting the whiskey on my desk.

"The commander lost one of his men today . . . shot up pretty bad," the captain answered in horrible simplification.

"One man, Thieu Ta," Thanh laughed. "Thanh lose hundred men . . . little brother . . . father . . . two sisters. Whole village burned . . . all killed except mother. That why Thanh fight with Thieu Ta. Lose one man? Thieu Ta, that is nothing. You have big victory today. We have drink. Captain, sir, you have drink."

"Victory? Thanh, do you know what happened today?" I asked, unstrapping my gun belt.

"I just come back from Phu Hoa—Golf. Just come back. Ong Tam very happy. Twenty-three VC killed by green boats, he say. Ong Tam say great victory on Bassac. He say Thieu Ta Sheppard great. What American word, *le guerrier?*"

"Warrior," Captain Laske answered.

"Yes, yes, WARRIOR! Thieu Ta, Ong Tam say VC very unhappy . . . lose too many comrades to green boats. Ong Tam send whiskey."

"But, Sergeant," I asked, pouring whiskey into three coffee cups. "Ong Tam is on the other side of the river. How could he know?"

"Thieu Ta, everyone know everything on the river. Ong Tam say you come, he will fight for you now he knows you are great le guer . . . no! Warrior . . . warrior."

Captain Laske lifted his cup: "Le guerrier!" he toasted.

"Le guerrier!"

"Le guerrier!"

And we emptied the cups. And another. And another. And time passed.

"Good night, Interdictor . . . Sergeant Thanh," Captain Laske said, bowing, wobbling slightly as he left the room.

"Captain!" I called to him. He turned. "Thank you!"

"Good to See You"

---•---

We obtained two 60mm mortars. Whining and begging paid off again. Unfortunately, none of us knew how to use them. We'd seen it done in the movies but could find no one who had ever shot one. I radioed Major Shellon from Tra On and asked him over for dinner in trade for instructions.

Lieutenant Norwick was up from the T for a "logistics" run. On a rotating basis, a 511 patrol coming off the river would divert to Tra Noc, ostensibly to pick up parts and supplies. Read that as get drunk and get laid. I would lend them my jeep and off they would go into Can Tho. Maybe a fourth of the time I'd have to go into Can Tho to bail them out of the MP stockade. That was okay with me. I'd built a rapport with the Can Tho MP advisors, keeping them supplied with whiskey and captured Viet Cong paraphernalia. It worked out; life was tough on the T. And these were my boys. The staff got wind of it once and, since that's what staffies do, tried to make a big deal of it. I lied and said I'd have some ass over it. That made them happy enough.

For Sergeant Thanh and his men it was a bit more difficult. One night Thanh and a few of his troopers tied on a good one. They tore up a bar and kicked some ARVN ass for not being aggressive enough. They were locked up tight and my American contacts could do nothing. This was purely a Vietnamese affair. I called in some favors.

We brought the subsector chief from Tra On into Can Tho to plead how courageous Sergeant Thanh and his men were and how much they had helped him. We presented Ong Tam and Co Bac from Golf to laud the men as the saviors of their village. It worked—being resolved with the good words of those we brought in and by me paying a fine of 20,000 piasters—about $170—from my secret funds. Money well spent.

The mortars were easy to use. The mortar was just a simple tube with a firing pin on the bottom. One drops the two-and-a-third-inch shell into the tube and when it hits the pin the mortar round fires out. Range is determined by the angle of the tube and the number of small firing charges one has rubber-banded to the shell. The tube, supported by two legs, had dials for fine elevation adjustments. It was not a mobile weapon.

Major Shellon told me about a counterbattery mortar the army had that tracked an incoming mortar round, adjusting itself to fire automatically back along the same trajectory. A bit discouraging to an enemy, I supposed.

We discarded the supporting legs and placed the tube on a sandbag in an ammo box. The gunner sat on the engine covers facing aft with the tube placed between his legs, controlling elevation and direction by hand. Another man affixed the firing charges to the round and on command dropped it into the tube. By judicious aiming a good gunner could continuously adjust his tube to fire on one area while the PBR sped by. It became a very skilled art and the good teams could drop up to ten rounds on a small area, such as a bunker, in twenty seconds. Only a few two-man teams were effective, but those that were, were magnificent. We practiced a lot. Lieutenant Norwick stayed on at Tra Noc to become familiar with the mortar.

"I gotta get back, Commander. Too much of this high living is messing me up for the real dangers of Dung Island."

"It's funny, Bill, it was rather quiet until you guys got down there."

He laughed. "Yeah, until you had to go through Khem Bang Co and stir them up."

"You think they might be cutting out a new crossing corridor?" I asked as we walked down the pier to the logistics boats that were preparing to get under way.

"I don't think so. Geography just isn't right with such a wide portion of the river to cross and so few canals on either side. I think it's just a PBR-VC hassle thing."

"Hardly worth fucking around for something like that, is it?" Five Eleven had been having a lot of firefights around Dung Island.

"I don't know, Commander. If they think we might put some troops in there and mess up their R&R center or screw up their training camp, maybe they'll have to keep more men there than they normally would. That's how I see it up here. Shit, I'm sure 512 doesn't stop any more crossings than we did, but all the shit you guys are laying on them keeps more of their troops occupied and away from up north."

First Class Petty Officer Bryan was standing on the pier waiting for us, his two boats banged up, badly in need of hull work. So was Bryan. "Ah, Commander, the boys and I want to thank you for last night." I had to go into Can Tho and bail them out of the stockade at 0300, five hours ago. I had bought them two cases of beer in payment for my first firefight with them.

"And we're sorry about your jeep," First Class Petty Officer Fern said, staring at his feet, looking no better than Bryan. "We didn't mean to wreck it."

"I see Romeo Patrol is at their best this morning," I said. "Willie, get your ass awake," I continued, laughing at the pathetic sight of the hung-over master gunner of the Bassac. "Can't you guys even have a few beers without getting fucked up?"

"Ain't our fault. Gee, Commander, we ain't never been the same since you made us go plum through Khem Bang

Co. We're just plain tuckered out," he teased. "We need your guidance, sir."

"I got your guidance, Willie—hanging. If you weren't such a good gunner I'd have court-martialed your ass months ago."

"Shut up, Willie," Bryan demanded.

They'd almost completed their loading of the mortar and boxes of ammunition for it. "Hear you got a Silver Star for that bit in Khem Bang Co, Commander. Congratulations, sir."

"You know how it is, Bryan, officers get the medals, enlisted men get the shit," I joked, but felt embarrassed by his statement. I didn't think I deserved the medal, the third highest in the nation, and more likely deserved a reprimand for going in after that junk with no support.

"You take it easy down there, Bill," I said, shaking his hand. "Hey, you guys, now that you know where we live, don't be strangers," I yelled as they pulled away.

"This is Lieutenant Don Rover, Commander, my relief," Lieutenant Simon said with that smug grin that men get when their reliefs were on board.

Don Rover was a big man, six foot, maybe six two. He didn't look like a combat trooper: He had a baby face and smiled as though butter wouldn't melt in his mouth. He gave the impression of being the good-guy type: an efficient but unexciting staff guy whose life would be devoted to making some admiral happy. At best a high-quota recruiter.

Five days later at the relieving ceremony, Lieutenant Rover was introduced to the men. Lieutenant Simon lauded River Section 512, I lauded Lieutenant Simon, and Lieutenant Simon said good-bye.

There was a new gun on the Bassac, and he started off on the run. He was constantly on the river. I surreptitiously administered much of the paperwork that he didn't even know about yet. In him I saw myself six months earlier. Six months—had I been here that long? I saw in him the same drive for action, the same lust for combat, the same push to get out there and do something. I counseled patience. We talked for hours as I tried to give him my wisdom, my experience. I had wasted time and lives and suffered agony reinventing the wheel. I had lacked a mentor and was not about to let that happen with Rover. Lieutenant Rover listened and learned, asking a thousand good questions.

On a Monday morning, Lieutenant Rover, Sergeant Thanh, and I drove into Can Tho to meet a Vietnamese major from the Soc Trang subsector. Thanh did not know the reason, nor did he question. In a small ceremony at the local ARVN headquarters, a tall ARVN major pinned the Vietnamese Cross of Gallantry on S. Sgt. Nguyen Thanh's chest and promoted him to master sergeant. It had cost me 10,000 piasters—$84.75—but it was worth a million to Thanh.

No current operations were planned, and action on the river was slow. It rained almost continuously, driving down in vertical sheets, distorting everything you could see in the limited visibility.

We were sitting in my office on the barge, going over old after-action reports with me pointing out the good and the bad features of each. I had classified our latest run through Titi with the battleship as extremely bad, bordering on gross stupidity on my part. The mental baggage still weighed heavily on me.

The watch officer from the ops center rushed into the office: "Tra On's under attack. They're being overrun! They want help!"

"Scramble four boats. I'll meet you on the pier!" I shouted to Lieutenant Rover, grabbing my combat bag and running for the pier. I was aboard the outboard boat warming up the engines and checking the fuel as the crews, Lieutenant Rover in the lead, came running down the pier. The sentry and I had already started the other three boats.

Lieutenant Rover and three crewmen came to my boat and we were under way before the other boats were completely manned. The second boat moved out as we turned around the stern of the barge. The third was just behind. We were midriver heading downstream as the lights on the fourth PBR cleared. The ops center reported the patrol at Juliet engaged and the patrol from the Tanh Dinh side diverted to assist.

"Handlash Two, this is Handlash. Be advised Handlash Two Actual aboard. Interrogative, who ordered the patrol to assist? Over."

There was a pause. I repeated the message.

"Handlash, this is Handlash Two. The ops center ordered. . . . Over."

"This is Handlash. Roger. Out."

"You see how they suckered us in on this one, Don?"

"Yes, sir."

"Ya gotta give the ops center some authority, but they must be made to understand that you must be informed of any deviations they make."

The tide was coming on high as we rounded five point five into the narrow east fork of Cu Lao May, heading for the barely visible fire over Tra On. The fourth boat joined up. We could see the tracers from the gunships working over the area to the north and east. I tuned to the army frequency and tried to give them a call. I could hear them but they couldn't hear me. The transmissions indicated that Tra On was being hit from both the upstream and downstream sides, in addition to rounds received from Cu Lao May across the canal, the heaviest push coming from the mainland side.

I could hear Major Shellon, the district advisor, expressing concern that the VC might cross over from Cu Lao May and attack from the water side. The helos replied that they'd blast anything that moved off the island. So would we, I thought.

"The pagoda, the pagoda!" a helo pilot yelled over the radio as tracers cut up at him from a large temple just upstream from the town. Major Shellon's voice reported, "Charlie's taken it, blast it . . . blast it."

We were getting closer but still couldn't raise Tra On or

the six helos up there. We were running as normal with no lights.

"There's a big boat down there moving fast" came the characteristic clipped, mushy voice from a helo's transmission. "I'll get it . . . I'll get it."

Lieutenant Rover and I strained to see any boats moving at high speed. We saw nothing. Maybe it was farther downstream. A helo broke off, heading for us. "Follow him," I ordered.

Tracers zipped at us from his flex guns, churning up the water and stitching holes across our bow. "LIGHTS! LIGHTS!" I screamed, diving for the electrical panel and jamming on the switches. We lit up like a Christmas tree. The other three boats followed our action. I didn't even know who crewed them.

"I guess we were the fast boat," Lieutenant Rover stated in a matter-of-fact voice, much cooler than I would have said it. "Pretty lousy shot, I'd say."

From the beach a blast of machine-gun fire took up where the helo left off. We were a beautiful target. The bullets didn't come very close but nonetheless we opened up on our attackers. I left the lights on.

"It's those navy boats," the helos yelled over the radio.

I tried the radio again. "Helo, Helo, this is Handlash, right under you—the navy boats, the navy boats. Over."

"Rog, navy boat Handlash. This is Maverick Leader. You're the dudes with the twelve point seven a while back, ain'tcha? Over."

"That's affirmative. You got tracers on your ass, Maverick. We're hittin' 'em now." Our guns opened up on Cu Lao May. In seconds the fire stopped. "Maverick Leader, this is Handlash. Can't raise Tra On. You got any instructions for me? Got four boats ready to go. Over."

"Wait. Out," he replied, and in minutes came back with: "Navy, the grunts say to hose down the island, then both sides of town. Copy?"

"Roger, Maverick Leader, but negative on the island. We

got four boats right across the other side. Don't want 'em to fire back at us. We'll take the sides. Over."

"Rog, navy, daddy grunt says come in to see him if you can. Out."

Lieutenant Rover sent the three boats with lights off to the end positions. We blinked our masthead lights on and off as we approached the rickety public pier. A blinking light answered.

"Chao, take me to Thieu Ta Shellon," I commanded the two Vietnamese RFs waiting for me on the quay. To Lieutenant Rover I said: "Pull out and wait in midstream."

"Well Shelly, looks like you gotta good one going." We shook hands. His were filthy, covered with blood.

The command post looked like something out of a World War I movie. Except for the helmets, it might have been. Rubble from the walls lay all about as if a hammer had crushed part of the building. The lone flickering, uncovered light bulb sizzling from the rain cast dim shadows on the crumpled plaster walls. Three Vietnamese soldiers burst through the door carrying a crying woman on a stretcher, her face gushing blood. Several other wounded lay around the room in various stages of pain, bandages, suffering, and filth. Mud covered everything.

"Can't you soldiers even defend a little bitty town like this?"

"Goddamn, Don, it sure took you long enough to get here. You stop at Can Tho for a quick piece of ass?"

A Vietnamese second lieutenant came over, put three x's on Shellon's map, and drew a line connecting them. It was well inside the town's border. I knew it was the VC line of advance. A bullet whistled in, splattering high against the wall. Plaster fell on me.

"Got the boats on each side of town blasting away."

Shellon didn't acknowledge. There was a muffled explosion from the direction of the marketplace. More wounded poured in. The helo pilots kept up their steady stream of undisciplined radio chatter. Two more had arrived on the scene, stating that Spooky was on the way. Visibility because of the rain was near zero, they complained.

"Look bad?" I asked.

"No, I think we can push 'em back," Major Shellon offered with a conviction I didn't feel that he really meant. The American advisors at the subsector level here had a tough time of it. They led a crummy life. They lacked command authority on their own; all deeds were accomplished as suggestions. The advisors' effectiveness rested solely on the rapport and feelings of the district subsector chiefs. Luckily, Shellon had a good one here. We had often had dinner together.

"What do you want me to do?" I asked him. "You know you caused me to walk out in the middle of a damn good war movie. And to top that your young buddies up there damn near waxed me."

"You sailors have a life of luxury up there at Tra Noc. Shit, I know, I just ate there."

"Where's your fancy counterbattery radar-controlled mortar system tonight? And besides, just last night the popcorn machine busted and at lunch the wine was improperly chilled. Don't talk to me about hardship," I retorted.

"Hell, only regular army gets the fancy stuff, not we frontiersmen," responded Shellon.

We both forced a laugh. The battle dressing on Shelly's head was turning dirty red. A flare from overhead lit up the area. Spooky was on scene, dropping his 200,000-candle-power magnesium flares. They floated down on gently swinging parachutes, trailing behind them a thick white smoke, the brilliant light blotting out all color. Distorted by the torrential downpour, the harsh light slammed through the doors and gaping holes in the roof.

The machine-gun fire was getting louder. We stared at each other. I wanted to yell at him to get his other three men and get the hell out of here. His eyes wanted the same, and as if our minds communicated, he said: "Shit, Don, it's my district."

"Shelly! This ain't Corregidor or the Bulge or any other godforsaken place that's worth a drop of your blood. Fuck it, Shelly, advise them you've got business in Can Tho."

"It's my job, Don," he answered, almost ashamed of the words.

"Yeah, I know. Whataya want me to do?" I answered, exhausted from my mental anguish for my compatriot.

"Well, Spooky seems to be hosing and the helos are working close in . . . not too effective at night. We . . . they got a lotta RFs out there. Could you take some of these wounded into Can Tho?"

I picked up the PRC-25 microphone and called in all four boats. In twenty-five minutes three severely overloaded PBRs shoved off for Can Tho. Chief Tanner was in command.

I took my boat and set up a blocking station between the town and Cu Lao May. If the VC planned to press the attack against the town from the island, they'd have to come through us. Also, if things really got out of hand, I'd be here to pick up the advisors. I didn't really think it would work. There'd be panic at the pier and no way could the advisors break through it. Given the caliber of Shelly's men, I doubted they'd even try.

I made Shelly agree that Tra On was not the Alamo or Fort Henry, and for him to sacrifice his life in combat was one thing, but sacrificing it for a few stinking buildings that the Viet Cong would abandon at first light anyway was quite another. He said he understood.

It was quiet on the river compared to the CP. There was no moon, but the ghastly light from the flares periodically made visibility excellent. I'm sure we were well silhouetted from the fires burning in Tra On. All the action from Cu Lao May had died down. The tide was ebbing. We'd run upriver for a short distance, then drift back down. Just the chatter of the helos and Spooky kept us informed of the action.

In twenty minutes the helos announced that the VC were pulling back. Spooky moved in closer and closer to the town. Finally, he rogered being released by Tra On and headed home. The helos had departed minutes before. It was over.

On the other side of the town, the helos were still working over the area pretty well. All the previous action on Cu Lao May had died down. There was nothing for us to do but wait. We waited and drifted. Time passed slowly. After twenty to thirty minutes the boat captain finally spoke. "Commander, the port backing gate's stuck."

The boats reversed by lowering a gate over the water jet exhausts. This forced the high-velocity stream of water under the boat toward the bow, thus backing her down.

"SHIT!"

The engineer bent way over the stern. "Hey, Boats," he reported, "need a big screwdriver. This thing's really jammed."

"There's a big toolbox up here but it's locked," the coxswain answered.

"How 'bout the chief's quarters?" I asked. The enclosed radio compartment was called the chief's quarters—supposedly a comfortable place and thus derogatorily implying that chief petty officers, the highest enlisted grade in the navy, always had it comfortable. They usually did not.

"It's locked," Don Rover answered.

Since we'd had so much trouble with pilferage lately, the boat captains had taken to locking up their tools. When we scrambled, we of course didn't have time to get the keys or the right boat captain to the right boat.

The boat lurched slightly and stopped. "We're aground," someone said.

"Let's push it off," Rover ordered, and four of us stepped off the boat into the murky water and shoved. The boat didn't budge.

"We could wait till the tide came up," Boats said. We called every boat captain Boats.

"Yeah, we could, and maybe get our ass shot off in the process," I replied.

"Hey, Horner," Rover called to the coxswain, "you get off and help, too. One more man might make the difference." The coxswain joined us.

"Tie a line around yourself," Rover told him. "If the boat pushes off too fast, it'll drag you with it and you can come back and get us."

I was ashamed that I hadn't thought of it. "Damn good idea, Don."

We pushed and shoved, grunted and groaned. It happens to everyone—the old adage drifted through my thoughts. Not to me, my old answer haunted. We pushed and shoved, grunted and groaned.

The boat moved, stopped. More, a little more. My hands pounded from the strain; brilliant colored psychedelic stars and pinwheels danced in my brain. The boat moved, stopped, moved, and with a slurping suck, broke free. We scrambled aboard. Horner started the starboard engine and we pulled into deep water.

All the firing had stopped; Tra On was quiet. The fires had burned low. Now it was really dark, with only the faint light from the stars giving any illumination at all.

"I just can't fix this gate without a wrench and a screwdriver," the engineer pleaded.

"Shoot the lock off the chief's quarters door," the boat captain said.

I drew my .38 and put it next to the lock. "I wonder where the bullets go when you do this," I commented to Rover.

"Don't know."

"They don't seem to have any trouble in the movies," I said.

"If the lock doesn't splatter all over us, it'll probably glance through the bottom of the boat," Rover replied.

"That'd be inconvenient," I offered.

"Yeah, the maintenance people get all pissed."

"Why don't we hold that toolbox over the stern and blast its lock off?" the boat captain volunteered.

"Good idea," Rover said as they walked aft with it.

"Shut down the engine. I don't want to miss."

We drifted upstream. The tide was coming in fast and Tra On moved rapidly down our starboard side.

"Hold her steady now." I put the flashlight right on the lock and brought my gun barrel two inches from it. "Which way do you think I should shoot—straight down or to the side?"

"Straight down," answered Rover.

"To the side," countered the boat captain.

We discussed it for two or three minutes. The boat was picking up speed. "This box is getting mighty heavy, Commander. Do something."

I pulled back the hammer, aiming carefully; I would go for a straight down shot. As I bent over to get a better view, we hit a submerged log and the boat lurched. I bumped the boat captain. He dropped the box and the huge splash soaked all of us.

"SHIT!"

"Hell! We'll go on one engine. Call Tra On, Don, and tell 'em we're leaving. Looks like the war's over. The other two boats should be back anytime."

"Engine won't start, Mister Rover," the coxswain reported.

"Radio's dead, Commander."

"Check the batteries."

"Batteries all shot up. I don't know how they lasted this long," the engineer said in a disgusted voice.

"Throw out the anchor, then. Hurry."

The forward gunner scurried down into the forward compartment and in a few seconds emerged in a panic. "We ain't got no anchor."

"We're in deep shit, Commander. That's real bad-guy territory we're drifting into," the boat captain offered.

"I'm more worried about those two trigger-happy PBRs on the way back."

"I reckon you're right," he said.

We drifted at two or three knots for ten minutes and then hit the beach with a thud. The low-hanging palms raked the top of the boat and slapped viciously at our bodies as we vainly tried to grab them. The branches cut our hands and knocked us over. Finally, after fighting them for five minutes, we clutched the boat to a stop. The forward gunner threw a line around a tree. We had made so much noise, I was sure we had alerted every Viet Cong for miles around.

And there we sat. We'd lost our mobility. If the Viet Cong attacked, we could fight to be sure, but the tracers zipping around would call in the PBRs wherever they were, and they'd come in blasting. An odd phenomenon of tracers in the night is that you can't tell which way they're going if you're at any distance at all from them.

I searched the jungle and the river with our starlight scope. This night-observation device (NOD) electronically amplified any available light by fifty thousand times. Where the human eye saw only darkness, the NOD would show an eerie green landscape, like something from a science fiction movie. If a campfire appeared during the search, it blossomed in the scope, temporarily blinding the viewer. After using the scope for only a few minutes, a green spot appeared in your vision, staying there for five to six minutes. I rarely used it.

We waited. It was like a tomb, with only the tide lapping against the hull to break the silence. A Vietnamese night bird mocked us and a strong wind rattled the high palm leaves and chilled our wet bodies.

The increasing rumble of diesel engines announced the coming of the two other boats. From a slight hum the noise grew until it overcame all else.

The coxswain drew out his .44 magnum revolver. "What're you doing?" I asked.

"Gonna fire a shot into the air to tell 'em we're here."

"ASSHOLE! Put that gun down before six fifties cut into us."

"Jesus! You're right."

"Flash your light, Commander," the rear gunner suggested.

"Christ! That's just as bad," Rover said.

"I don't see why," he replied.

"Dumb head," the boat captain answered. "How do the Viet Cong sometimes signal their crossings?"

"With a flashing light. And we shoot at the lights" came the apologetic answer.

"We'll let 'em go by. When they don't find us at Tra On, they'll be back looking for us," I said, and hoped.

The boat came into view. They were on step and moving fast. "Pretty, aren't they?" I said to Rover.

"Beautiful targets. Look at how big they appear. I don't know how the Viet Cong keep from wiping us out."

"Would you like to go against those eight machine guns and the helos they call in?"

"NO!"

Down the river they went until their roar became a murmur. We were alone again. Five minutes, ten . . . stretched to twenty.

"Where are those bastards?" the coxswain cursed.

"Don't know."

Five more lethargic minutes dawdled by. Then came the low trolling of four diesel engines. They were coming back. I prayed they'd keep a cool head. How could we signal them? What if the Viet Cong took the slow boats for a juicy target and opened up? Who was the patrol officer? Was it still Tanner? Were the crews experienced?

They were about two hundred yards from us. Their searching lights were playing along the bank. A small comfort, for where the searchlight pointed the two .50s followed. The light was mounted directly between the forward guns. I was sure they had their .50s double-cocked. At least if I were there, they would have been.

"Whataya think, Commander?" Rover asked, his voice betraying just a hint of nervousness.

The coxswain blurted: "You don't think they'll miss us, do you, sir?"

"I don't think so," I replied, mustering all the courage I could to hold my voice steady. Goddamnit, why do they ask me? I don't know. Hell! Why is the leader supposed to know everything? I was no more of a man than any of them. I was just as petrified. I wanted to cry. Don't shoot! Don't shoot! the whirlwind voice in my mind pleaded. I wanted to hide behind the armor plating. I wanted to run away.

I had to do something—anything. I was the leader. I blinked my flashlight. I was sending an SOS. That's all my fear-soddened mind would let me remember in Morse code. I hoped they could read the blinking light. I hoped they wouldn't shoot.

The two boats stopped. I almost swallowed my tongue. A series of light flashes came from one of the dark hulks.

"Can you read it, Don?"

"I think they said S-H-I-T."

My brain strained for the code. The dots and dashes jumbled in pained confusion. "What is Y?"

I could hear Rover say, "Uh . . . it's . . . uh . . . yeah, dah, dit dah, dah."

"Right!"

I flashed back, "ON YOU."

"Identify yourself!" came, I think, Chief Tanner's gruff command, sounding like a sweet angel's kiss coming from underwater.

"SHEPPARD WITH ROVER, HORNER, AND RANKIN!" Rover shouted.

I turned to Rover. "That's not a good identification. The Viet Cong could easily read our ID cards and give the same info." They were both drifting by us. Please, Viet Cong, don't shoot now.

"YOU THERE," another voice boomed. I heard the thunder of a .50 being double-cocked. "Who was the star pitcher for the losing team in the '65 world series?"

I knew it. Every damn baseball fan thinks everyone else knows that trivia bullshit, and everyone who doesn't is prima facie not a loyal American.

"Anyone know?" I asked, the anxiety nearly breaking my veneer.

"No!" came several replies.

"Satchel Paige!" was one apologetic answer.

"I don't think so . . . WE DON'T KNOW!" I shouted. The immense deluge of rain distorted our voices beyond recognition. They were drifting by.

"It's Raymond's voice," sang out Horner, the coxswain. "RAYMOND, you bastard, come over here and get us before I take that five bucks you owe me and jam it up your ass!" Horner shouted.

Silence from the boats. Their engines started and one headed for my flashing light. I knew that they wouldn't be able to see us until they were right on top of us. They'd snap on their gun-mounted light at the last moment. Don't be nervous, gunner—don't slip.

Fifty . . . forty . . . twenty yards. The light torched on, blinding us. "IDENTIFY YOURSELVES!"

"IT'S SHEPPARD, GODDAMNIT. Toss me a line, and turn off that fuckin' light before you get us all killed."

"Okay, okay, Commander! We had to be sure."

In short order they pulled us from our mangrove-entangled prison and we were on our way.

A lump waltzed in my throat. I was thankful it was too dark and too wet to see the tears trickling down my cheeks.

Search and Lounge

———●———

It was Wednesday, and we were moving into our new base on Friday. Across from the new base, separated by a six-hundred-yard channel, was a small island called Cu Lao Nei. The far side of the Bassac from the island was about a mile across and, to the best of our knowledge, controlled by the Viet Cong. We didn't really know, but if the Viet Cong could infiltrate Cu Lao Nei, they would have a perfect place from which to mortar our base. The local ARVN said that the island was friendly. I never believed the ARVN and thought that we should sweep the island.

I discussed the possibility of VC infiltration with Sergeant Thanh, and he concurred that a sweep would be a good idea. I suggested we do it in the morning.

"Island may have many Viet Cong, Thieu Ta. Better Thanh go alone with men," he said.

"No, Thanh," I replied with bravado. "The Bassac is my responsibility. We'll both go." I knew all about search and destroy missions. Hell, hadn't I seen a dozen of my movie heroes do it? It looked easy enough: Be watchful, be quiet, be decisive, go where the enemy thinks you can't. This formula has worked for centuries.

At 0600 the next morning my little amphibious assault force hit the beach at Cu Lao Nei. The six of us drifted in on a small boat beaching and waited for the dawn.

At the first hint of light we disembarked clandestinely. Unopposed, I hand signaled the point man to move out, low. I put my right index finger to my lips and whispered a barely audible shhh! We advanced with Private Tho in the lead, then Sergeant Thanh, me, Corporal Chi, and Private Phan, with Private Loc bringing up the rear.

We moved forward stealthily. My eyes missed nothing; my ears tuned to hear the smallest rustle. I scanned the long, undulating palm leaves waltzing in the sky over us. I looked ahead with piercing, knowledgeable eyes for the expected thin, near-invisible wires that would explode the insidious booby traps. I tried to perceive the telltale markings of disturbed earth that would announce the crippling punji stake pits. I searched ahead, I searched our flanks, I searched behind us.

I was ready. My dog tags were taped as I'd seen in a movie. A big rubber band held grass twigs around my helmet for camouflage. I held my M-3 grease gun loosely across my chest, ready in an instant to spray .45 slugs into any enemy. Three full clips of thirty bullets each hung from my belt.

Developed in the early forties to be manufactured cheaply with just a minimum of parts, the M-3 grease gun was dropped to resistance fighters in Europe. I imagined they caressed it for comfort just as I was doing now. The grease gun, called that because it looked like one, was an extremely reliable weapon that could be dropped in the water and brought up firing. It fired a standard .45-caliber round that had tremendous stopping power. Its only problem was its slow rate of fire and the weight of the .45-caliber slug. I was the only one on the Bassac who had one. I wondered where Chief Gathy had gotten it. I wondered about its history.

My bayonet, honed to razor sharpness and strapped upside down on my flak jacket, could be drawn in an instant. My helmet was buckled securely—no clanking straps to give us away. My .38 and four hand grenades completed my arsenal.

At the sound of a snapping branch I whipped my body around and almost fired at Corporal Chi. "Quiet!" I mouthed. I imagined that every lurking enemy eye on the island followed my every movement.

In about twenty minutes we broke out of the underbrush. We were at the edge of a wide clearing laid out into somewhat sloppy rice paddies. Two old men and a couple of women were working the fields no more than a hundred yards away. If they had heard or seen us, they didn't show it. Thanh motioned to the right as we inched our way slowly to the end of the clearing. Moving so deliberately was a tedious chore. My equipment became heavier with each step.

We came upon a grass hootch. My pulse nearly doubled. We waited, watching very carefully. The house seemed deserted. I motioned for two men to cover the far side and left two of them where we were. If the Viet Cong, hidden inside, made a break through the front or back, the flankers would catch them in a cross fire. If they fought inside, Thanh and I would get them. At an agonizingly slow creep Thanh and I crawled to the front. My knees were bruised and my trousers ripped. Damn, trousers were hard to get. In five minutes we were in place ten yards from the front door.

Thanh made a birdcall imitation, signaling his intent to close in. Another glance around verified that we were not in a trap. I tapped Thanh on the shoulder. He leapt forward, crashing through the front door. I waited a second, then hurled myself in after him. I envisioned four or five top-cadre leaders at a high-level meeting, scurrying around in confusion as we surprised them. The hootch was empty.

"Sonovabitch! They got away."

"No, Thieu Ta, house not lived in for long time."

"Shit!" I said in a loud whisper. I felt as if I were in an old Abbott and Costello movie.

We re-formed and continued down the island, pausing every few minutes to listen. Corporal Chi was now on point. A loud click from behind—I snapped around. Private Phan whipped his hand away from his M-16 as I turned. Sergeant Thanh grabbed his ear and twisted. Phan had clicked his safety off instead of easing it forward. The noise from the simple movement magnified by our tension was almost deafening.

We moved forward slowly. The camouflage dark green and black greasepaint I had put on my face held in the heat. It was the first time I had worn it and, though I looked ferocious, I felt a little foolish and even more uncomfortable. I had been trained by the navy to hunt submarines. What the hell was I doing here looking like a commando sweeping an island for enemy soldiers? I wished I hadn't started this stupid operation.

My eyes hurt from the strain. We moved slowly because of my fear of booby traps. A favorite of the VC was to pull the pin on a hand grenade and put the grenade in a tin can. They would attach a thin wire to the grenade and stretch it across a trail. When an unsuspecting man walked through and tripped over the wire, it would pull the grenade out of the can, the spoon would fall away, and that was it. To cinch the deal, the VC would sometimes use two cans with a grenade in each one and a wire tied between them. When the wire pulled out, two grenades exploded and that was the last thing you ever heard. Empty C-ration cans were the perfect size.

One plus for our side was the poor condition of the VC grenades in this area. Most were duds, resulting at best in low-order detonation. It was not that way up north, I understood. There was a story told of a grenade being tossed into a crowd of Americans at the Can Tho airport several months ago. An air force lieutenant threw himself over the grenade to save the people's lives. Nothing happened. The air force lieutenant just lay there, they said, with an odd expression on his face. He then got up and walked away. I wondered what he was thinking.

Corporal Chi raised his hand—we froze. Sergeant Thanh moved forward and in a few minutes came back. "Thieu Ta,

Thieu Ta," Thanh reported, "Buddhist temple and big house in clearing. Men talk and laugh in house. One man lay outside. Many Viet Cong, I think."

"We'll hit it."

"But maybe many Viet Cong, Thieu Ta."

"Surprise is on our side. If they've got time to carry on like that, they don't know we're here." I paused in consideration. Maybe it was a trap. Maybe they'd been tracking us since we landed. None of us were jungle fighters. Maybe we should get the hell out of here and let the real army do it. Shit, who was available to do it if we didn't do it ourselves? Surely not the ARVN. Anyway, it would take them days to organize and the VC would just move out and we'd have to do it again. We'd go for it now.

"Send two men, Sergeant Thanh, to circle the clearing, just to make sure that this is not a trap. Have them report back," I ordered.

In twelve minutes the scouts returned. "No Viet Cong around clearing."

"Same plan, Sergeant Thanh: two men on each flank; you and I will work our way around and bust through the front door together. You take the right, I'll take the left."

Thanh laid out their fields of fire and they moved out smartly to take their positions. I couldn't decipher much of what he said, but I did catch his last command of no shooting into or across the house or temple.

In six minutes we figured they were in position. Thanh and I moved in at a creep under cover of the small temple. My senses were peaked to a state of agony. Nothing escaped them. My footsteps sounded and felt like the clod of an elephant. My eyes and ears picked out the slightest rustle of a leaf.

We made it to the temple. The side of the hootch facing us had only one door and a window. I suggested to Thanh that we cut through the temple but he objected, so we inched our way around. When we reached the corner, we had twenty yards of open ground between us and the door. My trigger finger tingled. I had to fight the urge to stand where I was and fire my machine gun right through the thin bamboo walls. I loosened the pins on two of my grenades.

We listened carefully for intense laughter; we'd strike then. Hell, this was no different than playing kick the can when I was a kid. Even then I felt the same exhilaration, the same turbulence inside.

"Take them prisoner if we can, Thanh," I whispered. He nodded yes. "Understand?" I asked. He nodded again. I bet he did; sometimes Thanh shot a little too quickly.

Laughter. Now, I mouthed.

We dashed toward the door, made it, and paused, standing with our backs to the wall. "Ready?"

He nodded. We turned and burst through the door. "SURRENDER OR DIE!" I shouted in Vietnamese. Thanh was yelling at them to throw up their hands.

The men inside screamed. Four of them sitting at a table knocked over three whiskey bottles as they jumped up, hands in the air. A man lying in a bed swung upright, throwing his hands high. Two men hunkered down by a stove kept their position, slowly raising their hands. One man bolted for the door. My finger squeezed the M-3 machine-gun trigger; five bullets tore through the earth floor toward him. He stopped.

"Down! Down on the floor!" Thanh commanded. The one who had dashed for the door was too slow in obeying. Thanh cracked him across the back with his M-16 butt. I shouted for our men to come in. I was as happy as a whore in heat on payday. One man started to speak; Thanh slapped him across the face. "Quiet," he ordered. Six prisoners, hot damn!

The four flankers plunged in. Thanh beamed.

"Search the place. Get something to tie these bastards up with, and two of you stand guard outside. Quickly!" I ordered.

Corporal Chi yanked open a large metal locker. "Thieu Ta, look!" In the locker were six ARVN uniforms.

"Spies, infiltrators, eh? We got the bastards before they

could escape." One of them from the floor tried to speak again. Thanh jammed a filthy rag in his mouth.

"Here American radio, Thieu Ta," Corporal Chi said, laying a backpack PRC-25 at my feet. The PRC-25 was an FM transceiver and now the standard U.S. Army walkie-talkie. Private Phan brought six carbines and a .45 and laid them on the table. I was rifling through papers in the desk.

With a screech Private Tho erupted into the room. Ahead of him he flung two Vietnamese women. I whirled about, but before I could recognize him my hypersensitive nerves pulled my finger taut on the M-3's trigger. The thunder of three shots shattered his scream, "NO SHOOT, THIEU TA!" My finger went limp a second before the rest of me.

"YOU STUPID, STUPID BASTARD, THO!" I leapt for him. "You stupid bastard," I repeated, viciously ramming him in the stomach with my gun butt. He doubled over, a look of disbelief on his horrified face. He rolled over and lay crumpled in a corner, puking his guts out.

Thanh walked over to him and let loose a string of foul words just before he slapped him in the face.

The women lying on the floor sobbed softly. Thanh ignored them. I sat on a stool. My hands shook—I'd almost killed Private Tho. I looked down at my machine gun. It sat there, innocent as hell, in my lap.

The trussed-up prisoners said nothing. Thanh lifted one of them into a chair.

"Ask him where the other Viet Cong are."

Thanh started his interrogation. His voice changed from its normal pleasing singsong to a foreboding, demanding snarl. They talked for four or five minutes. Thanh back-handed the man across the face two or three times.

"Goddamnit, Thanh," I interrupted, "what's he saying?" The Vietnamese talk and talk but say little. They were yapping too fast for me to understand.

"He say he ARVN sergeant."

"What else?"

"That all."

"That's all? You've been talking for five minutes . . .

that's all?" I turned to the bound, obviously scared and uncomfortable prisoner. "What unit you from, soldier?"

He chattered off a reply. "What'd he say, Thanh?"

"He say he from artillery unit across from PBR base."

"Search him!"

Thanh rifled through his clothes and pulled out an ID card. "It say he sergeant in ARVN, Thieu Ta."

"Check the others." A quick search produced six more ARVN cards.

I picked up a radio frequency list from the desk drawer and checked it against the frequency tuned in on the radio. It was the local ARVN reporting circuit. "You know the call sign of the unit, Thanh?"

"Yes."

"Call the PBR base. Have one of your men go over there and call us to identify these men."

He did. We waited. Thanh moved the two women over to the bed. They sat there silently. I called Thanh aside and whispered, "Make them as comfortable as you can. If they really are ARVN, my ass is in a genuine sling."

I went over to Private Tho and helped him up. "I'm sorry, Tho, Jesus! I'm real sorry." It had been absurd—the worst outbreak of bad temper I had ever had.

"I sorry, Thieu Ta. I stupid . . . I not do again."

I walked to the door with him, my arm around his shoulder. "Stand guard, Tho. You're okay, boy," I said, smiling. He smiled back. I felt better. We waited.

In fifteen minutes the radio crackled out in the familiar voice of Private Lin. We listened, but except for the names on the ID cards, I couldn't understand it.

Thanh replied, then laid the mike on the table. I knew the answer. Christ! I knew the answer. The soldiers on the floor smiled the answer. Thanh's dropped face gave the answer.

"What'd he say, Thanh?"

"He say these men ARVN soldiers."

"Untie them."

My men obeyed quickly. This was crummy; we hadn't treated them too gently. If the goody-goody civilians ever got hold of this, they'd make a big thing of it. What's the old saying? The best defense is a good offense?

"Thanh!" I barked as I sat at the table. "Bring the sergeant over here."

A bedraggled, skinny man with betel nut–stained teeth and long black hair haughtily sauntered over. He had a smug look of disgust on his face. He chattered in a high, singsong voice too fast for me to understand. I reached into my pocket and pulled out my gold oak leaf rank devices. I made sure he saw them. He quit talking. His eyes grew wide. He looked scared again. I made a show of pinning them on my collar.

"SIT DOWN!" I hissed in Vietnamese, my eyes drilling into his. "NAME AND RANK?" I snarled.

"Sergeant, Sir, Sergeant Phue," he snapped back.

"Why aren't you and your men in uniform?" I demanded in my limited Vietnamese.

He answered, again talking too fast. I pretended to understand him. "Not good enough, Sergeant," I tried to make "sergeant" sound like an insult. I had to psych him. Maybe I could pull out of this one yet. I picked up one of the rifles from the table. Without looking at it, I tossed it to him.

"Why is this rifle dirty, soldier?" Chances were good that it was. He opened the breech slowly and looked up the barrel.

"I'm sorry, Thieu Ta." The "Thieu Ta" had a good deal of respect in its tone.

"How long have you been in the army, soldier?"

"Seven years, Thieu Ta."

"In seven years you should have learned not to be taken by surprise."

"Yes, sir."

"Get your men in uniform, immediately! I'm not going to report you, this time."

He jumped to obey, yelling orders to his men. He commanded the women to clean the place. There was a scurry of activity.

It had worked. Thanh came over and whispered, "Thieu

Ta do smart thing. Sergeant think he in real trouble." In five minutes the men were soldiers. I whispered to Thanh to tell them on the sly that I was a good man and trustworthy and for them not to worry.

Thanh smiled. The room we were in was large. There were four slat beds and two tables. A small cookstove was in the center, and a huge locker stood against one wall.

"He happy, Thieu Ta. He wants to offer you a drink. You should not say no. He lose much face already."

I agreed, after seeing that four guards, two of Thanh's and two ARVNs, were posted outside. The women served the warm whiskey as we sat around the table. One bottle disappeared. Then another. We were all happy now. The soldiers talked and joked. My facial expressions and laughter mimicked theirs. Each word caused the men to laugh harder.

"Let's get out of here, Thanh," I whispered. The physical and psychological ordeal of the day had exhausted me.

Two more young women came in with bundles of food. "Thieu Ta eat with us?" Sergeant Phue asked hesitantly. "Women fix good food."

Sergeant Thanh looked at me. "I think we should, Thieu Ta. It would be better."

Sergeant Phue insisted that no VC were on the island or had ever been. His mission here was to patrol the island and report any enemy activity. My opinion of the ARVN increased dramatically. Had all the stories and my prejudice given me such a false impression over the months? Granted, any VC could have taken them as easily as we did, and he should have had patrols out, but what the hell, it was boring duty. The poorly paid and more poorly led ARVN were not the soul of efficiency. Also, it didn't help much when they saw the great privileges being enjoyed by their officers.

Hell! maybe they weren't poorly led; maybe the officers were just saving their lives in a war they didn't care about. The dictator in Saigon wasn't too popular and I didn't see any benefits his government brought to the people. I don't think the people cared one way or another who led the country. Communism—what the hell was that? The people just wanted to grow rice and live the easy life of the delta. And from the stories we heard and read, the soldiers of the great American army up north weren't doing themselves too proud by their actions.

One could excuse these ARVNs. I could excuse these men but never my own for the same conduct. It didn't make me feel too comfortable about the security of the island but it was better than nothing. If the VC wanted to hit our base they could more easily do it from the mainland, just as they could torch Binh Thuy Air Base anytime they felt like it.

In sum, a wasted day.

"May I Be
of Assistance?"

———•———

Early in the summer, Captain Laske assigned the Seawolf helo detachments and the LST to my operational control (OPCON). Now I could move the LST to where it could best be employed, and where I felt it could do the most good. I no longer had to request permission from higher headquarters to deploy my forces.

With these extra forces came extra problems—not with the T, for its captain was a real, live, surface line officer, steeped in the tradition of obeying orders and performing his mission. The difficulties arose with the Seawolves, the naval aviators who were, by necessity, machine- and self-oriented.

When the helos passed to my OPCON, Captain Laske's guidance was succinct: "Sheppard, bring those helos under control; they're here to support the PBRs, not to fly all over the delta looking for something to shoot at. They're to be responsive to your needs and your needs only."

The road was long and scattered with ruffled feelings and innuendos of the stupidity of higher command (which included me). Ever so slowly, they complied, complicated no small amount by the helo detachments' OinCs being several years senior to me. The strides were slow and reluctant, until Lt. Comdr. Bill Marsh reported aboard to take command of the newly formed helo detachment at Binh Thuy.

Bill was a naval officer who incidentally was a helo pilot, not the reverse. He was a rare breed. We talked. I liked him. I wanted to be his friend, but you can't become friends with a man you might have to order to die. His assistant, Lt. Comdr. Chuck Sams, was of the same cut. Here was a team that understood. Here were two Bassac Interdictors. These men were to walk the riverbanks, talk to the people, see what a rocket does to a man's stomach.

Don Rover and these two went to work. I sat back and watched, and was proud. For the first time, with all due respect to those who preceded me, I felt that I had help in anything but brute force. They developed tactics; they molded the PBRs and helos into a close-knit, integrated fighting team. I no longer had to plan and work out everything anew. A new era had arrived on the Bassac.

Marsh and Sams spent most of their early days in the air. Their helos could be seen almost anytime over the Bassac as they became familiar with their battleground. Thousands of rounds poured out of their guns as they perfected their skill. Their rockets went where they aimed and their bullets laced the trees they chose. The detachment had their own maintenance force and sufficient repair parts.

Don Rover and his boats worked closer and closer to the target, until finally confidence grew to where the helo fire teams would lay their strikes twenty to thirty yards from the boats.

One notable tactic they developed, which later grew to be one of our most successful, was called helo hide. This tactic was dangerous, but when it connected the VC suffered heavy casualties. Either Bill or Chuck would set down his helo fire team at an outpost close to the mouth of a small canal. Meanwhile, Don would take two boats up the narrow channel at slow speed, just daring the Viet Cong to strike.

Up these small tributaries the Viet Cong did not have the heavy bunkers that dotted the Bassac and were vulnerable from the air.

The first time they used this tactic, the Viet Cong fell for it as though they were part of the plan and had rehearsed their part. Don was up the narrow canal at Hotel perhaps a half to three-quarters of a mile in when a couple of sniper shots cut close to his boats. He returned only a few rounds and continued in. Four hundred yards more and two machine guns blasted him. He engaged and called the helos. The Viet Cong, thinking that the helos wouldn't arrive for their normal twenty to twenty-five minutes, couldn't resist fighting; two boats in a confined canal were a lucrative target.

I could only imagine the enemy's shock when, in three minutes, seemingly from nowhere, two deadly helos were on top of them. The first operation netted five dead Viet Cong.

The plan also worked with the SEALs. We received intelligence on the exact location of some hootches where some VC would be spending the night. The SEALs inserted by strike assault boat (STAB) just before daybreak and hit the hootches at first light. The helos were idling on the ground at Golf. The VC, in panic, broke and ran. The SEALs followed in hot pursuit. Three of the VC ran into an open field and the helos were overhead. Lieutenant Commander Sams circled low over the running VC and with a few well-placed rounds from his side guns convinced them to stop. They did, throwing down their AK-47s.

Sams landed his helo next to them. Tension in his crew was running high, he told me later. This was their first time in direct eyeball-to-eyeball contact with the enemy. I could picture how they felt with adrenaline jamming through their veins. Sams ordered his left door gunner to "get 'em!" The door gunner, thinking "get 'em" meant to shoot them, fired, cutting a VC to pieces with his mounted 7.62mm M-60. Sams's scream of "NO!" came too late.

The door gunner was operating on instinct. He felt himself in danger and reacted accordingly. That is what adrenaline's for—flight or fight. Once the man's mind perceived that he was in danger, the adrenaline took over and he fired.

Sams loaded the remaining two very docile VC into his helo and delivered them to the SEALs.

I appointed Bill Marsh as my deputy for the Bassac. His tight control over flight operations of both helo detachments, his and the one on the T, earned him the somewhat facetious title of Bassac air marshal. He did his job well.

Operationally, he reported directly to me. But his road was hard, plagued mostly by guidance from his parent squadron—his administrative control, based in Vung Tau, just outside of Saigon.

The job of an administrative control parent squadron is mission accomplishment within the constraints of flight safety and machine endurance—an unarguable concept in peacetime and training. Many of the tactics worked out by the air marshal and his boys were looked upon by the squadron with a jaundiced eye. "You fly too low," they said. "Too dangerous to set down at an outpost," they preached. "Your strikes are too close." Some of this criticism came from the normal dislike of having their "birds" controlled by a nonaviator, especially a nonaviator like that "lunatic" on the Bassac.

Perhaps they were correct. Maybe looking down at the war from the next level up gave a sagacious overview that was all too often missed by the combat commander when machine-gun bullets and antitank rockets were tearing through their boats and only a fast helo coming in hot at treetop level could save their ass.

I was ambivalent; it was all too easy for me to criticize. A shot-down helo does one infinitely less good than one late on the scene and coming in high. But I had OPCON, and until my higher authority—Captain Laske—ordered me to stop, I'd continue.

I was fortunate that my administrative commander understood the situation, provided excellent support, and backed me up when my actions got me in trouble in Saigon. He ran wonderful interference for me and the other river division commanders. He took care of us. We were his boys.

Crimson Tide I

———————•———————

The men grumbled about the austerity of the new base and the loss of their small rooms to the large, barracks-style living quarters. We had no recreational clubs. The grounds were a sticky brown quagmire from the rain. The tropicalized, overhanging roofs and expansive, wirescreen construction of the buildings allowed wind-driven rains to fill their insides. Everything on the southwestern side remained sodden day after day. Ponchos and plastic sheeting nailed over the open walls protected us from the rains but cut off the cooling winds. The humidity caused metal to rust in hours and kept clothing always damp.

In bed, if you left a fan on, you'd be cold; if you turned it off, you'd suffocate from the clutching humidity. So from around midnight until seven in the morning we'd shiver. On the river we wore ponchos just to keep warm—we had no heavy coats. We always got wet anyway and never dried. Around our belt lines our constantly wet trousers caused rashes and open sores. Maybe the hot, dry weather was best.

Rains and discomfort aside, our mission continued. Captain Laske continued to brood about Titi Canal. He was ambivalent about it. On the one hand he knew the casualties we took in back of Tanh Dinh. On the other, he had not personally experienced any of the firepower they threw at us. I think he doubted the danger. One afternoon he told me to set up a patrol; he was going to make a Titi run. I argued against it. Titi was no place for a full navy captain. Captain Laske was much too important to be cut down by a sniper's bullet, or blown to bits by some well-placed grenade; he commanded well over nine hundred men.

Propriety demanded that he remain in a reasonably safe area to guide and direct. His warrior's blood demanded that he fight. He must have had a difficult time with his conscience, but his icy stare and "don't be ridiculous" ended the conversation. I asked if I could go along. "NO! I want nothing special." That ended that.

At dawn he got under way. The volunteer crew was easy to come by; action had been slow for the last couple of weeks. Lieutenant (jg) Sammy Merrick, a young but very experienced fighter, volunteered to be the patrol officer. I alerted Lieutenant Commander Marsh to have his Seawolves airborne and out of sight when the two boats entered the canal. I had him place the helo team on the T on five-minute standby alert.

I adjusted the regular patrol with Don Rover as the patrol officer, to be on station at the northern mouth of Titi just after Captain Laske entered. I told them to ensure they weren't seen by him. I pulled the patrol from RIVSEC 511 to come up to the southern entrance. I ordered all other patrols to stay in the middle of the river. I asked Sammy Merrick to try to stay in command, though I knew it would be impossible if things got hot.

I waited in the op center. At 0632, the patrol reported receiving light automatic weapons fire from the mainland. I could hear the chop of their .50s in the background of the transmission.

"Roger," I answered. "Seawolves available. Do you require assistance? Over."

A slight pause. "Thank you. Negative. Out."

I heard, "This is Seawolf Three Six. Roger. Out." I didn't

know if Marsh was in communication with Captain Laske or not. I wasn't going to ask. If the captain learned that I had prestationed helos, he'd have my ass. I was on the fringe of disobedience, but if he got into deep trouble, the helos being airborne might save ten to fifteen minutes. It could be decisive. I chose to take the chance.

Nine minutes later: "WATCH THE CHURCH! WATCH THE CHURCH! Swing wide. There's a dozen guns in there." Again, I heard the staccato *pop! pop! pop!* of the .50s in the background.

"Yeah, we see it," answered what I assumed to be the cover boat. His .50s also interrupted the transmission.

"Goddamn them!" I yelled. The men in the ops center gave me an odd look. "What about the Seawolves?" I screamed at the radio.

"We're clear. NEGATIVE! NEGATIVE! Getting it again" crackled over the loudspeaker. Damn Sammy Merrick! He knew I had the Seawolves standing by. Why didn't he use them?

"Handlash Two, this is Handlash Charlie. Getting it again from the island. Sounds like a couple of AK-47s. Shit's getting heavy—request scramble two. I say again, scramble two. My location just south of church. Over."

"Charlie, this is Three Six. Overhead zero five. Over," Marsh answered before I could key the mike to order him in.

"Roger, Three Six. Hit the mainland first, then the island. Be advised you'll be coming in hot. Out," Sammy Merrick answered in an unruffled voice. The kid was cool.

"You're getting it from behind, Three Six. Looks heavy. Pull outta there . . . now, now, now," Handlash Charlie ordered.

I turned to the watch officer. "Scramble Seawolf One Six from the T. Order Sierra Patrol in from the southern end . . . now!"

"Handlash Two, this is Charlie. I shackle mike november bravo kilo . . . break . . . alpha alpha foxtrot . . . break juliet. Over." What a tiger, shackling in the middle of a firefight.

I'm sure he had memorized some key codes just to show off for the captain.

The watch officer broke the code within seconds: "Two badly wounded, request medevac," he said.

I picked up the mike. "Charlie, this is Handlash. Be advised Seven Six on the way, ETA unknown . . . break, break . . . Sierra on the way from south . . . break, break . . . dustoff will be I shackle mike mike unshackle. Advise ETA when possible. Interrogative: Is one of them down a six? Over."

I had told Merrick that the helo medevac would be at Tra On and asked if Captain Laske was one of the wounded by referring to him as a six, the pay grade of a captain.

"Negative on the six. I am in communications with Sierra. We are attempting to disengage. Out."

I sweated. Even in the air-conditioned ops center, water dripped from my body. My hands shook. "I should be there . . . I should be there," I kept mumbling.

Eight minutes passed, a jumble of radio transmissions haunting me from Titi. "This is Seven Six. I see him . . . rolling in now. Sierra, Sierra, go left, go left. Three Six, watch your ass. This is Charlie, I'm pulling out. Cover me, cover me!"

Another eleven minutes. "Handlash, Handlash, this is Handlash Charlie. Exiting canal. Over."

I keyed the mike. "Charlie, this is Handlash. Roger. Out."

I went over to my office and had a sandwich and a warm beer, then walked down to the pier for the long wait. I tried to look nonchalant as the shot-up boats moored, two crewmen short. "How was the patrol, Captain?" I asked as he stepped off the boat.

"Sporty!" he replied. "Sporty!" There were bloodstains on his wrinkled blouse. He looked a little older than this morning.

"Sporty?"

"That place is bad news, Interdictor. We're going to have to do something about it."

"Yes, sir! We need troops."

"Yes, we do." We walked in silence to his office. At the door he turned to me, touching my shoulder. "Thank you, Don."

Two days later, strolling into my office coming off patrol, I was told that the captain wanted to see me.

"Yes, sir," I said, entering his office. "You wanted me?"

"Sit down, Interdictor."

Lieutenant Baker, the OinC of the SEALs, was there. "We've been discussing a little plan to hit the Viet Cong behind Tanh Dinh."

"We need troops," I interrupted.

"We'll use the SEALs. They're first-line combat troops."

"Captain," Lieutenant Baker said in a plaintive voice, "we're not trained for that . . . for frontal assaults. They'll wipe us out."

"Your objection noted again, but I think you can do it. It's really not that dangerous."

"Yes, sir, but I can't be responsible for what might happen."

What a horrible thing for a naval officer to say. Captain Laske's eyes narrowed. His face drained of color. Christ! Here it comes.

In a calm voice, not betraying anger, he replied, "I'm responsible, Mister Baker, for anything and everything that happens to the naval forces in the delta."

I imagined there had been a lively discussion on the subject. Lieutenant Baker sat in silence for the rest of the meeting. Special forces troops always had this problem when they came under control of regular troop force commanders. It seemed that the special forces troops, such as the Green Berets and SEALs, had their own sense of mission, which did not always dovetail with the overall commander's view. These special forces were taught that they were above such things, and it caused them no end of problems. Maybe they were right, I don't know. I did know, however, that the SEALs on the Bassac were not as effective in carrying out their mission as they could have been. Their mission was to support the PBRs.

Another factor that irritated most of us was their blatant manipulation of the system to collect extra pay. In the military if you were assigned temporary duty, TDY, away from your home station, you received a per diem allowance. This was to pay for any extra expenses that might be encountered because of the temporary nature of the assignment. The maximum time one could be on TDY was six months. Since we were all here on a permanent assignment, we were not eligible for TDY pay.

The SEALs, with the blessing of their command chain, assigned themselves in-country on TDY for five months and twenty-nine days, thus being able to collect the per diem pay. After this, they rotated back to the States, returning to Vietnam six months later, again on TDY. This per diem could add up to a substantial amount of money. We didn't fault the individual SEALs for this bit of chicanery, but we did criticize the thought processes that allowed it.

"So you see, Interdictor, the plan is simple: You take your PBRs through Titi. Where you draw fire we come in behind and land the SEALs to wipe 'em out. We'll use the Vietnamese RAGs for protection around the battleship."

"I don't think it'll work, Captain," I hazarded a reply. "The Viet Cong will fire at us all right, but when they see those iron monsters come in, they'll bug out. The heavies will never see them."

"That's one possibility. Get with the forces and polish out the details. Let me know when you're ready to brief.

"Oh," he said as we walked out. "Let's call it the Crimson Tide."

"Crimson Tide One?" I asked.

"Not bad for starters," he answered.

We raced across the Titi sill, our four PBRs still sluggish from our ammo load. The heavy stuff plodded slowly behind, rapidly dropping out of sight in the dawn's haze.

Four Vietnamese RAG boats circled the behemoth of a battleship as though she were a mother hen.

If we wanted to draw fire, the Viet Cong might as well be alerted. "Wake 'em up, Henderson," I yelled to the forward gunner. He triggered off a long blast down the canal.

Thirty seconds passed. The sun was coming up. Why'd we always have to kick off these operations so early in the morning? I'd be changing that.

"Hit it again, Henderson." Twenty more rounds roared out of his .50s, landing out of sight somewhere down the canal. Where were the sampans today?

We passed the first set of fish stakes. The fires that had been winking at us through the jungle were now out. Somebody was awake. The wind ripping across the bow chilled me to the bone. My teeth chattered despite my two shirts and flak jacket. A few drops of rain fell. A shot sounded in the distance—the signal.

I wasn't scared, not even excited. It seemed I was just going to work. An odd job to be sure, but nonetheless just going to work. The faces of the crew were noncommittal. I wondered how they felt; they surely didn't look scared.

"Another blast, Henderson!"

His guns spoke but only silence answered. The church was coming up fast. My body braced for the expected onslaught. Only silence. Past the first island we sped.

"This is crazy. Can't those Viet Cong do anything right? Come about! Those bastards aren't getting off free today."

The PBRs in column slipped around. I motioned to the Tanh Dinh side of the first little island we'd just passed and the coxswain headed for it. The other three boats followed around. I figured they knew what I was up to. I was going to bedevil the Viet Cong into taking a shot at us.

I figured the heavies were up to the fish stakes by now. We cut close to the small island and broke around the end, heading directly for the church before straightening out and heading back upstream.

Our "swift decoy force" ran fifty yards from the beach, presenting a juicy target for the enemy. Couldn't they see my red and white river division burgee pennant? I was getting anxious, from anger or fear. I didn't know which. Captain Laske's armada hoved into sight.

"COME ABOUT!" I ordered, and again we turned. Three shots banged out from the mainland, and the second PBR opened up. The rest of us held our fire. I reported the coordinates to Betray. There was excitement in his radio-talker's answer.

Captain Laske had most of his staff on the battleship—to teach them something, he had told me. As we came up to the church again, I could see the SEALs' battleship behind us, moving into position. They were softening up the beach with their .50s. If the Viet Cong stayed, they were in for a big surprise today; we'd never landed troops before.

We continued downstream. At the church, a machine gun took us under fire. We didn't fire back—that place was getting to me. I reported the firing to Betray. At the southern tip of the first island we took two sniper rounds and returned the fire. Five minutes farther down, a rifle grenade plummeted through the air, splashing harmlessly into the water between number two and three boats. It was a dud. Our .50s raked the beach in a futile gesture of revenge; we had no idea where the grenade had come from.

Hell! This plan wasn't working either. The SEALs were still at the first landing site. It would be impossible for them to adequately attack the ambush positions in time to do any good. We needed troops on every PBR.

We came about and headed back for the amphibious assault force. They were just extracting as we arrived. We received no fire on the way back. The Viet Cong were gone; they're clever fighters. As Mao demanded: When the enemy advances, retreat.

There were two hootches on fire at the landing site. The SEALs were backing off, calling in their defensive perimeter with them. In five minutes they were under way. Captain Laske gave me the thumbs-down, lack-of-success sign.

We cruised leisurely up to the fish stakes. I felt depressed;

the crew felt depressed. What had promised to be an exciting, fruitful day was turning into another dull patrol duty.

We were hoping for a break in the monotony. The men spent roughly half their time—seventy-eight hours out of a work week of one hundred sixty-eight hours—in an imminent combat zone. Not a combat zone like all of the delta, but a zone where you know there's a guy out there with a gun, and when he gets a bullet, or the nerve, or a reason, he is going to try to kill you. The thought grates on your nerves. It's like the moving ducks in a shooting gallery: Round and round they go and it's only a matter of time before someone with a dime is going to shoot at them. The ducks' time is split about the same as ours: Half the time they're underneath being pulled around, and half the time they're on the gun line.

Searching large sampans on a normal patrol was dangerous. We never knew what the bamboo-thatched roof on the sampan contained. In a couple of instances they hid a Viet Cong with a death wish and a shotgun. When a PBR crewman bent over to enter the enclosure, a shotgun blast greeted him, spreading him over ten square feet of Southeast Asia.

When a man lives under the constant pressure of violent death, an increase in this pressure is periodically welcomed as much as biting down on an aching tooth, just for the difference. Today we were biting down.

Betray reported extracting from the second landing area: no enemy contact. I could see smoke from the hootches they had set on fire. That was the way to do it—burn 'em out. If the Viet Cong couldn't live here, they'd be less of a threat. Here lived the cadre that moved the supplies to attack Saigon; here lived those who branched out to attack the towns and hamlets, indiscriminately killing women and little kids. This place was no better than a viper pit, a cancerous growth that must be destroyed. Here lived the Viet Cong 306th Division.

"What are you doing? What do you see, Malcolm?" I asked the boat captain, who was pointing a Remington Model 870 pump-action shotgun toward a hootch, saying, "Bang! Bang!"

"I got a bead lined up on a big water urn by the hootch over there. It would sure be inconvenient for those bastards if I put some buckshot into it," he said.

"Good idea, but wait a minute." I walked over to the radio. "Betray, this is Handlash. Am exercising the crew at target practice. Over."

"Roger, Handlash. No action up here. Out."

"At your pleasure, Malcolm!" I said, pointing to the urn. His answer was two quick shots. The urn shattered; water flew every which way.

"GOOD SHOT! You've become quite an expert. That looks like funnsies. Here, lemme try it!" I never did like the shotgun, even though for searching boats it was deathly intimidating. We had buckshot or flechette shells. The flechettes looked like children's tiny jacks; spinning through the air at close range and high velocity, they did a bloody number on the flesh they hit. Additionally, the flechettes stayed on course; they weren't thrown off by branches or foliage like the M-16 round. Five quick shots into undergrowth cleared it like a scythe.

He handed me the weapon. Shotguns intimidated me from my youth, when I saw a man commit suicide by blowing his head off. "Mister Brown . . . two doors down . . . lying dead on the ground," the older kids used to chant, taunting us younger ones. I was eight years old.

"Over there," he pointed. I took the shotgun, aimed, then handed it back. "Nope! Just don't like 'em." I drew my .38 revolver and fired. Missed.

From the stern came the ear-blasting stab of the .50, shattering the urn to smithereens.

"No one likes a show-off, Malcolm," I chided him. "I'd get it, eventually." I picked up my M-79, took careful aim, and put the grenade squarely into another urn fifty feet farther on. With a smug smile I turned to Malcolm. "Now that's good shootin', boy."

I radioed the other three boats, telling them to maneuver independently to exercise their small arms. Six shots rang out from them before I even got my finger off the mike button. We moved in close to better see the targets, amazed at the density of the hootches back there. Every other time I'd been this way we'd been moving fast, with no time for sight-seeing and certainly not this close. We shot water urns, benches, saws, bottles, and, of course, any sampans hidden under the trees.

The Viet Cong, if nothing else, were going to be pissed. Pissed! They were lucky I didn't have a napalm strike to call in. Napalm? "Hey, Malcolm, you got any pop flares?"

"Yes, sir," he said, bringing over two of the hand-fired illumination flares.

"You think you can put one into that hootch over there?" I asked. The flares were fired by removing the top cap, which contained a firing pin, placing this cap over the rear end, pointing, then giving it a sharp rap. I had never mastered it; they never went where I wanted them to go.

"I'll give it a try, sir."

He fired one; it went wild. He tried another. It went zipping right through the hootch. A good shot, but it traveled just too fast to set the hootch on fire.

"Lemme try this."

He pulled the pin from a thermite grenade and gave it a powerful heave. It landed squarely on the roof, igniting in a brilliant white flash, then harmlessly rolling off and dropping all of its savage inferno into a useless heap, only to boil water in a mud puddle. Thermite grenades could not be extinguished once ignited. They would burn underwater. They'd burn in a vacuum. We kept thermite grenades on the top of our classified material safes back at the base. In theory, in case of an attack we would pull the pin and set it back on the safe top, and the grenade would burn right down to the bottom of the safe, destroying everything within.

"Won't cut it, Commander. Lemme dash ashore and use my handy Zippo."

"Handlash, Handlash, this is Betray. We're skipping church and moving to end of first island. Out."

"Hey, I dunno, Malcolm, you get shot, I'd be in trouble."

"I'll go with him, Commander," Henderson shouted from his forward guns.

"I dunno."

"No Viet Cong for miles, Interdictor, sir, Commander."

"You asshole . . . okay! What the hell . . . but let's do it right."

I called the PBRs to join up and we moved out of Titi, rendezvousing in midriver. They were having the same problems: They couldn't get the hootches to burn. I called in Sammy Merrick and his two PBRs that were patrolling on the river side of Tanh Dinh. The patrol officers, Lt. (jg) Sammy Merrick and Chief Tanner, the six boat captains, and I laid hasty plans.

We designated two boats as the assault boats and put two extra men on each of them. These boats would run up on the beach and three men would jump off. Two of them would establish a flanking perimeter while the third doused the hootch with diesel fuel and torched it off with a cigarette lighter.

Before the men landed at a designated point, we'd hose it down with .50s. Prepping the area, it was called. Reconnaissance by fire, or recon by fire, was the official term. Generally it violated our ROE, but we had received fire earlier from the area and anyway this was a free-fire zone. To provide cover fire for the beached assault teams, two other boats would remain just off their sterns.

It wasn't much of a plan, and right away we had problems. There were almost fistfights over who would be on the landing party. A den of tigers. We set up a complicated rotation plan so that all but the coxswains would have a chance. We couldn't afford a grounded boat because of inexperience on the helm in close quarters. Of course, the guys who didn't go first grumbled.

Thus we started an entirely new and unprecedented phase of riverboat warfare.

The first assault team, with me on board, eased up close to the shore by the first targeted hootch. Our six .50s tore into it and the area around it with a vicious onslaught of high-speed steel. Fear of the unknown kept our triggers depressed. At this distance of only ten meters, the .50-caliber bullets shattered wood and dug deep holes into the muddy ground. Trees fell like twigs as the half-inch slugs splintered the trunks and scattered the branches.

We ran her bow up on the beach, and the two flank men jumped off. Waterborne American sailors storming an enemy beach—John Paul Jones looking down must surely be proud. The torch man followed, armed to the teeth with a pistol, a canteen cup of diesel fuel, and a Zippo lighter.

The two flankers moved into position, a wary eye out for booby traps and punji stake pits. There were none. They crouched and watched. The guns of the other assault team started pounding the shore a hundred meters down the line. My eyes didn't leave the beach; my M-79 pointed ashore to halt any intruding Viet Cong who might object to the destruction of his house.

The torch man ran into the hootch. Time seemed to stop. "GODDAMNIT, MALCOLM! Get the hell outta there and burn it," I screamed.

He backed out and with an affected flair splashed his pitifully small cache of diesel fuel on the front wall. He leaned over, glanced side to side, sparked his lighter, and fired the hootch. The diesel fuel burned in a little circle, started to die, then flared, and the whole front of the place burst into flames.

"Beautiful!"

Malcolm drew his pistol while backing toward the boat; the flankers moved back with him. They looked like professionals. Malcolm jumped on the boat, a wide grin covering his face. The flankers came aboard. The coxswain threw his throttles into reverse and, as the backing gates slammed over the pump discharge, two powerful streams of water shot under the boat, churning mud and tugging against the tenacious suction of the beach. The boat shuddered.

"ROCK 'ER!" the coxswain yelled.

We jumped from side to side, sallying ship. It moved a little, then more, and with a deep, sucking rasp broke free and backed into the canal.

"Burn, baby, burn!" Malcolm chanted.

"You crazy, man?"

"No, sir! See this?" he said, holding up his three-fingered hand. "There ain't enough Viet Cong hootches in this whole damn country that I can burn to make up for two missing fingers." He'd had them shot off nine months before. His logic seemed incontestable.

The second group just pulled off as we approached. Their target had been much larger than ours. Billowing smoke from their fire lifted a hundred feet into the air. Lieutenant (jg) Sammy Merrick's greens were muddy. He had gone ashore on the first raid. His crew was jubilant; they gave me a thumbs-up, and I returned the salute.

We moved on to the next target, which we hit simultaneously. I hoped the Viet Cong knew that the PBRs were doing this. Viet Cong eyes from Tanh Dinh, I'm sure, followed our every move. Either they didn't have the resources or the guts to hit us. Probably the former. The Viet Cong rarely lacked for courage. They were a good enemy; they fought hard for what they believed in, with few resources but their beliefs to support them.

Why did we fight so hard? We could carry out our stated mission by sitting fat, dumb, and happy in the middle of the river. My mission didn't call for storming the beaches. Look at those silly bastards; they're enjoying it. Those kids couldn't even pronounce Vietnam eighteen months ago; now they're throwing their lives on the line for its freedom and self-determination. Hell? I don't think so. I think they fought for kicks and in reverence to that great American fetish of doing right those jobs worth doing.

We pulled off and hit a fourth, then a fifth. We rotated

boats and men. Merrick and Tanner and their men took turns going ashore. I wanted to go; I wanted a turn, but waited impatiently.

Captain Laske, as senior officer present, was responsible for what I was doing. He was there and in command. He, therefore, took full and unequivocal responsibility for every bullet shot, every man wounded, every man killed, every boat lost. He was in command and he was responsible and he got the credit. It has always been that way in the navy and God willing it always will be.

I had neither permission nor authority to conduct these burning raids. I was clearly violating my ROE of don't shoot unless fired upon. If someone were killed on the beach or if I lost a boat, there would be hell to pay. The navy is as cruel to the commander who exceeds his authority and fails as it is in praise to the one who exceeds but wins.

If I failed here, propriety demanded that I be around to stand up at the green table of my court-martial and say that it was I who ordered this operation without authority and without briefing my superiors. But, Christ, I wanted to go ashore.

The eighth and ninth hootches flared in appreciation of our devastation. Smoke hung low over the jungle in the windless skies. Storm clouds were gathering to the south. This game might have to be called for rain. Betray called on the radio. "Interrogative smoke clouds your area. Over."

"Betray, this is Handlash. Have raiding parties burning hootches. Over."

"This is Betray. Say again. Over." I repeated the transmission.

"This is Betray. Wait. Out."

I waited. I could imagine the radioman reporting to Captain Laske. What would the captain's reaction be?

"Handlash, this is Betray. Extract troops. Report my location immediately. Over."

I guess I'd find out. I pulled in all the men and shuffled them back to their own boats, then sent Sammy Merrick back to his normal patrol. The other four PBRs in a line column raced full speed for the battleship. We were going to have to make this look good.

Because I had shifted boats continually while observing the assault teams, I had hauled down my burgee pennant. The burgee pennant can be flown only when the commander is actually aboard. I ordered it raised.

If I was going to get my ass chewed, it would be under full colors.

Hootch Roast

———•———

Captain Laske's armada was standing off the southern tip of the little island. On the beach opposite them a couple of hootches burned. We came in fast, on step, sweeping around the four iron RAG boats just to look good. We turned for the battleship and, as my boat approached, the after three PBRs broke off in fancy sharp turns, whirled around, and in perfect coordination slid into flanking positions. For no good reason I took off my helmet and put on my black beret.

We were going to make a high-speed approach. My boat came in fast. This was going to be a difficult but mighty fine looking bit of seamanship. At the proper moment (Oh coxswain, please don't screw it up!) the coxswain had to throw his throttles into reverse—he did. For a split second the two boats were at the same speed. I stepped leisurely onto the deck of the battleship; Malcolm hauled down my burgee, the coxswain jammed his throttles full forward, and the PBR flashed forward and away. Beautiful, just beautiful! How can anyone chew a guy's ass out whose men can do something like that?

"Show-off," someone whispered as I marched toward Captain Laske.

"Sheppard, sir, reporting as ordered."

None of these gyrations had escaped the fighter pilot's eye of the good captain. His face was void of expression.

"Interdictor, what the hell are you up to? What were you doing up there?"

"Prosecuting the war, sir, carrying the battle to the enemy, hitting him where he is most vulnerable, taking—"

"Don't gimme that bullshit, Interdictor. What were you doing?"

I laid out the whole operation for him, with details on exactly how we made the insertions and how we covered each play. His staff gathered around us. They made comments, some derogatory, under the protection of his rank. I had that horrible feeling of being on trial. My fear of rebuff had turned to anger under the stabbing eyes of my impromptu jury. Assholes! Except for the captain, none of them had one one-hundredth as much combat experience as my men or me. Most had none. My judge—the captain—sensed the audience, sensed the caution and restraint his staff projected. His warrior's blood would have none of it.

"Good show, Interdictor, but be careful."

"Aye, aye, sir!" I nearly yelled. I snapped out a salute and jumped to the main deck, waving my boat in.

"Can I go with the Interdictor, Captain?" I heard someone ask.

A moment's pause. "Yes."

Jackie Boushay, a tall, somewhat gangly lieutenant junior grade on Captain Laske's staff, popped up beside me, saluting. "Request permission to go along, sir."

I returned the salute. "Permission granted," I said, slapping him on the back in admiration of his request. Boushay had been in-country for only two months and this was his first time on the river. I hoped he understood what he had just volunteered for.

Malcolm again brought the PBR in at full bore. It was flashy, and a miscalculation could result in a disastrous high-speed ramming. From the corner of my eye, I glimpsed the battleship's occupants bracing for a hit, but not the captain.

Just as the PBR's bow passed the stern of the battleship, Malcolm released the whip antenna he'd been holding down with my burgee on it. It flashed into view just as the strained-faced coxswain jerked his throttles back with split-second timing. The speed differential dropped to zero. Boushay and I stepped aboard. The two boats hung together for a second. Malcolm tapped the coxswain on the shoulder and the throttles flashed forward. The boat banked to starboard like a fleeting fighter jet, righted itself, and nimbly spirited forward. We held on for support.

Giant plumes of water shot from the sterns of the other three boats; they were already under full power to join up. We weren't going anywhere in particular, but damn, we were going in style. They glided in, in column, as we roared south down the canal. I loved those guys.

"Commander, Handlash Romeo from 511 has been trying to call you. I told him you were busy."

"Okay, thanks. Slow 'er down, 'bout half throttle."

"Handlash Romeo, this is Handlash. Over."

"Roger, this is Romeo. Have talked with Handlash Charlie. Request permission to join operation. Over."

"Romeo, this is Handlash. Interrogative your patrol area. Over."

"This is Romeo. No sweat, Command—I mean Handlash. All quiet. I have cleared with One. Over."

"This is Handlash. Permission granted. My posit, middle of Titi. Over."

"Roger! Be your location one zero. Out."

It was Lt. Bill Norwick, one zero, ten minutes. He'd been at the bottom of the canal just waiting. We ran downstream to meet him. We came about as he hoved into sight. His two boats joined up astern and now, six in column, we raced back to the hootch roast.

The fifteen-man SEAL group was ashore on the mainland blowing bunkers and burning hootches. We steered wide to the left, carrying us close to Tanh Dinh. A light machine gun laced across the third boat. He fired back, as did number four and Norwick's boat.

"All units, this is Handlash. Ignore area. I say again, ignore area. Follow me . . . break, break. Betray, Betray, this is Handlash. Machine gun on Tanh Dinh just opposite us, three hundred meters south of you. Request you engage. Over."

"This is Betray. Roger. Out."

The last boat in column got another burst and a large rifle grenade explosion popped just off his stern. Norwick hauled his two boats out of column, swinging in for the attack.

"Romeo, Romeo, this is Handlash. Break contact, break contact. Rejoin. I say again, rejoin. Over." There was a pause. I repeated the message.

"This is Romeo. Roger. Out."

Just up from the church we stopped. I called Romeo alongside. I had Chief Tanner's patrol circle around in case of trouble.

As they were tying up, I called Lieutenant Norwick over to my boat and in a low voice said: "Goddamnit, Mister Norwick, when I say ignore something—when I give you an order, you fuckin' well better obey it. You understand that, mister?"

His eyes and face dropped as if I had slapped him. "Yes, sir!" he said, saluting meekly.

"You know Mister Boushay here?" I added to break the tension.

"Sure, hi, Jackie. You here for a piece of the action?" he said as they shook hands. His perpetual smile returned to his face.

"What's the matter, Bill, can't you 511 people stir up enough action around Dung Island?" Every time I saw someone from 511, I felt guilty for not spending more time down there.

"We bugger the hell outta 'em, Commander, but not much action."

"I keep telling you people, Dung Island's a rest camp," I replied.

"Yeah, well, why don't we take a little spin behind Con Coc Island?" he said.

"Bullshit! Once was enough for me. But don't say it too loud or the captain will take you and that battleship of his back there."

I filled and lit my pipe. Willie, the self-proclaimed ace of the Bassac and savior of Romeo Patrol, smiled his shit-eating grin at me. Bryan, his boat captain, glared at him. "He's not allowed to talk, Commander, whenever an officer is within twenty feet. You know what I mean."

Bill Norwick laughed, adding, "I couldn't believe it when Sammy told me what you were doing back here. He's really pissed at you for sending him home. He dropped down to see me before he left."

"Christ! He'd been on patrol for fourteen hours already. Tell him I'll discuss it with him when he outranks me."

I glanced to the stern of Bill's boat and recognized two men from Merrick's patrol. "Hey, what the hell are you two guys doing here?"

"Ahh . . . we didn't feel like going in and missing all the action and . . . uh . . . ahhh . . . decided to stay out with Mister Norwick, and we just sorta ended up here. Odd coincidence seeing you here, sir, eh, Commander?"

"And how did you plan to get back to Binh Thuy?"

"We'd work it out somehow, Commander. Sammy was going to do the same thing, but he thought you might not take kindly to him leaving his patrol."

"He thought correctly. Now here's the plan." I laid out what we were doing and how we were doing it. A sniper rifle cracked from Tanh Dinh; the bullet zinged into the side of my boat, hitting an ammo can with a loud clatter. Chief Tanner answered back in a flash with his .50s.

"Okay, you got it, Bill? Let's move. I'll point targets for you." Bill stepped over to his boat, and we started again where we had left off. I stayed offshore, directing the insertion of the other boats. We were playing it more boldly now, using three boats on the beach at one time and covering them with only two. At the seventeenth house, shots rang out. "The team's getting it," the radio blasted out.

There was a wild exchange of shots. I didn't know who was shooting at whom. Bullets splashed into the water.

"Extract all troops!" I ordered over the radio. I was forced into inaction. I couldn't fire.

"All boats hold your fire, hold your fire unless you have a definite target," I commanded over the radio.

A hootch blazed into flame. Two boats backed off the beach. A cover boat moved in next to the remaining beached boat. Light machine-gun fire clamored from their direction. An M-79 grenade exploded in the background, then another and another. What was going on? I started in but realized it wouldn't help. The other three boats pulled around me as we formed a semicircle about the two beached boats.

More rifle shots; a hand grenade resounded through the jungle. Huge flames shot up from the hootch. Two more M-79 explosions, and then the jarring din of four .50s blocked out every sound. One boat pulled off and slid aft, then the second one.

Norwick gave me a somewhat unenthusiastic thumbs-up as their stark faces looked back at the jungle. His .50s quit. We started an M-79 barrage. I called Norwick over. "Bad guys in there?"

"Man, it's a different war when you don't have a boat with a throttle to kick in the ass."

"Any wounded?"

"No."

"You get any of them?"

"I doubt it."

"How many were there?"

"Two or three thousand, maybe."

"Scared?"

"Shitless!"

Moving downstream a little, we hosed down the area and Boushay took another party ashore. They were unopposed. We were in sight of the church with its neat little village. We were up to where the SEALs had started. I could hear their gunfire in the distance.

I called my officers and Chief Tanner in for a quick conference. "Let's hit that whole village around the church," I proposed.

They agreed and we laid the plans. "Ensure that no man deliberately fires a single bullet at that church. Make sure . . . damn sure!" I admonished.

Four boats beached, forward .50s blazing; two boats took flanking stations with all six of their .50s going. At this point-blank range the half-inch slugs all but devastated the village. The fourteen .50s tore up furniture, plowed up gardens, collapsed hootches, and generally left the village in shambles. The rest of us rained down 40mm grenades, hoping to clear the bunkers.

On my signal the barrage stopped. We waited. If there was ever going to be opposition, it would come now. Silence.

We moved out. Lieutenant (jg) Boushay took four men forward and established a perimeter around the opposite side of the church. His total combat experience had been gained today, but he had guts and a cool enough head to handle it. I gave him my four best men. Two more men moved to the flanks on the beach. Tanner and Norwick with two men each moved out fast behind Boushay's guard; each carried a bucket full of diesel fuel.

The village was built in a U around the church, with the bottom of the U away from the beach. There were two or three rows of hootches along each side—in all about fifty.

Methodically the sailors started their burning, ducking in to check each house before igniting it. They used their fuel sparingly; fifty houses had to go. I moved up to check the church. I advanced cautiously, my eyes peeled for booby traps. I peered in the window. The place was filthy, with half the pews torn out and piled across those that weren't. The cleared area was a storehouse: Huge bags of rice were stacked in one corner, lumber in another.

There were three- and four-tier chicken coops next to the rice; chicken manure was all about. Three small pigs rooted in the rice sacks. A dead, still-warm cooking fire with pots and pans was in the center. The place stank. The ceiling was covered with soot. Under the two front window openings lay several rounds of empty machine-gun brass. The walls were a foot and a half, maybe two feet thick. We'd have a hell of a time getting the enemy out of here in a fight.

A lone rifle shot ricocheted off the side wall of the church. No other firing. "Over there," someone yelled, followed by the spurt of an M-16, then only the crackling of the flames.

The men were working faster now. Boushay was pulling in his guards as the burning progressed back toward the canal. Hell! I had to burn a hootch.

"I'll get this last house, Chief Tanner," I yelled as he ducked out of one he had just lit. I moved over to Willie, who was guarding the flank on the left. I had my black .38 pistol drawn from its English World War II canvas holster. I had four hand grenades clipped by their spoons onto my flak jacket. Next to them I had my M-16 bayonet strapped upside down. (To draw it faster was the theory I hoped I'd never have to test.) My helmet straps were buckled across the back to prevent my neck from being snapped if a concussion explosion occurred beneath me (another theory I didn't care to test).

"See anything, Willie?" I asked. It was a stupid question; if he had, he would have blasted away at it. Willie stared at me.

"Jesus Christ, Willie, you can talk to me." Bryan must have put the fear of God into him.

"No, sir, haven't seen anything."

"Whataya think, Willie? This oughta teach those mothers not to mess with the PBRs," I said in a rather haughty voice.

"This place is a sawmill, Commander."

"Yeah, you move around in back while I check it out."

Kicking open several boxes, I checked their contents— saws, nails, glue, and other woodworking tools were all I found. One huge, circular, foot-driven saw was well oiled and mounted in a long bench. I kicked open another large rectangular box. "Willie! Come in here a moment. Look at this!"

"Goddamn! Rifle stocks—there must be fifty or more in here." We dumped them out into a pile of wood shavings.

"Go back on guard; I'll finish this."

"Gee, Commander, I didn't think officers ever did any work," he chuckled.

"They don't. Now shut up and get your ass out there."

I piled more wood on top. I took a large hammer and banged against the teeth of the big saw blade. They wouldn't use this again. I got some paper and, in my best Boy Scout tradition, constructed a fire base under the large pile of wood.

I stepped back to look. Hah! A neat job, Sheppard. I took out my Zippo and leaned over to ignite the paper. Click. Nothing. Click! nothing. Click! A small glimmer of flame and then out.

Sonovabitch! Sonovabitch! Out of fluid. Stupid, Sheppard, stupid; your chance and you blew it. I walked out to Willie. My other men were pulling back unopposed. He jumped when I called his name. "Gotta light?"

I felt like a fool. He burst out laughing. "Don't push it, Willie, just shut up and give me your lighter."

I went back in and finished the job. I stood there for a moment watching the flames build higher and higher, then backing out the large door, I set fire to the straw on each side of it.

I walked around to get Willie. In only these few seconds the flames had engulfed the entire back wall. "Let's go, Will—"

Crack! Crack! Two rifle shots slammed into a tree next to us. We threw ourselves to the ground, shinnying behind a fallen log.

Another shot cut into the log I was hiding behind. My blood ran cold. Another shot churned the dirt just behind me. The sniper was firing high. I couldn't crawl backward. I had no place to go. I pulled a grenade from my jacket, yanked out the pin, and lobbed it over the log. There was small chance that it would do any good, but it was something. Its explosion was shattering—it hadn't gone very far.

"Willie, you see anything?"

"Only mud. We're in deep shit, Commander."

Deeper than he thought; what if a snake showed! He put his M-16 over the log and pressed off a short burst. Two more enemy bullets hammered into my log.

"I don't think he can see you, Willie. You got any grenades?"

"No! Damnit."

I tossed him two of mine and watched as they rolled away from him. He scooched them in with his rifle. The sawmill behind us was a full inferno by now. The heat was becoming unbearable. We had to do something; that place could collapse. Boy! This had been a stupid idea. I swore I'd never get off another boat, assuming I ever got back on one. Where in hell were all my men? Several shots came from behind us.

"Hey, Commander, you fire a couple of rounds from that toy you got and I'll try to make it to that mound over there."

"It's not a toy!"

"Okay, you jump up and blast him."

"It's a toy," I conceded. "Okay! Ready, Willie?"

I tossed out my last grenade and when it blew I put my pistol over the log, jerking off four shots. Willie leapt up, firing his M-16 from the hip as he dove for the mound of dirt. A burning timber fell across my log, landing inches from my head. I pushed it away with my pistol.

"See anything?"

"Yeah, he's behind some trees in a little bunker."

I reloaded my toy. I watched Willie peer over the mound, pulling a pin from a grenade. He may do some good from his position. I was pinned down. This whole thing would have to be Willie's play. He plunged up, tossed the grenade, and made a dash for a huge palm tree. Two bullets followed him; a third took a half-inch gash out of the tree a scant hair behind him. Willie leaned against the tree, panting like a dog.

I crawled to the end of my log castle; two more burning timbers from the sawmill fell behind me. Maybe I could make it to Willie's old log. At the end of my crawl, I took a stick and wrapped a rag around it that had been lying next to me. I eased it up into the open.

BURRAT! BURRAT. A light machine gun spoke, disintegrating my stick. I dropped it, yanking my hand back violently. Assholes! They fell for that old Indian trick. So what?

"There's two of them, Commander."

"I think I can get 'em with a grenade," he wheezed. I could see the sweat trickling small rivers of mud down his face. He eased the pin from the grenade. A burst from the Viet Cong machine gun peppered his tree. I still couldn't see anything.

"Willie, where are they from me? I'll fire just before you throw."

"They're about twenty yards away at your one o'clock position."

"Okay, stand by."

I pushed the rag out again. When they blasted it, I raised up my pistol to fire, and from the river came the sweet thunder of a .50. One of the flanking boats had moved into position, observed our predicament, and fired. Sweethearts! Willie stepped from behind his cover and in an underhand motion lobbed the grenade into the air. He whirled behind the tree with his arm still up in the air.

Three . . . two . . . one . . . KAPOW!

"It got 'em!" Willie yelled, plunging forward into the explosion smoke. I jumped and ran for him. He leapt atop the bunker, his M-16 on full automatic, and sprayed straight down into the hole.

"C'mon, Willie, let's get the hell outta here."

The bodies were bloody shreds. "Good job, boy—thank you, mighty good job."

We picked up the broken weapons and ran back to the boats. Tanner was just finishing the house next to the ex-sawmill.

"Where the hell you been, Commander? What's all the shooting?" Lieutenant Norwick asked.

"Where the hell have you been?" I countered.

"Burning hootches! That's what you told me to do! This place is getting unfriendly."

"C'mon, let's get outta here."

Keeping a sharp eye on the hootches, we moved toward the boats as we backed away from the burning village. Jackie Boushay pulled in his troops behind us. The men were finishing the second-to-last house on the right side. Jackie and his boys moved into position in front of them, keeping up their gun play to hold the snipers down while Norwick finished. I sent Willie to tell two of the boats to keep the left side under fire. A crewman came scampering up from the boats with an M-60 while another carried a huge box of belted ammo. I directed them over to Boushay. In seconds Jackie had it in action against the snipers. Tanner was helping Norwick douse the last house. I was standing there yelling at them to hurry.

There was a lull in the firing of the .50s. I had sent another boat to fire on our right flank. They were slicing up the jungle fifty feet from us. I borrowed a lighter and lit a cigar.

There came a woman's wail from inside the hootch. In a flash Norwick and Tanner bolted in. This whole thing was getting complicated. They came out dragging a small, ugly woman with betel nut--stained teeth.

"No Viet Cong! No Viet Cong! No Viet Cong!" she sobbed.

"Where Viet Cong now?" I asked in Vietnamese.

"No Viet Cong ever here."

"She's lying, Commander. I'll get the answer out of her," Willie snarled. He started for her, reaching out to grab her shoulders.

I cracked him hard across the arm with my .38. "Keep your hands off her, Willie, she's a prisoner."

"Look at this, Commander," he said, holding one of her arms. "That creamy colored stuff on her hands is plastic explosive."

"You're sure?"

"I've worked with that crap for years."

"You damn sure, man?"

"I ain't shittin' ya, Commander."

I pushed my .38 into her throat. "You make bomb?" I asked.

"No! No! Don't kill me!"

A sailor came out of the hootch waving a Viet Cong flag. "It was hidden in a drawer with this paper," he reported.

Bill Norwick doused the last of his diesel fuel on the hootch. "NO BURN! NO BURN!" the woman pleaded, wailing, as dark brown juice from her stained saliva slobbered down her chin. She dropped to her knees, screaming, as my .38 jammed against her throat and twisted her neck to a painful angle as she went down. A young gunner yanked her back up. As I opened my mouth to speak, she spit. My cigar sizzled out from her slimy attack; my tongue recoiled from its taste.

"Shoot the bitch, Commander. She's a goddamn killer."

"You burn house, comrades kill you," she hissed at me.

"What about it, Commander?" Norwick yelled.

Boushay was next to us now, his M-60 red-hot from the firing. "Let's go, Commander," his voice seemed to demand.

"NO BURN! NO BURN!" she pleaded again. Both Tanner and Norwick lit it off. "NO! NO!" she screamed. "Baby! Baby!"

She made a break for the house. Boushay grabbed her. "Where?" he demanded.

"Tunnel, tunnel under house."

Boushay threw her down and dashed for the house. It was a blazing oven, the straw and bamboo burning with a fantastic heat.

The woman lay in a heap on the ground, sobbing, "Baby, baby."

After what seemed like hours, but was only seconds, Boushay dashed out, carrying a naked child and dragging a young woman. Two men ran over, picked up the girl, and roughly carried her over to me. I had the sickening feeling I was some ancient barbaric warlord ravaging, plundering, burning. Was this Mrs. Sheppard's little boy, Donny?

The girl was fighting against them. If she broke and ran, would I shoot her? They were having a deuce of a time holding her. Boushay held the baby in his arms. Behind him the hootch was a blinding-hot pyre. Slowly we moved back toward the boats, our work here done. The .50s blotted out all but the loudest shouts. Tempers ran high. The girl kept screaming as two sailors dragged her toward me.

They held her up in front of me. Her eyes focused on my face. Her screaming stopped. "Sheppard!" she snarled.

It was the girl we couldn't catch in the sampan. The one I couldn't shoot. She twisted, breaking loose, bolting for me. In a blur she yanked my bayonet from its scabbard and drove its point viciously and uselessly into my flak jacket. The force knocked me back, although it felt no worse than a sharp rap. The bayonet, viciously twisted out of her hand by Willie, who had grabbed her, dropped to the ground.

"Move out!" I yelled. Enemy bullets were coming too close.

The sailors pulled the old woman down to the canal. The tide was running out and the clifflike bank was now three feet high. Boushay jumped down beside her and put the baby in her arms. We were almost to the boat, dragging the young woman behind us.

She shrieked in Vietnamese far too fast for me to understand. Curses such as "Sheppard die!" however, came out all too clearly. At the boat I pointed down to the old woman and baby huddled together, secretly hoping that the men would throw her down the embankment. I took a last glance at the woman. She was attractive despite her screeching, snarling hate.

"Sheppard bastard, die," she blasted out coherently in English. And in a last gesture of hate, she spit at me again. I moved; it missed my face, hit my neck, and oozed down my blouse front.

That cut it! Grabbing her by the hair, twisting it, I backhanded her across the face. Her jaw mushed. With my hand still contorting her scalp from the tremendous pressure on her hair, I brought her six inches from my face.

Looking into a wild, distorted study of psychopathic hate, I cleared my throat, grabbed her chin with my other hand, and held her steady. Blood from her mouth trickled over my hand. I spit in her face. She tried to scream. I forced her mouth shut and spit again. With my hand still yanking her hair, I pulled her down the bank behind me and tossed her next to the old woman.

"Sheppard bastard, die," she screamed as four husky arms pulled me up the four-foot siding to the bow of the boat. Our boat had a towline attached aft, and two other PBRs strained to pull us out of the mud. Ten more minutes and we'd have been there till the next high tide.

My ears pained from the concussion of the .50s firing inches above my head as I crawled back to the coxswain's flat. Bill Norwick in a last act of destruction threw a line around the large bamboo poles supporting drying fishnets, yanking them into the water as we backed. The nets were already aflame. He dragged them to midstream, then cut them to splinters with close-range .50s fire. We moved out fast. The entire village was a frighteningly beautiful display of orgasmic, flaming destruction. If a job is worth doing, it's worth doing well.

I sat on the engine covers as we ran full speed out of Titi to the Bassac. We'd been ashore only sixteen minutes; it seemed like sixteen hours. Bryan shoved my knife back up into its scabbard.

"Thanks."

"Don't women like you, Commander?"

"It doesn't seem so. I had the same trouble in high school. Willie saved my ass, Bryan, the kid's all right. Cut him some slack, okay?"

"Betray, this is Handlash. Have completed operation. Am exiting canal. Over," I reported.

"This is Betray. Roger. Out."

It took both hands to light my pipe. I gazed at the flame from Bryan's lighter. Proud of yourself, Sheppard?

It started to pour. I didn't move. Maybe God's rain could cleanse my conscience.

To the Victors

———————◆———————

I could glean no intelligence that our burning raid had any
effect at all on the VC 306th Division. I traveled down to Tra
On to see Major Shellon. Tanh Dinh was in his subsector,
and if anybody knew anything he surely would. We had
lunch with Captain Thuy, the subsector and district chief,
but the best he could offer were platitudes and praise for my
men. I didn't need that; I needed intelligence.

A few days later an army major came visiting from
Saigon. Just looking around, he said. We hit it off quite
nicely. He wanted a PBR ride and, since I was going out on
patrol anyway, I took him with me. We had a sporty time,
with two evading sampans and a firefight up a small canal
supported by Marsh and his Seawolves. He took a wound to
his upper left arm; a Purple Heart for a Saigon warrior. To
celebrate, I gave him a black beret and the rusty CHICOM
rifle we'd confiscated from one of the sampans.

Drinking together at dinner that night and later in my
room, I bemoaned the lack of intelligence. He stared at me.
"You poor bastard" came his reply. "You ever had an
intelligence billet, Don?"

"No, I've always been on ships."

He looked around the room, then got up to ensure that no one was listening at the door. He opened it and looked down the hall. He glanced searchingly out the louvered windows as if looking for someone lurking outside. He looked like a poor actor in a grade B movie. He sat on the bed next to me and with a conspiratorial grin and low voice said, "It's all bullshit, Don." He was a little drunk.

"Bullshit? What do you mean?"

"I've had two previous tours in intelligence, my first with the Army Security Agency and the other with the Defense Intelligence Agency, the DIA. Now I've got the same type of billet in Saigon.

"Now listen, Don, I shouldn't even be telling you this because you're obviously not cleared nor have an institutionally defined need to know, but I'm sick of this shit. You of all people have the absolute need to know about the intelligence available in your area; your ass is on the line. There's plenty of intelligence available: satellite pictures, VC voice transmissions, infrared searches, and so forth.

"Your very questions today prove out my feelings that we're failing in providing support. I'm trusting you not to tell anyone that I've briefed you or even mentioned or hinted anything to you."

Intrigued, I answered, "You've just met me today, but you know I'm good for it."

"Yeah, you seem okay, but you're a victim of the community. They won't let you know because you're just a lowly combat commander who's not cleared nor has the muscle to force the issue," he went on, glancing around continuously as though we were children preparing to raid the cookie jar.

"I don't understand what the hell you're talking about," I answered. "What community?"

"The intelligence community: the CIA, the DIA, the NSA, the ASA, and even your own naval intelligence and every other shit-ass intelligence-gathering group or agency. They all hang together when faced from the outside, which is you, and on the inside they don't talk to each other very much. They do all their work sitting on their asses. All of them—I should say us; I'm one of them—don't really get very much from all our fancy agents, networks, analysts, spy planes, satellites, and electronic equipment.

"The community hasn't predicted one significant event in years, but there's a lot of local, quick-reaction stuff you could use if you got it fast enough. But that won't happen because everything has to be analyzed first, and each group's secrecy prevents them from working together."

His voice was breaking, his head nodding. He drank straight from the almost-empty bottle of scotch.

"And the compart . . . part . . . mental . . . ization and the need to know makes for a very sluggish bu . . . bu . . . reaucracy, keeping coordination to a minimum and making outside interpretation near impossible. Shit! Everyone wants to publish their own stuff in hard-cover form for posterity and self-aggrandizement . . . making it . . . making it . . . much too late for you and gener . . . ally useless to everyone else." He continued drinking and shifting his eyes as he talked. "My arm hurts so goddamn much," he slurred.

His voice became lower and lower. "I'm sorry, Don, goddamn sorry, that we've failed you and people like you." He was crying, shaking my hand. He took another swallow. "I shouldn't be talking," he muttered, falling back in his chair unconscious, the bandage on his arm staining red.

Can it be? I thought, throwing a blanket around him and collapsing into my bed.

I didn't see him in the morning. He didn't know I had my own intelligence network financed by a kindred spirit from the 9mm Browning automatic pistol agency. I pondered his words, but who could I ask? I was sworn to secrecy. I pushed it out of my mind as my patrol with Sergeant Thanh and four of his men aboard headed southeast to a spot between Kilo and Juliet.

A former Viet Cong, now government, sympathizer had agreed through Ong Tam to spot some VC hootches for us.

Thanh and his men landed just before sunset to capture an old woman reported to be in charge of the southeastern portion of the Can Tho crossing corridor. The landing and attack went smoothly, and although the woman wasn't there, her husband was. We killed him in the short firefight that ensued and took two of her helpers prisoner. We torched the hootches and captured two CHICOM rifles, an AK-47, and several documents. Sergeant Thanh and his men were ecstatic.

Unfortunately, there was an economic imbalance here. I paid the informer 2,000 piasters ($17), cash on delivery, for his information, whereas Thanh's men received 3,500 piasters ($30) for the entire month. I hoped they didn't know.

"Well, Interdictor," Captain Laske said four days later, walking into the corner hideaway cubicle I called an office. "Looks like the Viet Cong are playing hell again with your boats in Titi."

"Mildly put, sir," replied Lieutenant Rover, who was with me. He was referring to yesterday's excursion through Titi, which had cost us a PBR. It was a standard run-through, like we were making every few days. I was fulfilling my promise to Major Shellon to take his assistant, Captain Gordon, out on the river for a little action. Captain Gordon was due to leave country in two days.

Ten minutes into the canal, an angry red hole erupted in Gordon's forehead. Not a sound was heard before he crumpled, dead at my feet. Seconds later a rocket exploded in the side of the third PBR in line. Only its rapid sinking saved the boat from being completely burned. We took heavy casualties rescuing the crew and getting a line on the boat.

Lieutenant Commanders Marsh and Sams were right in there with us. On their first strike, Marsh's helo took a hit, slightly wounding his copilot. On their second run from rearming at Binh Thuy, another round smashed up through the floor, tearing a small wound in the copilot's leg, but still not enough to take him out of action. The Seawolves were short of pilots and the copilot said he could make it. He had arrived at Binh Thuy only that morning and was still pumped up by the action. We needed the helos to suppress the fire as we tried to rescue the PBR. We couldn't afford its guns falling into the VC's hands.

On the third sortie a bullet tore through the windshield, exploding his gun sight. The copilot took the shrapnel in the face. He was medevacked to Saigon and was on a plane to Japan by 1800. Three strikes, you're out; his was the shortest tour on record.

Only three feet of the now-vertical bow still showed as we got it in tow and out of there.

"You ready to go back in?" Captain Laske asked.

"No, sir, my assault teams aren't ready yet."

"How soon?"

"Week . . . ten days."

"Well, let me know. Wanna call it Crimson Tide II?"

"Okay with me, Captain," I replied with no great interest.

"Make it so."

"Aye, aye, sir."

Captain Laske was a man of few words. He had just returned from running the battleship through Khem Bang Co with four PBRs from the T. They shot up the place but received few rounds in return and no casualties. I had opposed the operation based on the narrowness of the upstream end. He concurred and agreed to enter from that direction, thereby negating any objection I could voice. I chose not to go. I was just too tired.

He left my office and Don Rover and I went back to the huge aerial photograph of Titi. We were targeting the area for destruction. What I couldn't get done with an air strike with napalm, I was going to do with sailors and diesel fuel. Even at this moment the SEALs were training PBR and base support sailors in assault tactics. We had been doing it for two weeks, ever since we had destroyed the village around the white church.

I had formed what we called mobile assault combat elements, or MACE teams as they became known. An officer led each of these seven-man teams. There were six teams, all volunteers, with more volunteers than openings. A SEAL assigned to each team was the trainer and advisor; when he deemed necessary, he had the authority to take command. The SEALs were professionals at this, and rank be damned.

The Viet Cong knew we were coming back. We had told them so. We told them if the PBRs were shot at again, we'd destroy the area. Two days after Crimson Tide I, a psyops team I had requisitioned from Saigon went into Titi in a mike boat escorted by four PBRs. They broadcasted for the wounded to come out for treatment, come out and Chieu Hoi, come out, come back to the government. Come out or be destroyed was our message.

The mike boat returned with three wounded sailors, testifying to the Viet Cong's answer. They hadn't believed us.

The sun was just over the tree line as fourteen PBRs invaded Titi with the pure power roar of twenty-eight high-speed, high-compression diesel engines announcing our visit. The helos had already been working over the area for an hour. During the night, I'd moved the LST up to the southern tip of Tanh Dinh Island; Lt. Comdr. Bill Marsh, in command of all four helos, had been cycling them off the ship, two at a time, over the area in continuous firing runs. I wanted the Viet Cong chased off. I had come to destroy, not to fight.

We had lettered each target and numbered each MACE team. There was one team per two boats. I simply had to call out a numbered team and a letter. The assigned boats would move in and land their team. Four of the men would move out to perimeter positions while the other three carried out my orders: Burn! If it wouldn't burn, smash it or blow it.

I ordered the teams in randomly. One time we'd move up, then back, then across. The Viet Cong, if they were watching, and I hoped they were, could not anticipate and set a trap. Just for good measure, the helos would lay a strike in on any likely area. The two 60mm mortar teams laid in a barrage on concentrated areas we encountered.

We worked smoothly, unopposed. One assault team, including the mortar boys, stayed with me in reserve. In case of trouble I could rapidly throw in extra strength. Saigon had tacitly indicated that if I failed, I'd better give my soul to God, for they'd have my ass. Sailors belong on boats and boats belong in the main river, was Saigon's message. I didn't agree and I was in command of the Bassac. Captain Laske thought it was a fine plan and that was all the license I needed.

I was proud of my men. I was proud of myself. I recalled a long-ago movie when I was a child, a movie about Sherman marching through Georgia. Today, I was Sherman. I was not ashamed. We'd told them what would happen. They were the enemy; they had killed my men. This was vengeance. With no place to live they might give up. Wouldn't this clear Titi for friendly river traffic?

The black smoke from the burning hootches drifted high into the sky; sometimes, like an omen, it blotted out the sun.

Occasionally, I lost track of who was where. At the peak of the operation all five teams were ashore and spread out; bookkeeping became a chore. I wanted to be with one of the teams but my job was here. By innuendo, I was criticized periodically for leading instead of commanding. There could be no complaints today.

"Team Four, this is Handlash. Your new target, Oscar. Over."

"This is Team Four. Understand, Oscar. Roger. Out."

"Team One, this is Handlash. Your new target, Papa. Over."

"Handlash, this is Team Six. Request new target. Over." And so it went.

The enemy wasn't here but his booby traps were. He was ready for us. Constant reports poured in of grenade traps and punji pits. Four men already wounded were eagerly replaced by regular crewmen. Casualties would have been higher save for the trained eyes of the SEALs and their skilled disarming of the grenade traps. They ensured success.

I continually conferred with individual team officers for updates and to disseminate information from the others. We discovered that there were far more hootches than anticipated. They might be invisible from the air and water but not from the teams' torches. It was taking fifteen to twenty minutes to destroy each target instead of the planned five to ten. The men were indefatigable; as for me, the nonparticipating combat intensity strained my nerves to the breaking point.

"RECEIVING FIRE, RECEIVING FIRE!" came the near-panicked voice over the radio.

"Who! Where?" I yelled back stupidly. A panicked yell will panic others. The operation had been too smooth.

"Where, goddamnit, Handlash Unit, where?" I demanded, and cursed myself for this uncalled-for outburst.

"Handlash . . . ahhh . . . Handlash, this is Handlash Echo . . . no, I mean Team Five. We're at . . . ahhh . . . target November getting fire."

"Roger, this is Handlash," I spoke with deliberate calm. "Is your MACE team ashore? Over."

"Yes, sir . . . yes, sir, but I can't see them."

"This is Handlash. Hold your position; do not fire. I say again, do not fire your guns! I'm on the way. Out."

"Yes, sir . . . yes, sir. Thank you . . . ahhh . . . Out."

My coxswain was already at full speed. "Tip of the small island there," I pointed.

"Yes, sir, I know."

Who was at target November? Yes . . . Jenkins—good officer; he could handle it. We wouldn't arrive for at least seven minutes. The coxswain kept pushing his throttles forward though already hard against the stops. You know it doesn't help but at least you're doing something, not just waiting. I guess pushing throttles helped. I knew that clicking the safety of my M-79 on and off was something substantial that really helped.

"Team in sight, Commander. They're coming back fast," the radio blurted again.

"This is Handlash!" I emphasized the Handlash. That guy had really blown his cool. "Roger. Out."

I saw the boats back off the beach. "Team Five, this is Handlash. Are all your men aboard? Over."

"This is Team Five. Affirmative . . . we have one prisoner. Over."

"This is Handlash. Roger . . . break, break . . . Seawolf Seven Six, you copy? Over." Seawolf Seven Six was from the T.

"Roger, I copy. We're on the way."

"Roger, Seven Six, hit the island where you see my smoke. Out." I closed the beach and threw a purple smoke grenade.

"I see a purple . . . Handlash . . . rolling in now."

We pulled alongside Jenkins's boat in midcanal. "Anyone hurt?"

"Yes, sir, Smith got one in the shoulder, and he," Jenkins pointed to a tall, well-built Vietnamese, "he's got one in the arm and in the leg."

"How much fire did you receive?"

"Ten, twenty rounds, mostly wild."

I gave the boat captain, whose strained voice I'd recognized, a disgusted stare. He became interested in the deck at his feet. We transferred Smith to a boat to be taken into Can Tho. Two men had just finished bandaging the Viet Cong's leg and arm.

"Sergeant Thanh! Ask him how many men are in there."

Thanh knelt down beside the man and they chatted. I waited.

"He say . . ." Thanh turned back to the man and said something else. The man spoke again. Thanh backhanded him hard across the face. "He say . . . ah . . . for Thieu Ta to kiss his ass."

I pulled my bayonet and knelt beside the man. Saying

nothing, I flicked the blade through the bandage on his arm. Its tip parted his skin as it cut through the bloody cloth. He screamed. I wiped his blood from my knife on his shoulder. "How many men are on the island?" I asked. He scowled, saying nothing.

Thanh put a hand on each side of the nasty, open wound. I looked him dead in the eye as Thanh slowly pulled apart the jagged three-inch cut. Thanh's fingers turned red. The man screamed. Thanh let up.

"Tell us!" Thanh barked, slapping him again in the face.

"Commander! Stop!" came a plea from behind me.

"I . . . will . . . never . . . talk," the man said, in obviously memorized English.

"Kill him, Sergeant," I said in Vietnamese, handing Thanh my .38 revolver.

Thanh slapped it against the man's forehead and pulled back the hammer. The Viet Cong's eyes crossed as he followed the position of the revolver. Thanh flicked the barrel ever so slightly to the right and fired. The flash etched a cruel burn across the man's temple as the slug passed an inch away from his head, splashing into the water.

"Kill him, Sergeant," I commanded in Vietnamese.

Thanh slowly moved the ominous barrel of the black revolver between the man's eyes, rested it on the bridge of his nose, and squeezed the trigger.

Click! the hammer resounded, falling on an empty chamber. I had previously removed all but one round.

"NO! NO!" the prisoner screamed, jabbering, pleading incoherently. I couldn't understand him.

Thanh looked around and winked as he handed me back the .38. "He say two, three men, but they scared and hide in jungle till we go. They have three machine guns but too frightened to shoot."

"Bandage his arm," I ordered.

"Jesus Christ, Commander! I thought you were going to kill him! My God!" the coxswain said.

"Asshole!" I replied as I pulled the gun open to show that it was empty. "It's a trick. I show 'em I'm a mean mother, then Thanh goes to shoot 'em. They think Americans are soft and won't let the Vietnamese soldiers get to 'em. It works every time . . . the old Mutt and Jeff trick."

"Wow! This shit's too heavy for me," he replied.

"Can I go back and hit my target, Commander?" Jenkins asked.

"Permission granted. Throw the Cong on my boat . . . be careful."

I called off the helos as Team Five headed back for the beach, then lit a cigarette and placed it between the prisoner's lips. He looked confused. He took a puff, coughed, and spit the cigarette onto the deck. The after gunner, angry at sharing his station with the prisoner, picked up the cigarette, yanked back the prisoner's head by his hair, and jammed the cigarette into his mouth. The VC started coughing, spitting out the cigarette again. The gunner roughly repeated his move.

"When the commander gives you a cigarette, asshole, you'd best smoke it," he snarled, pulling out his knife. The Viet Cong got the idea and puffed clumsily on the dangling smoke.

I sent Thanh to see what was going on. He came back: "He say he not smoke before."

"Well, make him smoke . . . maybe he'll get lung cancer."

The sun was low; our pyro lust had been venting for five hours. Targets were getting slim and the men tired. I called Don Rover and passed control over to him. One insertion had to be mine. I'd saved a juicy target just for myself, and in we went. I had been rotating a different MACE team onto my boats about every forty-five minutes, to give them rest and to ensure that all teams could exercise their skills.

The boat beached with a thud, and with a quick, wary glance the flankers moved out. In sixty seconds we burners followed, the SEAL in the lead. Four steps from the boat the left burner dropped, screaming, into a punji pit. "Dumb shit!" I yelled as the SEAL and I helped him out. "Any half-blind idiot can see these sons of bitches. Don't move, don't try to help us, goddamnit. We'll do it."

We slowly pulled him up. The other burner came over. "Get back . . . torch that hootch," I ordered. The nasty, half-inch-thick bamboo-spiked punji stake pulled out of the ground; it was embedded maybe two inches into his upper right thigh. I could smell the human excrement smeared on it. (I wondered how they put it on.) I yanked out the stake and helped him hobble back to the boat. "Get him into Can Tho, right now." We had boats standing by for medevacs. I threw the punji stake in with him. "Here, give this to the doc. They may want it."

I moved back to the hootch, glancing down at the punji stake trap on the way. It was a square hole about three feet on a side and four feet deep. Twenty to thirty sharp bamboo spikes projected from the bottom—ugly-looking thing. The pits would be much more effective if camouflaged better. The Viet Cong were sloppy at this; with just minimum caution the pits could be avoided.

When I got back to the hootch it was well up in flames. Shit!

"Hey, Commander!" the torch man yelled, "there's a little woodshed over on this side. I saved it for you."

"Thanks, but if I can't play with the big boys, I won't play at all," I feigned a whine.

He laughed while he doused it with diesel oil. The heat from the big hootch became unbearable, and the SEAL ordered us back. We moved slowly, with a sharp eye for traps. Most accidents happened during a sloppy withdrawal. My eye caught a clothesline with a bra hanging from it. I yanked it off the line and shoved it into my pocket. It'd look good on the trophy wall.

"C'mon, let's get the hell outta here," I yelled.

I breathed easier on the deck of my boat. Looking back at the long, sleek formation of fast patrol boats following me out of the canal, I felt good, satisfied we'd done a good day's work.

We came to destroy, and destroy we did. To the victors go the spoils: a limp brassiere.

The Handling
of Ensign Martin

———————•———————

"An ensign! What the hell do you do with an ensign?"

"I don't know, Commander, they just said you were getting one" came the voice of the chief of staff of RIVRON 5 in Saigon.

"Listen, do me a favor, see if you can get him sent to another river!"

"Well, actually he's assigned to Captain Laske's staff for further assignment to you. There's nothing I can do about it. Besides, Sammy Merrick was an ensign when he went on the river."

"That was different. Merrick had a year aboard a destroyer before he showed up. What's this ensign's name?"

"Martin, sir, Ensign Martin." So ended the phone conversation to Saigon.

"Interdictor! We're getting an ensign. Take care of him; teach him something," Captain Laske ordered.

"If you can teach an ensign to stay out of the doorway before he makes jaygee, you've done a fine job," I replied. "Gimme a break, Captain."

"BUPERS is trying something new, sending ensigns right from the academy. This guy's a test case. Don't get him killed."

"Why do I get all the shitty jobs, Captain?"

"Because I like you."

"Oh?" So ended the conversation with the captain.

"Commander, that new ensign just checked in," Yeoman Stills said with a smirk.

"Buzz off!"

"Yes, sir." So ended the conversation with my yeoman.

"Martin, sir, Ensign Victor Martin, academy graduate, reporting for duty, sir." He stood there in all his Annapolisian glory: stiff as a ramrod, eyes boring straight at a point six inches over my head, arms arched at the perfect angle, feet at the precise forty-five-degree angle, stomach in, chest out, head up, greens pressed, shoes shined.

I imagined that he and his fellow ensigns had practiced reporting to their first commanding officer many times. (I did.) He did it beautifully.

I stood up. "Sheppard, sir, Lieutenant Commander Donald D. Sheppard, mustang. Sit down!"

"Yes, sir."

"What can you do, Mister Martin?"

"Anything the commander desires, sir."

"Please don't use the third person."

"Yes, sir."

"Can you get me a flamethrower?"

"If that's what the commander desires."

"Please do not use the third person."

"Yes, sir."

"Get me one, then."

"Aye, aye, sir."

Ensign Martin, perhaps twenty-three years old, was suave and self-composed, bearing an uncanny resemblance to the American concept of the generic movie star hero. His young handsomeness made me painfully aware of my homely aging face and body. He had a strong aquiline nose and a pencil-line mustache. He carried himself well and sat straight. He looked me squarely in the eye when he spoke. I liked him.

"Did you volunteer for the PBRs?"

"Yes, sir . . . even begged."

"You'd have been better off for your career if you'd gone on a destroyer first."

"Yes, sir, everyone tells me that."

"Why did you want this duty?"

"I've always wanted to fight a war, like the PT boats in World War II. This is the closest thing."

"Yes, I reckon it is."

"Excuse me, sir. Why did the commander . . . ah . . . you volunteer?"

"I've always wanted to fight a war, like the PT boats in World War II. This is the closest thing."

I stood up, he followed suit, and we smiled at one another, shaking hands. "I wasn't mocking you, Mister Martin. My reason for being here is the same as yours, and I wish you luck. But don't let it bite you in the ass. Glad to have you aboard."

Ensign Martin was an aggressive fighter. He took every other patrol; twelve out of twenty-four hours he spent on the river. He learned fast and fought hard. His firefight total soared. He wanted medals, as have all warriors. He already wore jump wings that he had earned on a summer cruise. Unfortunately, COMRIVRON 5 in Saigon learned of his exploits and, afraid for the program of sending unseasoned naval officers into combat, ordered him off the river.

I learned that the order came from the Commander, Naval Forces Vietnam (COMNAVFORV); he had gotten his direction from the Bureau of Naval Personnel (BUPERS) in Washington. Ostensibly they were concerned that if Ensign Martin got killed or badly wounded, the program of sending ensigns straight out of school into combat billets would be suspended. It didn't ring true to me.

Captain Laske had recognized Ensign Martin's value and fumed, but no amount of complaint to Saigon or Washington could budge them from their order. On the third time around we obeyed. The long, grasping tentacles of staffdom reached out and clutched him in. He was assigned mundane, prosaic little tasks and stood watch in the ops center, which only caused the war to teasingly mock him. He had to sneak every hour he spent on the river. I went out of my way not to know about it.

He became disillusioned, disenchanted, embittered. He came to fight; Washington, the navy, and Saigon robbed him of his opportunity, robbed me of a fine patrol officer, robbed the war of a tiger and, no doubt, the navy of a brilliant young officer.

There was nothing I could do. My futile efforts with the hierarchy of Saigon only got my ass chewed. Captain Laske refused to discuss it. Lieutenant Rover couldn't understand the bullshit. It broke my heart to see Martin sit alone at night in the O club drinking. I knew how he felt; I knew. He was a younger version of Don Sheppard. I wanted to put my arms around him as if he were a child and say, there, there . . . things will be okay.

Perhaps, however, the order saved his life, for he had a propensity to charge machine-gun nests. Until ordered off the river, he periodically reminded me that he hadn't forgotten the flamethrower.

The handling of Ensign Martin was my greatest complaint.

My second complaint, and one of the most foolish pieces of staff work I had ever seen, was the order to remove the big black painted numbers from the hulls of the boats.

It started somewhere in the bowels of Saigon, when some trying-to-do-good rear-echelon tactician reasoned that since boat crews were assigned specific boats, they might well fall into a pattern that the Viet Cong could detect and use to destroy them. Logical thinking, save that all river sections had ten boats and thirteen crews. At least one boat was always out of the water for repair, so the odds were tremendous against a given crew having the same boat for more than two patrols in a row.

Control of the boats with no numbers in any but a two-boat operation was difficult to ludicrous, giving rise to such precise military commands as: boat heading downstream that just passed the second canal, do so and so. Or boat that just crossed in front of me (my boat always marked with my burgee) take station astern my boat . . . no, no, the first boat, not the second, no, no, not both boats, just the one with the paint scraped off the port quarter.

Patrol officer identification took time. "Handlash Delta, where are you? Over."

"Off your port quarter. Over."

"I'm turning; when were you off my port quarter?"

"Two, three minutes ago."

"There's four boats there."

"Where are you now? Over."

"On the right."

"Your right or my right?"

"Your right. Off your port beam now."

"Screw it. Come alongside."

I got so frustrated and angry I just wanted to cry. I couldn't make Saigon understand. They, in their infinite displaced knowledge, knew that they were saving lives and had done a good thing. They just couldn't see what a stupid order it was. We circumvented it in a somewhat unkempt-looking way—by flying different patterns of colored rags from the radio antennas.

Now the commands were somewhat more ordered but not much: Two Red Rag Boat, do so and so, or Yellow Rag Boat, come about. But even this was too cumbersome. Screw 'em, I put the numbers back on. Such were the hazards of war.

The problem of burning enemy hootches continued; we just couldn't find a decent way to do it. Thermite grenades either burned through the roofs too fast or rolled off and ignited harmlessly on the ground. The pop flares, even when we could hit the straw hootch, shot right on through and left only two small holes for their passing. Landing with Zippo lighters and diesel fuel was too dangerous. We found that burning the houses in the Viet Cong areas from which we received fire was effective in harassing the enemy. Intelligence reports spoke of the infuriated Viet Cong and their vows to sweep the Bassac clean.

This was okay with us. If they didn't fight, we couldn't kill them. We had them psyched—they made rash moves. Our VC body count grew; it was our measure of success. We never really knew if we were helping the big war up north, but this was our own little war, and we did what we thought had to be done.

I sat in bed one night cleaning my .38 and dry-firing it at the rotating blades of the slowly turning overhead fan. I was thinking how lucky I had been for not having diarrhea. It had a severe debilitating effect on our men, rendering those who had it almost useless. On the river the victims were a distinct hazard, always wanting the boats to stop. The medics had pills but generally they were ineffective.

I lit a damp cigar, marveling how I could even consider smoking such a foul-tasting thing. I flicked the still-burning match through the air toward the wastepaper basket. Its flame arced beautifully, landing squarely in the center and instantly igniting the crumpled papers. I was dashing over to smother it when the idea hit me: flaming arrows!

After the fire was out, I sent a message to the recreation supply people in Saigon asking for a couple of bows and several arrows. They had anything anyone might want—nothing was too good for the boys at the front. In a few days, to my surprise, some fine equipment arrived, along with snide remarks from all around me. The Wright brothers had detractors, as did Billy Mitchell, Elvis Presley, and even Henry Ford.

The arrows, unfortunately, were too short. By the time I got cloth wrapped around one end, I couldn't get enough pull for any distance. The maintenance shop, between giggles, turned out several four-foot-long, quarter-inch shafts. To these, Stills, my yeoman, and I weighted one end with tightly wrapped cloth, and glued light cardboard feathers to the other. They were ready.

We went outside to try them. On a base as small as ours, there wasn't much room to practice. The Seabees had neglected to build an archery range or even a swimming pool.

We used the main street. Stills, now known as Sitting Bull, would shoot five. I, now known as Commander Cochise, shot five. Then we'd walk to where they landed and shoot back the other way. Though we tried to be careful, a few went astray. The troops, though we watched for them very carefully, crossed at their hazard. This was war, boy, war.

Then we tried fire.

The arrow tips were soaked in diesel fuel, strung in the bow, lit, and fired. The first one arced beautifully through the air. I was beside myself with joy. At its apogee, however, the tip, having burned through the wood, fell off, and it and the shaft fell to the ground. We tried again. It happened again.

Roars of laughter from a not large audience accompanied each shot. Bet if I put one up their ass the guffaws would stop.

We tried wetting just the outside of the tightly wrapped rag. It worked. The arrow sang through the air, landed point down into the ground, and burned. Another shot by Stills—this time the fiery missile arced seventy-five yards, then stuck into and ignited the big cardboard box we were using for a hitherto unhit target. The raucous laughter turned to cheers.

We ran actual combat tests the next day: Two PBRs snuck into the upper end of Titi. It was godawful quiet. I hoped to find an unburned hootch. The area looked like Dresden. My men had done their work well, but there was one small hootch left just past the entrance.

Pulling up close to the bank, I strung the bow. The crew made bets on its worth. The arrow flamed through the air, but hit a branch and dropped to the ground. Shit! Another shot. I missed. The next one arced high, stuck squarely into the thatched roof, flamed momentarily, then flickered out. Shit! I handed the bow to the boat captain.

"Here, you try the sonovabitch," I said, trying not to let my disgust show through.

He fired, and hit a branch. He fired again. This time it was perfect. Seconds after the arrow struck, the house was ablaze. Beautiful! Beautiful! It works! We moved down Titi until we found another hootch. The engineer tried. Two arrows destroyed it.

Three rifle shots smashed the water behind us. An eerie zing announced a piece of steel cutting close overhead. We turned in, attacking with our .50s. One run. Then another. We pulled out fast as Three Six, skimming low over the canal, released his 2.75-inch rockets against our attackers. Mighty unfriendly place. Didn't they appreciate our slum-clearance efforts?

A few officers humored me and took the bow and arrow on patrol. "Burn hootches in hostile areas that fire on you, but don't go ashore," I admonished. We had only modest results.

Anyway, the weather was turning nice again. It gently rained every evening just in time to cool things down to eighty degrees or so. There were no more torrential downpours to fight. Sleep became pleasant when you didn't have to lie in a pool of sweat or a puddle of water. During the day, cool winds sang from the southeast, slowly hauling to the right. We could breathe again.

The next week I received a call from Saigon; it was Ensign Martin. "Commander, I've got the flamethrowers." There was a pause while I caught my breath.

"You shittin' me, boy?"

"No, sir, I'm at Than Son Nhut, but they're too much to get on the milk flight. What'll I do?"

"Can you get them to the heliport?"

"Yes, sir."

"I'll have a helo there in an hour." I met them with a truck as they touched down on our helo pad. Ensign Martin beamed. I could've kissed him. But so many boxes?

"What the hell you trade for these, a PBR?" I asked.

"I'd rather not say," he answered.

"I'd rather not know."

Ensign Martin worked on the flamethrowers for a week. No one knew anything about them. Ensign Martin cautioned us not to discuss it with the U.S. Army. All we had was one small instruction book, three sets of tanks, two gun units, and an air compressor.

We worked hard. We didn't realize that the care and feeding of backpack flamethrowers was such a time-consuming and difficult job. The theory of operation was simple: One tank is filled with jellied gasoline, the other with extremely high pressure air. The air pushes the jellied gasoline—napalm—through the nozzle at a rate determined by how hard and how long the trigger is depressed.

Just before the full-pressure napalm-air mixture roars out, a flint device is sparked—much like a cigarette lighter—igniting the jellied mixture starting out the nozzle. The maximum time available before the jellied mixture empties is a scant nine seconds, or maybe, with judicious handling, five two-second bursts.

For all their shortcomings, the flamethrowers could prove invaluable in MACE ground operations. Ensign Martin had done his job well.

Death of a Pig

———•———

Each patrol is an entity unto itself. From the initial briefing until thirteen or fourteen hours later, weary, perhaps blood-stained, you get back and write up your postpatrol report or, if you're in the crew, refuel and rearm your boats. Patrols are similar only in that they all contain intense boredom, slow-festering heartache, and periodic high adventure. The physical strain of searching sampan after sampan in the blistering heat or torrential rain, and the ever-present dissonance of buzzing, biting insects, tears at your body and scrambles your brains.

Couple this with the fear of getting your head blown off every time you come alongside a sampan. Add to it the night when every flicker of light or sound could announce death, and one can see that patrolling is not a pleasant way to spend one's time.

The OinCs set daily patrol objectives under guidance from the river division commanders and overall directions from Captain Laske. On the main, however, the section OinCs ran the show. I, as a division commander, became directly involved only during special operations or when acting as a normal patrol officer. For the first six months of my tour I took around three patrols a week, but as our operation became more complex I found I could ill afford the time.

Bill Marsh's and Don Rover's tactics of running up the small canals to bait the enemy, then hitting them with helos, worked so well that we were now using the PF troops from the outposts. Thanh was in all his glory here. No longer was he just a grunting foot soldier. In these operations he was, de facto, in command of two to four PBRs and two helos. Quite a responsibility for a master sergeant untrained in multiple-force command and control.

Five of these operations had been conducted successfully, each becoming more aggressive, each driving deeper into the sacrosanct domain of the Viet Cong. Don Rover led most of them, and his score of enemy KIAs increased dramatically.

Reports were in from one of Ong Tam's agents: A small group, ten to twenty, of the enemy had moved up to the outpost at Foxtrot. Thanh and Don Rover went to see Ong Tam at Golf to arrange for troops. With no pressing immediate duties hampering me, I went along for the ride. It would be good to see Ong Tam again. It had been three weeks. He was the only man on the Bassac I felt could be my friend. I became awfully lonely sometimes, and being with him eased the pain. He understood, for he had the same problems. Often I would have a patrol drop me off and pick me up hours later.

Ong Tam was an excellent chess player, and the hours we played together were a tonic for both of us. The PBR sailors thought it was Co Bac and Co Hue who attracted me to Golf. It was an easy thing for them to believe—the way the two ladies fawned over me when they walked me back to the boats or when they mysteriously appeared when my boat tied up. I was just macho enough to let everyone think that, to think of me as a stud. I didn't want it known by either my men or the Viet Cong that a good deal of our intelligence originated in their classrooms.

Ong Tam was to go on the raid, and at the last minute I

decided to join them. I took only the role of an M-79 gunner. Rover was too good for me to interfere. During the attack, several VC broke and ran, but five were killed in the initial strike.

The acrid smell of gunpowder still hung over the five humanlike forms lying at our feet as we got off the boat. One of the forms wasn't dead: His blinking eyes pleaded for help; his lips moved but no sound came out. His hands clutched, relaxed, clutched again.

"Shoot him, shoot him!" came the singsong chant from the Vietnamese soldiers circling him. The man looked plaintively to me for salvation. The soldiers looked to me for guidance. Ong Tam's eyes waited for my decision. Don Rover watched.

Bastard! my mind spoke to the half-dead Viet Cong. Don't look at me; what can I do for you? You don't even have any legs left . . . you're dead. Die! Get it over with. I wanted to scream but I didn't; I couldn't. I just stood there watching his blood pump out over the clinging mud of the jungle clearing. I stood there watching, fighting to keep my vomit from betraying the wretchedness I felt.

"Shoot him, shoot him!" the eerie Vietnamese murmur resounded in my ears. I wanted to run. I wanted to cleanse myself of this savage butchery. "Shoot him, shoot him!" echoed in my brain.

I gave no sign, no command. I turned away. I looked back, nodding my head down no more than half an inch. Ong Tam looked at me, smiling, as he drew his pistol. One shot and a scream.

The operation had started in midafternoon; we'd gotten under way just after lunch, Don Rover in the lead. We cruised slowly up the narrow canal as bait for the ever-watchful Viet Cong. Ong Tam and ten of his PFs followed a half mile or so behind. Thanh and six other small-framed Vietnamese soldiers, secreted three to a boat in the chief's quarters, rode with us.

Once jumped by the Viet Cong—an almost sure thing

here so deep in their territory—we would keep them engaged with our .50s while Ong Tam moved up on the double. When he was almost on them, we were to land our six Vietnamese soldiers up canal. It was a box from which the Viet Cong could not escape. The back of the box would be closed by Marsh's helos standing by at Golf.

The low rumble of the trolling engines magnified by the low-hanging mangroves on each side of the canal announced our coming. There wasn't much color here, only the dirty brown somberness of bamboo-thatched hootches and the dark green of the jungle trees. Our olive-drab patrol boats dawdling up the shallow, muddy waters of the canal added nothing but an occasional white swirl. Our brilliant American battle ensigns stood out in sharp contrast to the mundane surroundings.

It was coming on 1400; the burning sun had already turned our combat greens wet and smelly. There was no breeze; the oppressive jungle lay over us like a suffocating blanket.

From the north side, a rifle shot rang out, followed almost immediately by the short BURRAT of an AK-47. Four bullets ripped through our fiberglass hull; one splattered against the armor shield, spraying deadly shrapnel throughout the boat. A Vietnamese soldier screamed. My right leg felt a sting. Our .50s fired back. The coxswain stood the boat on its side as we wheeled about, swinging in for the attack. On the beach I could see muzzle flashes through the small firing ports of a bunker; our .50s ricocheted harmlessly off its thick, hard dried-mud walls.

It was the same old story. We couldn't touch them in their near-impregnable fortresses, but today we had troops!

"Victor One, Victor One, this is Handlash Two," Rover radioed Ong Tam. "Have made contact, one bunker, up two hundred meters from your position. Am landing troops now. Out."

Again the boats pivoted, braving the firing bunker as we sped past to land our six Vietnamese up canal. Rover had to maintain contact. He didn't want the quarry to melt into the jungle. Thanh's men were barely off before Rover came about swiftly.

They were still there, this time in greater fury. Their bullets cut over, churned the waters beside us, and made ugly, jagged holes in our boat. We fired 40mm grenades. The tracers from the .50s painted beautiful yet grisly light patterns dancing through the jungle. The helos laced down the area behind them. The Viet Cong didn't know it but they were trapped—they were men waiting to die. Their bunkers weren't built to withstand a land assault. They were built to knock our boats off the river. And I was sick and tired of being a patsy for their ambushes.

"Handlash Two, this is Victor One. Bunker in sight; we fight now. Over" came Ong Tam's calm voice from the PRC-25 I had given him.

"Roger, Victor One. Do you see other troops? Over."

"Yes, am going to fight now. You no shoot now. Over."

"This is Handlash Two. Will not shoot now. Out."

We continued down canal, out of the kill zone; it was Ong Tam's show now. I could still hear the helos keeping their area hosed down. Seconds passed, then minutes—five . . . ten. I fought down the urge to call on the radio to find out what was going on. Ong Tam and Sergeant Thanh knew their jobs. Don Rover knew what he was doing. If they needed me, they'd ask.

I heard a grenade explode, followed by a short machine-gun burst, then several rifle shots. Rover ordered the boats to head back. I would have done it sooner just to prevent the VC from crossing the canal. Three more grenades in quick succession reverberated across the water.

Rover cracked the coxswain on the back. "Hit it, let's go." The throttles went forward; the boat leapt ahead.

"Come quick, Handlash. Viet Cong run."

"On our way. Out."

In seconds we were back in the kill zone; no bullets this time. We passed through, whipped around, and came in again.

"They're breaking!" screamed the after gunner as his

.50-caliber slugs chased the two running Viet Cong across the water, over the beach, and into their hapless bodies, painting them a splashy crimson. Then silence.

I could see Thanh on the beach. He moved in with his men, surrounding the bunker. He was shouting into it but I couldn't make out his words. Ong Tam, with his men, appeared for a moment, then disappeared into the jungle.

"Don," I said, nodding my head to the beach. Rover pointed, and the coxswain pushed the boat toward the beach. Rover secured the helos. They made a low victory pass over our heads, lifted over the jungle, and disappeared to the south. The boat ran smoothly onto the beach. I stepped off, carrying my .38.

Thanh's men at the bunker moved around in quick, excited steps. They jabbered back and forth like little children at a carnival.

Thanh shouted, "Come out, dogs!" but there was no answer.

I walked toward the bunker. Ong Tam's ten men reappeared, all shouting recognition as they saw me approaching the bunker. "Thieu Ta, be careful," Ong Tam said with a wave.

Thanh's men let out a howl. I whirled. A half-naked figure bolted from the bunker, dashing for the jungle. Fool. Six machine guns, like piranhas, ate away his flesh. He crumpled in a heap.

A dull, distant thud testified to deep explosions from three hand grenades tossed into the bunker's small tunnel passageway. Thanh sent two men in to investigate.

"Gather the bodies," I ordered, and Ong Tam's men set about their ghoulish task. One man came backing out of the bunker pulling a rope, a naked Viet Cong in tow. The soldier entered again and dragged out another. The bodies always seemed to have their trousers pulled off.

"Tunnel go somewhere from inside," the other trooper reported. "No more bodies left. Blood leads into tunnel."

We lined up the bodies in a neat row—five of a kind, a good hand. We'd leave them there—an example to others.

"Thanh! Ong Tam! Send your men out to search for the tunnel exit. Hurry!" Rover ordered. Both gave quick commands and their men fanned out. They'd tasted blood—the sweet smell of the kill.

I reholstered my .38 and lit my pipe, turning away from the bodies. The tobacco's sharp taste bit my tongue. Killing was a depressing business. I sent Rover's PBRs up the canal a bit just to check. He looked surprised that I didn't get back on the boat, but said nothing but "aye, sir."

"I check tunnel, Thieu Ta," Thanh said, disappearing into the narrow passageway.

I watched the smoke from my pipe drift up through the trees. The air was still. The gunpowder fumes irritated my throat. It dawned on me how stupid it was to sit here by myself. Stupid? I didn't even have a radio. I wanted to leave. I shouted for Thanh.

I watched a pig come out of a hootch; he was muddy and fat. He snorted along the ground. "HA! You won't last long once the soldiers see you." I don't think he understood me; he didn't look up. He sniffed around the bodies; his movements became faster, frenzied, as he found the one with no torso and drove his head deep into its bloody, open stomach cavity.

My insides drew up, my throat constricted; half-digested jelly donuts spewed out of my mouth. I grabbed a large bamboo pole and brought it down with all my strength on the pig's back. It squealed, driving its head deeper into the stomach. I hit him again, and again, and again. His squeal tormented my eardrums. My frantic effort only spurred on the disembowelment—he was tearing the body apart. I drew my knife and jammed it into his side. He stopped. I jammed it in again. He gave what would pass for a pig's scream and bolted off.

I sat down again away from the bodies, wiping the blood from my knife and hands. I'll never eat pork again. What a lousy way to make a living. Only an occasional yelling came from the men sweeping the jungle. A slight breeze came up, ruffling the high, splintered palm branches. The soothing sound and the contrast between their dark green dance and the cloudless brilliant blue sky was peaceful. It didn't seem so bad sitting here watching my pipe smoke curl up in weird patterns among the low-hanging leaves. I was tired.

My mind relaxed . . . I didn't look up . . . the carnage drifted away. What a beautiful spot for a picnic.

In the hootch across from the tree where I was sitting I saw a movement in the window—a flash of black? My imagination? No! It had been there. "Thanh!" I called. "Thanh! C'mon out, we're going."

He crawled out of the bunker. Turning my back toward the hootch, I whispered: "There's someone in the hootch over there, behind me. We'll circle around and hit it."

Thanh nodded and we walked casually toward the jungle, chattering about nothing. Behind the hootch I drew my .38, motioning Thanh to circle around the other side. We moved slowly. Great beads of sweat rolled off my forehead and down over my sunglasses. I felt my greens getting even more soggy. My toes squished in my boots. My breathing sounded like a wind tunnel, and stepping on a twig like a falling redwood.

Low and slow, boy—don't mess it up.

The breeze stopped. The bitter odor of burned rice stung my nostrils. The pig, Viet Cong blood all over its face, rolled lazily in a mud puddle, blood oozing from its stab wounds. It was silent. It was dying. Bastard pig!

I could hear nothing in the hootch. Thanh rounded the far side as I approached the door. He started to pull the pin from a grenade. I shook my head not to and pointed to my lips, using pantomime to motion for him to speak.

"COME OUT!" he yelled.

I couldn't make out the soft reply. I shrugged my shoulders.

"He say he afraid we shoot."

"No! No! Come out, we won't harm you," I said, attempting to make my words soothing and believable.

There was a slight shuffling inside. The door opened

slowly. I pulled the hammer back on my revolver. Damn! I wished I had my M-3 grease gun.

A figure of a young boy burst through the door, bolted ten feet, spun around, and tossed a grenade at our feet. My eyes transfixed on the ugly, rusty thing.

"GOOD LORD!" I screamed. Thanh dove for me, knocking me down. I rolled over. My .38 went off in a wild shot. The boy stood straight, a look of horror on his baby face.

Terror ran rampant through my mind, my soul crying, I'M GOING TO DIE!

My right hand, with the pistol in it, lay pointing toward the twelve- to thirteen-year-old boy. He had his hands over his face. I squeezed the trigger; his right shoulder squirted blood.

I rolled again. I wanted to die. I waited for the ear-shattering death blast of the grenade explosion, the darkness. There came only a muffled crack.

I jumped to my feet, springing at the boy as he tried to pull the pin from another grenade. I was four feet from him when my pistol exploded into his stomach. He opened his mouth to scream; blood gurgled out. The grenade dropped. His face contorted in pain.

We collided. He spun around, dropping to his knees. The impact twisted me, knocking me to the ground. The grenade lay inches from my face. He lunged toward me, his hand grasping for the grenade.

Our eyes met—his wild, crazed-animal look stopped my heart. I fired again, and his face turned into a bloody, macabre, expanding bubble. It grew; his features became indistinct in bulbous distortion. I fired again. The bubble burst—disappeared—his hand clutching the grenade.

I fired again.

I lay there for a moment. Thanh was still rolling. I started to cry. He came over and helped me up. I couldn't stop the convulsive shaking of my body. I vomited over myself.

Thanh put his arm around me, then he took my pistol and, as if I were a child, led me away.

We passed the pig . . . it was dead.

The
South China Sea

———————•———————

"Pull off into Golf, Quantrill," I ordered. I had an errand to do. I had been off the river for a week or so and this evening was on my way to the T to attend memorial services. Two of 511's men had bought the farm in a firefight off Dung Island.

Memorial services depressed me. I considered them no more than pagan rites chanted by some sanctimonious high priest who never knew the man. Canned and shallow, phony eulogies of the wonderfulness of man and his likely reception of heavenly reward disgusted me.

The two PBRs tied up smartly at the village piers. "Chao, Ong Tam," I said, extending my arms around him.

"Chao, Thieu Ta."

We passed the time sitting in his house sipping beer cooled over chunks of ice. I arranged to have two cases of beer sent down to my men, with the admonishment that only half of them could drink more than two bottles apiece. Ong Tam refused my money.

"Chao, Thieu Ta" came the honey-soft, sensuous song of Co Bac.

I stood up, bowing slightly. "How do you know when I come here?"

"It is a small village. We all love Thieu Ta here."

I wondered what she meant by love? She spoke English well, but slight innuendos of the language escaped her. I smoked a cigar that Co Bac lit for me. She acted the perfect hostess, pouring the beer, holding an ashtray, fanning me. We talked of her schoolchildren.

"They are at recess for the rest of the day in honor of your visit," she replied to a question on their whereabouts. "They, too, enjoy the American Bassac Thieu Ta's visit."

"When we go another raid, Thieu Ta, kill many Viet Cong?" Ong Tam asked. His standard dress of white shirt and black trousers was as always immaculately clean and pressed. I wondered how he managed.

"Ong Tam, you go on too many raids already . . . too dangerous. You must let your men lead."

"Like you, Thieu Ta," he laughed.

We played chess for two hours, with him winning three out of the four games. We were fast players, both taking the game quite seriously. "I must go, my friend, there is a funeral on the big ship." I gave him an envelope containing 25,000 piasters, a little over two hundred dollars.

"It is much money, Thieu Ta. Do you feel that you get . . . what is word? . . . value for this much?"

"You spend the money well, Ong Tam. Your information is of great value to my men on the river and to our countries."

We walked in silence toward the waterfront. Ong Tam's face took on a rare, somber look. "Thieu Ta must be careful of Tanh Dinh Island. I hear of what you are doing. The Viet Cong very angry. You know, Thieu Ta, the 306th Battalion is there. They have sworn to kill you. You must be careful," Ong Tam pleaded.

"Yes, Ong Tam, I know."

"Thieu Ta, do you know Viet Cong offer big reward for your death? They offer 25,000 piasters. Many people in Can Tho and on your base do not make that much money in a year."

"Do you believe that story, Ong Tam?"

His outstretched hand stopped me. He looked up into my

face. I had never seen him so serious. "Thieu Ta, it is true, I have heard with my own ears in the little villages." Ong Tam often moved inland in disguise, mixing with the crowds, gaining intelligence, and so did several of his men. The monthly money I gave him paid for the expenses on these trips.

We had another beer at the marketplace while Quantrill, the senior boat captain of Hotel Patrol, gathered up the halves of his crews he had let come ashore. Ong Tam had moved six captured CHICOM rifles aboard the boats while we drank. I'd later trade them for food and building materials.

"I thank you for the case of whiskey you sent down last week, Thieu Ta. I passed it to my outposts and soldiers; they are happy with you."

"It is nothing, Ong Tam. I am happy with them. When will you come to Binh Thuy to visit me? We'll have a big party; there are many girls in Can Tho, Ong Tam, or do your two wives keep you busy here?"

"Yes, two wives keep me . . . what you say? occupied . . . yes, occupied. But I must visit, and soon, Thieu Ta. Also many girls here. You must spend the night as our guest," he smiled.

"Yeah, I know. Thank you, Ong Tam."

We both laughed, walking arm in arm to the pier. We both knew that if I spent the night, the Viet Cong would surely attack, destroying the village.

"Chao, mon ami," he said.

The coxswains kicked over their engines as I stepped aboard. "Ready to go, Commander?" Quantrill asked.

"Yeah!"

"You look beat . . . where's those little gals who always come down to see you off?"

"Busy or tired I guess. Let's make it."

I sat on the engine covers with my helmet on my lap as we sped downriver. From Juliet three sniper rounds cut over the boat. The after .50 slammed back ten to twenty.

"You wanna engage, Commander?"

"No! Screw it." Six months ago I would have roared in fighting.

"Wow! A firefight," yelled the new coxswain.

"Shit, man, them sniper rounds don't count . . . only some farmer. Barely heard the bullets zing by," the engineer said, spitting a chaw of tobacco into the river.

"Wow, my first firefight," the coxswain repeated.

"It wasn't a firefight, goddamnit, Barfield. You'll bloody well know when you're in a real firefight. It'll come soon enough. Wait'll you go with the commander back behind Titi, or with Mister Rover when he races into one of those small canals he likes so much. Then you'll see a firefight," Quantrill said in disgust.

Had we become so stereotyped? "How long you been in-country, son?" I asked, disgusted with myself for calling him son, as though I was in some hackneyed war movie.

"All week, sir."

"You old enough to drink?"

"Not in Montana, sir, but I can here."

"How long you been in the navy, Barfield? You shave yet?" I had just met him this morning when we got under way.

"Almost a year, sir. Yes, sir, I shave every week."

"You don't have to call me sir all the time. Take an easy strain, boy, you've got a long way to go. Why'd you volunteer for PBRs?"

"It sounded adventurous, and I can go anywhere or strike for anything I want after my tour."

"I didn't know seamen were being accepted for the PBR program. What did you think of the PBR school in the States?"

"Okay, but from what I hear from the guys at the base, it ain't that way at all."

"Well, judge for yourself, and in a month please come see me and let me have your opinion. Okay?"

"Yes, sir. Sir?" he asked after glancing around. "Is Mister Quantrill really a relative of that Civil War guerrilla from Kansas? He said he was."

"Don't call him mister. Call him Boats or whatever he wants you to call him, but mister is not correct," I admonished. "If he says he's a relative, he is."

"Gosh, sir, I ain't never talked to an officer of your high rank before."

"I'm not of high rank, Barfield, just a lieutenant commander. In Saigon I would be no more than a messenger boy."

"Barfield, quit bothering the commander, he's got more to worry about than your rambling," Quantrill said, coming up forward from talking to the after gunner.

"Yes, sir, Mister Quantrill."

Quantrill raised his eyebrows, nodding his head in dismay. "Seamen on the boats . . . what's the world coming to?"

We rode in silence for ten to twenty minutes. "You're a fire controlman, aren't you, Quantrill? Don't see many of you technical ratings around here. Mostly boatswain's and gunner's mates."

"Yes, sir, but the fleet was getting mighty short of those guys, so they opened it to some techies like me and some 'outstanding' seamen, like Mister Barfield there. I've only been here four months but the older guys were telling me how bad it used to be with shortages of men and repair parts and stuff."

"It used to be bad," I answered, "but we've got enough of everything now . . . life's a lot easier. We used to have to cancel a patrol sometimes just because the boats were in such bad shape. Next week we even have three new boats arriving."

"Is it true you're shifting 512 to the T pretty soon?"

"Yes, I'm afraid so for 512, but 511 thinks it's a great idea."

"Shit! By the way, Commander, what happened to Tango Patrol down there?"

"They drifted too close and too long off Dung Island and, from what it appears, a Claymore mine triggered off right next to them."

"Oh shit!"

"Two men died instantly, and Ponce, the patrol officer, is in real serious condition. He's in Japan."

"What's a Claymore mine, Petty Officer Quantrill?" Barfield asked.

"An evil piece of shit you hope you never see the convex side of."

"Your great-granddaddy would probably have given a better answer to one of his men," I whispered.

He looked at me ashamed and, turning to Barfield over the engine noise, said: "Remember those things I pointed out around the perimeter fence on the base and told you to stay away from and I'd tell you later what they meant? Well, those were Claymore mines."

"I ain't been near them, sir."

"Don't call me sir. Well, those skinny, bent things the size of phonebooks weigh about ten pounds each and contain a pound of C-4 plastic explosive. When they're triggered remotely by wire or by a trip mechanism, the exploding C-4 throws out six hundred little steel balls, shredding everything out to one hundred fifty feet within its fan-shaped, sixty-degree burst arc."

"Wow! Those are the things you told me that the convex side always goes toward the enemy. Why do they call them mines if they're not buried?" Barfield asked.

"I don't know, Barfield, they just have two spikes you jam into the ground and then run your wire out. Now pay attention to your driving. Look, see that clump of weeds? Go around it. In Hotel when the Jacuzzis jam, the coxswain goes over the side to clear 'em."

We easily skirted the clump of weeds and floating logs as Barfield's deft hands guided the speeding PBR. Quantrill nodded his satisfaction. Barfield had already seen the clump. "You know Willie from Delta Patrol on the T, Commander?"

"Afraid I do."

"I think we got another one there," Quantrill said, pointing to Barfield.

I laughed. "We could do worse, Quantrill, we could do worse."

"Willie's calling himself 'Wyatt Bassac, Commander Saver' nowadays. He said he saved your ass when you and he were trying to take out a bunker with a .38 pistol. That true?"

"Wow!" shouted Barfield, turning back to look at us.

"The river, Barfield, look only at the river. You're the coxswain . . . always watch the river, Barfield, and you'll get us all home safely. The rest of us will watch everything else. You tell me what you see, but you always watch the river," Quantrill lectured.

"Yes, sir."

"Well, it's sorta true but we had a bit of help with frag grenades, Willie's M-16, and a couple of fifties in the end. I'm afraid Willie has a way of embellishing things a bit."

"I'm getting my own .44 magnum soon, Commander. Petty Officer Quantrill said it was okay as soon as I learned how to drive the boat," Barfield said, keeping his eyes dead ahead.

Two fast-moving helos approached us head-on at near-zero altitude. Passing over us they pulled up in a tight turn to the southeast. "Handlash, this is Seven Six. Welcome to the Lower Bassac Hunting Club. You slumming today or lookin' for some action?"

"Down for R&R. Got an NFG [new fuckin' guy] aboard lookin' to cut his beret. Anything interesting? Over."

"On the big mother saw a few troops milling about. I'm sure they took a shot at me . . . interrogative tube aboard. Over."

He was referring to Dung Island and to the 60mm mortar. "That's affirmative . . . point the way." Quantrill's Hotel Patrol was the best mortar team and as a matter of practice always carried it with them.

I nodded to Quantrill. "Stand by your guns," he ordered.

"Handlash One, this is Handlash with Hotel. Seven Six has interference upside big mother. We are joining with tube. Over."

"Roger, Handlash. Be advised, Captain says, seven-boy curry and baked Alaska for dinner tonight. Regret no wine. Be careful. Over."

Good man, the captain of the LST. Seven-boy curry with baked Alaska for dessert was a wardroom favorite throughout the fleet. I hadn't had it for years. It was basic curried lamb and rice plus seven different condiments. In the old days in India, seven young boys carried each of the seven condiments to the guests on a tray. If you served fewer than seven condiments and therefore used fewer than seven boys, you were considered cheap or poor.

"Roger, Handlash One, we won't be late. Out."

Seven Six put in a strike just ahead of us. A rifle round zinged through the boat just ahead of the coxswain's flat, leaving a jagged hole inches from Barfield's face. We swung parallel well out from 150 yards and opened fire with the mortar. Quantrill placed the shells unerringly as the helos spotted the fall of shot. We turned and made another pass. Our forward .50s and all the guns on the cover boat blasted away. Another round struck the armor plating inches from Quantrill and his loader's head. It splintered and I saw two small red splotches on Quantrill's neck. I felt a sting on my left leg and heard Barfield yelp.

We made two more passes. The recoil of the 60mm mortar was tearing up the sandbag in the ammo box we used to absorb the recoil. In normal use the ground absorbed this shock, but here on the boat, the hull, through the sandbag, took it. We could fire only about fifty rounds before everything was torn up, including the after-deck platings.

We took two more hits on the boat before I called Seven Six to break up the party. I didn't want to be late for the ceremony—wouldn't look good. "Good show," Seven Six reported, adding: "A game of chess tonight, Handlash?"

"Rog, Six. I eat rotor heads." I criticized myself for such sloppy radio procedure. I found I was using it more and more. The fleet would straighten me out soon enough. I was hoping for an executive officer's assignment on a destroyer. I'd best square away soon.

In midriver we tied up together. Sand was everywhere from the intense mortar firing. "Hate this part," Quantrill kept muttering. We dressed the slight wounds we received, then cleaned the boat. My trousers had blood on them. I didn't like having them stained when I went aboard the T. The T represented the real navy to me and I wanted to look sharp. Also, it didn't help the men's morale to see blood-stained clothing. I had brought another set of clean jungle greens, but shrapnel had hit my bag, shredding them. Shit!

The bottom of Barfield's left ear was gone. He hadn't said a word during the fight. The left side of his blouse was nearly black from the blood. "Was that a firefight, sir?" he asked Quantrill.

"That was a firefight, boy," Quantrill answered, picking up Barfield's brand-new black beret and cutting the holding ribbon in back. You owe us all a beer."

"WOW!"

Quantrill reached into his combat bag, withdrew a small package, and handed it to Barfield. Barfield opened it with surprise. "It's a .44 magnum . . . I . . . it's chrome-plated. I . . ."

"Keep your eyes on the fucking river, Coxswain."

"WOW!"

As I had feared, the sunset memorial service was maudlin —the pomp and ceremony impressive, but maudlin. Lieutenant Henry took it poorly. He naturally carried in his mind the responsibility, the guilt for their deaths. They were his men. He must write the letters home. Inside, I cried. Why hadn't I kept them in the middle of the river where doctrine demanded—where they would still be alive?

The rest of the evening I spent quietly playing several games of chess, having the captain's delicious dinner, and watching a good movie. Then Lieutenant Henry walked into the wardroom and handed me a message: At 2345 First Class Petty Officer Raymond Ponce died.

I left the wardroom and walked the decks. The night was

still, with only the sounds of sailors working on PBRs in the well deck breaking the soft rhythm of water passing by the ship from the shifting tide. I ended up on the bridge, sitting in the captain's chair, staring upriver at the Bassac.

The almost-full moon painted faces on the rippling water. Hazy faces danced through the clouds. Hundreds of faces drifting in and out of my view, and I knew every one of them. They tried to avoid my eyes but it didn't work; when our eyes met they died and I grew a little taller for each one.

I didn't recall leaving the bridge.

I was taking out the 0800 patrol. "Beautiful day, Commander," said the boat captain, Boatswain Mate First Banford, just to make conversation as we got under way and headed upriver. He was older than the average boat captain and was on his second consecutive tour.

"Yes, it sure is." I'd never seen the sky so blue nor the water so clear, nor felt my mind so calm. We checked a few sampans but found nothing more exciting than vegetables and firewood. Even the traffic was light. I pointed back toward the South China Sea, to the wide mouth of the Bassac from which we had just come.

"Your people check out there much?" I asked Banford.

"Once a week or so . . . not too often. Nothin' much down there but big ol' fishin' junks."

"With maybe recoilless rifles hidden underneath?" I interjected.

"Never found anything," he said.

"Let's take a look."

The two boats hummed in agreement as we headed out to the South China Sea. I always felt comfortable with the sailors from the T. Their boats looked crummy due to the difficult maintenance conditions on the ship, and their uniforms looked horrible most of the time because the T didn't have adequate facilities, but damn they were good fighters.

"Looks mighty calm. Should be a lotta fishermen out

there. Oh! Commander, thanks for taking care of my boys and me last week up in Can Tho. Don't know what got into us."

"Whiskey," I laughed, "in case you don't remember."

"Let's get that first one there," I said, pointing to a big fishing junk quite a way out. Banford radioed in our change of patrol stations.

"Are you still happy with your choice of extending for another tour?" I asked.

"Yes, sir, call me crazy but I like it here. It's the first time in my career that I feel I'm actually doing something worthwhile. Is that odd, sir?"

"No, Banford, I feel the same thing. Lot of the guys do."

"Also it's a financial thing. I'm coming up on twenty and my wife and I want to get a place in the Idaho mountains. Never been able to save enough money before. But here, what with the extra combat pay and no income tax, we'll be able to get ahead. God knows, there's not much out here to spend it on."

"You're right," I agreed.

"Also, sir, I've had trouble for years making chief. When I'd pass the test there wouldn't be enough in the quota to make it. It seems when I didn't pass the test the quota would be greater. Boatswain mate chief has been closed out for many years. Out here I gotta lot of time to study and everyone helps me a lot. And you know all you have to do out here is pass the test and you get the chief's hat—no quotas or bullshit."

I nodded.

"With the guaranteed duty assignment," he continued, "especially for those completing their second tours, I'll get a cushy recruiting assignment in Boise and start my second career."

"What's that?"

"Snake husbandry," he replied.

"What the hell is that?" I asked.

"You raise snakes for a living." I shuddered inside, turning away.

We were approaching the large fishing junk. We glided over the water as if the sea were a sheet of glass. I could actually see the image of the boat and myself in reflection. I looked like a stranger.

"Weren't you in that Coast Guard cutter mess awhile back, Banford?" I asked.

"No, sir, but I heard about it as it was happening."

"Tell me, I haven't seen any official report."

"It was a royal fuck-up, if you'll excuse my language, sir. We had gotten word that a steel-hull trawler was going to try to make it into the Bassac and we positioned the PBRs down here around the mouth of the river. We waited for several nights but nothing happened.

"Around the third night the patrol on the northeastern side of the mouth reported a strong radar contact heading south just outside the entrance. My patrol—I was the boat captain on the cover boat then—was stationed on the southwestern side. We only had slight and fuzzy radar contact, what with being so far away.

"Well, as the story goes the patrol and the radar contact got closer and closer together. The patrol in the center of the mouth was ordered to head slowly northeast to assist if necessary. I could hear the tension in the voices of the guys as they reported the steel hull getting closer and closer.

"We were ordered over to help but also at slow speed, so as not to alert the steel hull. It turned into the Bassac, hugging the shore. The PBRs waited for maybe ten, fifteen minutes and then when the moon cleared a cloud they opened up with their fifties.

"The steel hull returned the fire but the speed and maneuverability of the PBRs made it useless. By that time the middle patrol joined the fight and all four of them pounded the steel hull. But the steel hull got in some damn good shots, tearing hell outta the first two PBRs," Banford continued.

"It was coming on first light and they all recognized that they were both shooting up friendlies. It was a real fiasco, Commander, a lot of people killed and wounded. The Coast

Guard cutter didn't really have a chance. None of them had any combat experience and here they were going up against experienced close-in fighters with boats ten times faster and more agile in close quarters.

"Afterward everybody started blaming everyone else. It was damn simple to us: We had poor intelligence and no way to communicate with the ships on the Market Time operation. The Market Time ships had never been instructed not to enter the rivers, the assumption being, I guess, that they were too big to even think about it."

"Well," I answered, "we have clear doctrine and communications procedures now. It's a shame they came with such a high price. There never was a steel-hulled trawler, I understand."

"No, sir, there wasn't. Can you imagine?"

The coxswain made a beautiful approach to the large fishing junk. He was a natural. The fishermen were friendly, even offering us tea. We spent a pleasant ten minutes discussing the vagaries of the fishing trade. It cost me a pack of cigarettes and three boxes of C rations.

We pulled smartly away, then searched with equal gregariousness a few more of the large junks in the fishing fleet.

"There's a big one way out there, Commodore," Banford said.

"Commodore?" I responded.

"Yes, sir, in the navy that I came from, anyone who flies a burgee like yours is a commodore. Aren't you one?"

"Well, I just don't know for sure. It doesn't mean shit one way or another out here anyway."

I had my binoculars on the junk. The five or six men aboard worked feverishly to pull in their huge net. It came up loaded with fish, then swung over an open hatch, where a crewman pulled a rope tied around the bottom. This opened the net, letting the fish fall into the hold.

We hailed them on the power megaphone at some distance. They paid no attention as they kept to their chores. The water around our slow-moving boats churned in an odd rhythmic motion. We moved in closer to the fishermen. A snake's head popped out of the water, then another, and another. The whole sea around us undulated with snakes. A shiver ran through me. I stood nearly paralyzed. Banford clapped in childish glee.

"Sea snakes, Commander! Look, look, ain't they beautiful? Thousands, just thousands. I've never seen one, just read about 'em. Damn! Just look at 'em. They come up from around Australia every year to spawn. Then they go back."

"You outta your gourd, man?" I asked in shock.

"No, no! Snakes are my hobby. I just love 'em."

"From now on stay away from me. You're nuts!"

"Those snakes are one of the most deadly in the world—'bout the same as the krait and tiger. Makes a water moccasin look like a kitty cat. A man can live maybe three, four minutes after getting bitten by one."

"Let's get the hell outta here."

"Wait! I wanna catch one."

"Like hell you are, Banford. Get your ass up into that coxswain's flat."

"Ahhhh, Commander."

"You're crazy, Banford, fuckin' ass crazy."

"I'm gettin' out of the navy," he sulked.

"GOOD!"

I yelled over the power megaphone to warn the fishing boat but they had noticed and were pulling away. The cover boat was tossing concussion grenades over the side to kill the snakes. My flesh crawled up and down in horrid synchronization with the water's churning. The coxswain eased the boat about through the deadly quagmire. Blood squirted through our grinding propulsion pumps as the intakes sucked up the vipers, ramming them into the impellors. We were moving by the force of meat and blood instead of water. The boats were sluggish, answering their helms poorly.

We prayed our way back toward the river. It took fifteen minutes before water replaced the slimy goo slamming out of our pumps. We drove at high speed up the river, paying no attention to anything but getting away from the nightmare. No one spoke; our faces were without expression, our movements slow and aimless. Only that idiot Banford seemed to exhibit any meaningful activity, and that was writing in some stupid notebook.

As we passed the entrance to Khem Bang Co on Dung Island, I moved the boats in close and ordered all guns to fire. We had received no rounds and it wasn't a free-fire zone but I didn't give a shit. If it hadn't been for the Viet Cong on the island, we wouldn't have had to be in the South China Sea or the lower Bassac or in the delta or anywhere in this godforsaken country.

A half hour of firing cleansed us. We moved to the widest part of the river and drifted there until the patrol was over.

Never, never will I come down here again, I vowed.

Bong Bot

———•———

The order of shipboard life slowly brought me back to sanity. Banford and his crew seemed no worse for the experience. There was little for me to do on the T and I felt more in the way than a help. I took to riding recon runs with Seven Six whenever we weren't playing chess. I just didn't want to go back on the river.

The air-conditioned interior of the T and its routine happenings, such as the sounding of the bells to indicate the half hours and the boatswain's pipe call for reports, and for sweepers and for meals, were pleasant to hear. This, with the myriad other things that denoted life on a U.S. Navy ship, was a tonic to me. It was a symbol of my earlier days and hopes for my future. What if I got killed or crippled? I would never have a destroyer command.

For all but me, life on the T was arduous. Despite the low-key soundings of taps and reveille, no one slept easily or very often. The boats were coming and going at all hours of the day and night. The noisy takeoffs and landings of the two helo gunships shattered the silence. Meals were always available at all hours. The PBRs were always under repair, being gingerly lifted by crane in and out of the well decks as the severity of the damage demanded.

The ship's engineering plant was constantly running, providing power for its mission and allowing the captain to continuously shift his anchorage to avoid some courageous sapper detecting a pattern. Supplies of ammo and fuel were constantly being received and expended to the helos and the boats. Rain or shine, night or day, the work never let up.

Months on the T with no break, with no hope of touching land, was the fate of the T's crew. At least the PBR sailors had some action to break the boredom and they had the logistics runs, as did the Seawolves.

The Seawolves were doing it now. Lieutenant Commanders Marsh and Sams were operating off the T for a week or so. "How do these things fly, anyway?" I asked through the intercom while we sat on the flight deck warming up the engines. They were taking me back to Binh Thuy. I had been on the T for a week and a half and figured I'd best get back to the upper Bassac.

"You black shoes couldn't understand even if I told you," Marsh snickered. By black shoes he meant nonaviators. This referred to the uniform regulations just before and during the early part of World War II when only aviators could wear khakis and brown shoes. We all wore them now but the designation stuck. Aviators were called brown shoes.

"Try me, I finished grade school."

"Well, Don, there are four controls you use: the collective, the throttle, the foot pedals, and the cyclic control stick. By working all four simultaneously we can go up, down, sideways, or backward or forward."

"So, how does it do it?" I asked, helping the left door gunner set up his ammo loading for the flight.

"I should get extra pay for holding school on you surface types," Marsh chided in good humor over the intercom.

"Shit, you already do, with all that flight pay and working only a few hours a day."

"Hah! We earn every penny. You know what they say, aviators don't get paid more, they just get paid faster. Well, the basic control is the collective, here between the cockpit seats. As we pull up on it, the angle of the rotor blades changes, going from flat to tilted, giving lift. With this we raise off the deck. One problem: As the rotors bite into the air they need more power, so we advance the throttle, here, built into the top of the collective like a motorcycle throttle. The more we pull up, the more power we need. We hover when the lift is equal to the weight of the bird. Light on the skids it's called when we're getting ready to take off.

"The helo would spin under the rotors if we didn't have that little-bitty prop in the back. It counteracts the main rotor torque—it's how we steer with the foot pedals. If we want to change heading, we push one of the rudder pedals. The pitch of the little blades changes one way or the other, depending on which pedal we push. The torque of the little prop working with or against the main rotor turns the helo the way we want to go. You getting all this?"

The radio broke in over the intercom: "Six, this is One, ready in five."

"Rog, One. I'm holding basic flight instructions for our exalted leader right now . . . break, break . . . you copy, tower?"

"Affirm, we're at your convenience. Out."

The rotor blades overhead were making their slow whoop, whoop, whoop as Marsh continued. "To move in the horizontal plane, we use the stick between our legs."

"I know you guys would like to use the stick between your legs a lot more. Is that what Seven Six is doing in Can Tho right now?"

"Quiet in the classroom, sir, or you'll sit in the corner. With this cyclic control stick we can tilt the entire main rotor system to point in the direction we want to go. If we tilt it forward the rotor plane tilts forward and pulls us that way; if we ease the stick back, it tilts the rotor plane backward and we go astern. Sideways for left or right. In other words we have to use both hands and both feet, all at the same time in strict coordination, to pull you boat jockeys out of the shit you get yourselves into."

The deck siren blasted, sounding flight quarters. "Seven Six, Tower. You have a scramble two, say again a scramble two off northern tip big mother. Sierra on station. You are cleared for immediate takeoff. Over."

"You copy, One?" Marsh asked.

"That's Rog, ready" came Sams's terse reply.

"Tower, Seven Six. Light on the skids . . . airborne. Out."

We lifted, stayed stationary for a moment, then moved forward. As we cleared the tiny flight deck, the helo dropped five to ten feet. I saw Marsh's hand pull up the collective and twist the throttle. The engine and rotor blades answered his command and climbed, turning to starboard away from the T. Seven One was right behind us off our port quarter.

"That little drop there, Don, was due to a loss of lift that we get from the interaction with the ground. Translational lift, we big boys call it. Once we cross over the ship's side, our indicated altitude picks up an instant thirty or so feet, thereby losing the cushion that the T's deck had given us. At night it's a real bitch 'cause you can't judge it as accurately. But that's why only the finest can be Seawolves and the rest of you marvel in awe at our derring-do."

"So noted and duly impressed, Mister Marsh. I will so indicate on your already outstanding, upcoming fitness report."

"Blessed be the black shoes."

We came in low and fast. "Sierra, this is Seven Six. Your location zero five. Whataya got? Over."

"Rog, Seven Six, this is Sierra. Been catching some shit from the end of Khem Bang Co. Seems like a few forty-sevens. We got a couple of rocket rounds at us, all wild. Thought you could take a look behind canal. Over," came a calm voice I didn't recognize.

We continued upriver for thirty seconds, came around tight, and barreled in toward the narrow entrance to the canal. My mind jumped to my first firefight months ago when I had turned back into that creepy water to assist Romeo Two as Willie laid his fire on each side of the screaming PBR. A sampan was crossing. The copilot lined up his sights and triggered off his side flex guns. The sampan blew up and disappeared in midcanal. A bullet tore through the after compartment where the side gunners and I were sitting. It exited, tearing a hole in the overhead two inches from the left gunner's head.

I was firing an M-79 out the door while the gunners fired on both sides of the canal. Another sampan pushed out as we zipped by. Seven One behind us destroyed it with one rocket. We made two more firing passes with no rounds received.

"Rog, Seven Six, looks good. That's it . . . thanks for the assist," Sierra radioed. Our radio procedures were getting sloppy. I made a mental note to tighten them up.

We turned, heading for Binh Thuy. "Whataya think of the army's helo pilot policy, Bill?" I asked while scanning the riverbanks with my binoculars. Both 512 patrols were searching sampans as we passed over them.

"You mean getting those high-school kids to fly?"

"Yeah, I understand they take 'em right out of high school, teach them to fly helos only, then send them over here after making them warrant officers. You think that's a good way to do it?"

"Well it's probably sacrilegious to say this, but I think it is a good way to do it," he answered. "The air force and navy pilots have to be commissioned first, then go through flight school and learn to fly fixed wings for eighteen months, then transition into helos. It takes a long time before we can do any real work, and it makes training pretty expensive. With the army, shit, almost right away their helo pilots are operational, with Uncle Sam paying them a lot less. I figure after it's over they'll just kick 'em out, with no great loss to the infrastructure."

"I've worked with that Maverick bunch out of Soc Trang and they're damn good . . . not as good as you guys, of course. Maybe they're just adequate when I think about it," I laughed into the lip mike on the flight helmet I wore.

"Maybe they're just not old enough to know how to be scared," the copilot chuckled.

A voice from a door gunner chimed in, "I've applied for a transfer to the army flight warrant officer candidate program. Looks like I might make it. I think it's a good idea."

We set down at Binh Thuy and I was waving good-bye as Don Rover met me. "Commander, I've got a couple of young lions who want to talk to us about an operation."

"The dynamic duo?"

"Yes, sir."

"How things been going?"

"Pretty quiet. You hear about the RAG boat?"

"A little—what are the details?"

"Two nights ago one of the larger boats was out for a night spin for no good reason. They lost an engine and while they were trying to fix it they drifted pretty far downstream. A PBR patrol had just passed them and I reckon the VC figured it was clear. There was no moon. Sure as shit a big sampan came tooling out of Juliet and ran smack into the RAG. The sampan damn near sank while the RAG sailors shot hell outta 'em. The Raggies captured the sampan—can you believe it?"

The young lions were waiting in my office as we came in. "Commander, Mister Rover, we got a real neat operation. Will you see what you think of it?" Lieutenant (jg) Merrick said as he and Ensign Martin placed a large map of the southern section of Tanh Dinh on my desk.

"Always like a good operation. Whataya got?"

"Well, first off, sirs, begging your pardon, we want to do this on our own . . . we want to lead this ourselves," Sammy Merrick said, trying a smile that didn't work. "We just want your authority and your blessing," he chuckled nervously.

"Okay," I said, shrugging my shoulders in mock apathy. "If you don't want your big daddy to take care of you, you can be on your own, if the operation is sound and Mister Rover here concurs."

The four of us strained a laugh, but Merrick's words cut into me like a surgeon's scalpel. Glancing over to Don Rover, I knew he felt the same. He had reminded us of our error of overprotective leadership. I always felt that I had to

lead every dangerous mission. I had overcome this somewhat with Don Rover, trusting him with the responsibility,
but he in turn had not passed it down. Our junior officers
rarely got a chance to command.

The movie *Twelve O'Clock High* with Gregory Peck
flashed through my mind. His failure to delegate and his
overprotective attitude toward his men had cost him a
nervous breakdown. I was just as guilty, maybe more so,
since I realized my error.

"See this canal going into Cau Ke?" Ensign Martin
started briefing as if I were completely unfamiliar with the
area.

"We are familiar with Bong Bot Canal, Mister Martin," I
replied.

"Yes, of course the commander is. Well, as you've
said . . ." He stumbled over his words; I had unglued him
and was sorry for it. "This is probably the terminus for the
supplies crossing the Bassac. Well," he blurted, "we'd like to
take four boats up the canal and engage the bastards. They
won't suspect us and we should be able to get in, get a good
hit, and get out before they realize what happened."

I'd often considered doing this myself but dismissed it as
too dangerous. Damn them for coming up with this. They
stared at me, waiting.

"You think it's too dangerous?" Merrick asked.

I ignored the question. "Seawolves?"

"Bill Marsh with his fire team will be standing by."

"How many boats you say?"

"Four would probably do it, Commander," Don Rover
replied. It seems that Rover was more in on it than he
wanted to let on.

"Volunteer crews?"

"No problem!" they answered.

"And you, Mister Martin, you know my orders concern-
ing you."

"It's over, sir, I'm embarrassed to say, but it was personal
and politically generated in Washington and had nothing to
do with me being straight out of the academy. It's over. I can

go back on the river. You can check yourself if you want," he replied.

"I will, and I guess I should have more respect for you and your efforts to get back in the war," I said.

"No, sir, you shouldn't. It was a family matter that shames me and I know the trouble you've gotten into, taking my side of it."

"Shit like that happens. Forget it . . . welcome back." He smiled.

"Pretty bad country back there," I said, attempting to put things back on the track.

"Yes, sir, we can hack it," Sammy Merrick replied.

We stared at the map in silence. I wanted to say no. They knew I did. I recalled that I had refused this same operation to Bill Norwick three months earlier. Merrick and Martin probably could make it okay—surprise and all that. It would be a good hit. Merrick had enough experience to pull it off.

"Mister Rover, comment?"

"Dangerous, Commander, but I think they can pull it off. We haven't been back in Titi for a while."

I pondered the risks against the gains. I didn't want to give permission for them to go alone, and if I sent Don Rover it would show a lack of faith on my part.

"You guys realize anything significant that might help you on this raid?" No answer. "Look at the map and the village of Cau Ke. See anything?"

Ensign Martin answered, "Only that Bong Bot Canal branches off and heads into Cau Ke, and—"

"The artillery fans, gentlemen, the artillery fans from the 105mm fieldpieces from the Cau Ke batteries. We don't operate much where artillery can help us, but up Bong Bot Canal you're covered. Anybody think to talk to the subsector advisors up there?"

Sheepishly they replied no. "Mister Merrick, Mister Martin. You guys know how to call in and spot artillery?"

Don Rover broke the embarrassed silence. "It's rather simple, gentlemen. Out here they use the gun target line method; this means that you simply give the artillery commander the coordinates of the target and he lines up to shoot. From the initial request for supporting fire until you hear 'first round on the way' usually takes about fifteen minutes, then—"

"I know, sir," Ensign Martin broke in. "It's called gun target line because all spots are given in relation to the line between the battery and the target."

"That sounds like a canned piece from an army lecture, Mister Martin. You take a summer session with the boys in green?" I asked.

"Yes, sir, two years ago." I nodded for him to continue.

"It's important that you know where the battery's located because you call for left and right and up and down adjustments based on his location." Ensign Martin smiled as if he expected a gold star from me.

"Go to the head of the class, Mister Martin, you're correct, but in live situations it's not that simple. First of all you can't really see where the rounds are exploding, and in the excitement you may well forget that all spots such as left one hundred and drop fifty are given in meters and in relation to the artillery battery's location, not yours. A big mistake we make on artillery is to think we can call it in accurately. We've had some hairy shit go down when we invariably call it in too close to the boats.

"Once you're satisfied that the rounds are falling reasonably close to where you think they should be, call for 'fire for effect.' You'll then get all the 105s they've allotted to you.

"Don't expect too much, maybe ten rounds max. The subsector chiefs usually like to keep as many rounds as possible for themselves in case of an enemy attack. They don't take kindly to PBRs requesting fire missions. They figure we can run away, and they're right, but us being inside Bong Bot could change their mind.

"Don, get the Bassac air marshal to fly you over to Cau Ke and talk to the advisors and feel them out. I don't know the guys over there. From the geography it looks like Bong Bot is the only access to the Bassac, and the subsector chief may not even want us in there. The VC could bottle up his village and keep him from selling his produce in Can Tho."

"Do we need his permission, Commander?" Don Rover asked.

"Just for the artillery, but it's a courtesy to inform the advisors. Don't give any times or details, however; they might get into VC hands. You know the sievelike security the Vietnamese have."

"Does that mean you approve the operation, Commander?" Sammy Merrick asked.

The bastards had me trapped. "Okay! Make it so," I answered finally. "Ya gotta name?"

"Well no, not yet."

"Jesus, you guys, don't you know shit? The name is the most important part of an operation. How can we talk about it if you don't have a name? What can the reporters write about? How can I recommend you guys for medals if I can't say what you participated in?" I chided them jokingly.

"Think up a name quick, Martin," Merrick ordered.

"It has to have two short words, they must be chauvinistic, and they must describe the operation," I instructed.

"How about First Hit?" Ensign Martin said.

"Too simple," Merrick replied. "How 'bout Quick Hit?"

"Too simple," Martin replied. "How 'bout—"

"How 'bout you two getting out of here and letting me get back to work. I wanna sit in on your briefings—lemme know."

They walked out still arguing about the name. Don Rover got up to leave. "You been sandbagging me on this, haven't you, Don?" I asked. "It looks like something you'd think of."

"Why, Commander, would I do something like that?" he laughed.

At 0600, four days later, Merrick's and Martin's operation kicked off. Marsh and his fire team had come back from the T to support it. Don Rover and I sat in the ops center trying to be cool while we stared at the silent radios. To me it was like the first time my oldest son rode his bicycle around the corner out of sight.

Captain Laske had blessed the operation and personally saw the boats off. I knew he probably would be on a few flights with Bill Marsh to observe. The watch officer, a pimply-faced jaygee named Ramsey, who had been on the Game Warden staff for about six months, sat at his desk eating canned peanuts and drinking a cold soda. "Pretty dangerous op, eh, Commander?"

"Could be."

"You sure wouldn't get me on one of 'em. Those guys are crazy. They don't have to do that."

"Yes, I know."

"They had to turn down volunteers after a while. Even three of our staff men went. They have six men on a boat," the watch officer continued.

"Quite a few, eh?" I answered after a few moments of silence.

"Hell, Martin doesn't even have to go on the river. He's supposed to be on watch right now. I'm standing in for him!"

"You're a good guy, Mister Ramsey," Don Rover sneered.

"Why not? He pays us back two for one and throws in twenty bucks to boot. Good deal for us."

The radio broke our conversation: "Handlash One, this is Bravo. COMEX, COMEX. Over."

I picked up the mike. "Bravo, this is Handlash. Roger your COMEX. Good luck. Out."

"Guess that's it, eh? Think they'll get out okay, Commander?" the watch officer droned on.

"No!"

Ramsey opened another can of soda and offered it to me. "No, thank you." He offered it to Don Rover, who just looked at him.

"How come you didn't go?" he asked me.

"Too dangerous." He thought on that for several minutes. I was weary of his conversation.

"I just don't see why Merrick and Martin do it."

"Because, goddamnit, Mister Ramsey, they're naval officers! That's why. Now shut up, just shut the fuck up!" I said as I got up to walk to the head, just to get away from him before I really lost my temper.

A static silence from the radios was all the report I received as I returned. Ten more minutes passed.

"Ah, Roger! This is Three Six, rolling in for the attack now. Out!" an excited voice suddenly boomed through the crackling static.

"ROLLING IN FOR THE ATTACK? What the hell's going on? What're the boats doing? Where's that goddamned Merrick?" I yelled at Rover as if it were his fault that I wasn't with them.

The watch officer answered what he thought would be instructive. "Sounds like there's a blind spot in Bong Bot, Commander. We can hear the helos . . . they're high, you know. Those boats are blocked by lotsa jungle. Radio waves can't make it through. They—"

"Can't you shut up, for Christ's sake! I'm familiar with radio wave propagation!"

The radio crackled again: "Okay, Bravo, we'll come in again lower. Watch those fifties. The ricochets are coming close." Seconds passed. "Roger . . . ah, say again number wounded. Over."

Silence.

"Okay . . . is your fire still burning? We'll try to help you get out. We've taken several hits . . . rolling in now." I heard his machine guns open up before his mike button closed.

Silence. How many wounded? Is the fire out? What fire? JESUS CHRIST!

"Merrick, you bastard! I'll court-martial your ass when you get back!" I yelled into the speaker. I felt helpless. I was helpless. I should be there, damnit! I should be there. I gave Don Rover a withering stare.

"Roger, understand . . . heads up . . . heads up. First round on the way" came a strange, hissing voice over the speaker.

"Roger, Cau Ke. Drop fifty . . . right two hundred."

I heard an explosion over a momentarily open mike before I heard: "Cau Ke, add twenty . . . left twenty . . . fire for effect . . . and thanks. Out." I recognized Merrick's cool, modulated voice over the radio.

"Come here," I barked at the watch officer to relieve tension in me. "Scramble one the helos from the T. Send Echo Patrol from Juliet over to the mouth of the canal, on the double. Come on, asshole, move! I'll alert Pedro."

He jumped to the mike fast. "Sorry, Don, I know I should let you take care of this. I'm sorry." He shrugged his shoulders in understanding. I called the air force helo rescue unit at Binh Thuy; their helo call sign was Pedro. Everyone called them that.

"Yeah, listen, Hank," I said to their OinC, an air force major, "some of my boys are in deep shit down in the canal just south of Tanh Dinh. Bong Bot, you know the spot? Okay, swell. I don't know how soon they'll be out, or anything, just that they're in trouble. Okay, thanks, Hank. Bill Marsh is overhead down there. Yeah, Seawolf Three Six is his call sign. There should be two more Seawolves on scene in a few moments. Be careful!"

I looked up at the watch officer. "Everyone's on their way, Commander," he reported. "No luck on raising Bravo or Three Six."

I poured a cup of coffee, trying hard to keep the cup from shaking. I wasn't too successful. I placed the cup on the chart table while staring at the large map of Bong Bot Canal.

Stupid! I swore at myself. You shouldn't have let them go in alone. "It's okay, Commander, they're big boys down there. I know how you feel," Don Rover said, thinking he was comforting me.

"Do you, Mister Rover, do you?" I answered, ashamed before the sentence was finished.

My elbow bumped the cup, tipping the scalding liquid down my right leg and shattering the cup on the deck. The dividers I was holding flew out of my hand as I jumped to avoid the splintering glass. My left hand caught the dividers point on. Blood squirted out as I extracted them. I went and sat in a corner.

"Mister Rover," I said, stretching a Band-Aid over the fanglike holes, "you've just witnessed the story of my life."

And we waited.

"Seawolf Three Six, this is Pedro Nine Four with two birds. Do you have a mission for me? Over."

"Affirmative, Pedro. Four boats in Bong Bot pretty badly shot up. Seven wounded."

"GOOD GOD!" I gasped, "seven wounded?"

"Only four seriously. Can you carry? Over."

"Affirmative, Three Six. What is your position? Over."

"I'm flying cover with Seawolf Seven Six, fire team from the T. With any luck the boats'll be out in zero five . . . wait, they're getting it! Break, break . . . rolling in now!"

Silence again.

"To the right, Seven Six. Break right, Seven, break right."

A mike somewhere was left open; the muted swish of the rockets and the melodious clatter of the helo's machine guns filled the ops center.

"Bravo, this is Seven Six. We'll lace down the beach in front of you. Roger, understand fire out. Pedro is waiting outside the canal."

"Three Six, Three Six! This is Seven Six. My starboard door gunner just got it . . . bleeding badly."

Silence.

"Roger! Seven Six, break off. Fly him to Can Tho. Come right back. Over."

Click, click, answered the mike button.

"Bravo, this is Three Six. Two boats heading upriver fast. Do you want them to come in?"

Silence.

"Roger, understood, negative . . . break, break . . . PBRs heading south at Tanh Dinh. This is Seawolf Three Six. Interrogative call sign. Over."

"Three Six, this is Handlash Echo. Request instructions. Over."

"Echo, this is Three Six. Bravo is in the canal fighting his way out. He says stay at exit to cover his withdrawal. Over." The mike button closed. The hiss of our radios was the only sound.

"This is Pedro on station."

"Roger, Pedro. This is Three Six. First boats thirty seconds from exit. Don't know which boats have the wounded yet."

"Yeah, got 'em in sight."

Sixty more horrible seconds crept by. I kept filling my pipe, lighting it, knocking it out, and filling it again.

"Care for a Coke, Commander?" the watch officer asked.

"Oh! Ah . . . no, thanks. Got any coffee?"

"Bravo Two, this is Bravo. Head for the Pedro. Bravo Three, you stand by. Over."

"This is Two. Roger. Out."

"This is Three. Roger. Out."

"Bravo! It's Bravo! They're out! Goddamn! They're out," I sang, grabbing the mike to talk to him. But then put it down. They're busy, Sheppard. Relax!

"Hold your course steady, PBR, steady," Pedro's calm instructions came over the air. "How many do you have? Roger, understand two. Steady . . . lifting now . . . steady."

I could envision the stretcher being lowered by the helo down onto the PBR. It was a tricky maneuver. The boat and the helo had to be on the same course, same speed. A misjudgment or freak change in the wind or current could spell disaster. Who was the coxswain?

"Bravo Three, this is Bravo. Go under the other Pedro now. Out."

"Bravo! Bravo! This is Echo. We're getting it from the canal. Attacking now. Out!"

"Echo, this is Three Six. I copy, heading in now. Break, break. Seven Six, this is Three Six. I'm getting mighty dry. Interrogative ETA. Over."

"This is Seven Six. We're thirty seconds out. We'll take the second pass."

"Roger. We're going home to rearm and drop wounded. Will refuel hot and be back if you need us. Lemme know. Out."

"Handlash, Handlash, this is Pedro Nine Four. Pickup complete, four souls. Over."

"This is Handlash. Thank you. Out," I answered, pleased that I finally got to say something.

"Bravo, Bravo, this is Echo. Got two wounded last run, not serious. Goin' in again."

"This is Bravo. We'll join you but we're mighty low on ammo. Over."

"Roger. Don't know what's in there, Bravo, but you sure pissed off somebody. We'll fall in behind you. Out."

"Bravo, this is Seven Six. We're drawing mighty heavy fire from down there. Over."

"Don, get your people outta there right now," I interrupted over the radio.

Rover picked up the mike and broke in during the first lull. "Handlash Bravo! Handlash Bravo! This is Handlash Two Actual. Break contact. I say again, break contact. Return home plate. Over."

"This is Bravo. Roger. Out" came a somewhat relieved reply.

"Echo, Echo, this is Handlash Two Actual. Transfer your wounded and escort Bravo to five point five. Out."

"This is Seven Six. Returning my home plate. You boys sure play hardball up here. Out."

It was over. Marsh would be landing in a few minutes. "I'll be at the helo pad. Call me when you get an ETA on Bravo," I instructed the watch officer.

"Yes, sir. Your boats didn't see much of the center of the river today, did they?"

"Whataya mean by that, Mister Ramsey?" I snapped.

"Nothing . . . nothing, sir."

I fumed as I walked out of the ops center. What did that

puke know of war—just what he heard on the radios, that's all. Middle of the river? That asshole.

I arrived at the helo pad with a corpsman just as Bill Marsh set down. I opened his door and helped him unstrap. His left leg and arm were bleeding. The corpsman unstrapped the starboard door gunner. Dried blood spotted the rear deck. The gunner had a tourniquet just above his right knee. "Just a scratch," he said.

"Yeah! That's what all you heroes say," the corpsman grunted, lifting him out of the helo.

Marsh's pale-faced, glassy stare told the story. I'd seen it too many times. His reflexes secured the helo's engines. My eyes focused on the copilot's bloody gloves moving about the cockpit to shut down. Blood was already dry on his flight suit. His machine-gun trigger and rocket sight were a gooey mess. The copilot just leaned back in his seat, looking as though he wanted to cry.

"You okay?" I asked him.

"Yes. Yes, sir, I'm okay."

"Lost a little blood," Marsh chimed in. "He's okay. They got it on the first pass. Couldn't bring them in . . . boats needed us. I gotta little shrapnel on the last pass."

The pilots of the trail helo joined us. In silence we walked the twenty feet to the trailer they used as a ready room. Another corpsman looked at Bill's arm and leg. He applied large compress bandages. "Ambulance on its way, sir," he announced. Bill opened a can of soda. I had many questions but they could wait. The all-too-familiar aura of near death counseled patience.

I finished a cigar. The ground crew chief came in. "Door gunner's not too bad—no bones hit. Copilot has a pretty bad arm. The ambulance is here."

"Thank you, Chief," Marsh replied.

"Those two helos got a total of twenty-seven holes in 'em, and between both, only thirteen rounds of ammo left. Pretty hot day."

"Yes, it was. Get 'em ready to go as fast as you can, Chief.

Lemme know," Marsh said as I helped him into the ambulance.

"Aye, aye, sir!"

The trail helo pilot was new to the Bassac. I didn't know his name. He lit a cigarette. "Well, Commander, I personally counted more than fifteen dead Cong. It's not like this on the other rivers. I think we musta run into the whole Viet Cong 306th Battalion. Lotta lead flying round down there. Those PBRs did a real fine job."

"Yeah, reckon they did. Thanks for your help," I replied.

A messenger came in. "Sir! Bravo's estimating twenty minutes. Said he'd need an ambulance and a couple of corpsmen."

"Thank you."

"And, oh yes, Pedro called and said the troops he picked up were shot up pretty badly but they'll make it with no problem."

"Thank you. Tell the watch officer I'll be on the pier."

I walked slowly from the helo pad. My spirits were high—no dead or crippled, just a little pain. At least fifteen Viet Cong dead, boats making it back on their own . . . a damn good op.

I tried to look casual leaning against a pier stanchion. Don Rover waited with me. Neither of us spoke, but each of us knew that we should probably have been out there.

Merrick stood tall in the lead boat as they pulled up to the pier. He was wearing a smug, shit-eating grin, but the rest of his face betrayed the hurt inside him. The corpsmen were on the boats before the lines were over. "None of 'em too bad, Commander," Merrick reported, with a snappy salute of a bandaged arm. "Martin lost an engine. He's about ten minutes behind. He had the fire aboard."

"Boats look like sieves," Don Rover commented. "Pedro says the guys he took out are okay. You figure out a name for the op yet?"

"No, sir."

I slung Merrick's combat bag over my shoulder as we walked toward my office.

Ong Tam

———————•———————

For several days after the Bong Bot hit, action was slow. Though I couldn't tie it directly to the raid, I was sure that there was some connection. Merrick and Martin had moved into the Viet Cong's living room and shaken hell out of them. I realized now that the entire area must be destroyed. Just hitting Tanh Dinh was not good enough. I must push the VC back from the river.

I would move in everything I had on the Bassac. To this end, and to execute a still-nebulous plan, Ensign Martin was training flamethrower crews. Those chosen enjoyed a high status among the combat crews and took a lot of jealous ribbing, but these "pyros" walked tall. They were the best I had. It was no surprise that the four pyros were the same men who were first to volunteer for every dangerous mission.

The visitor population at Binh Thuy increased after word of the big raid. Everyone wanted to say that they had met the heroes of Bong Bot in the flesh. Ensign Martin was a tiger among tigers. Watching tigers train, however, grew boring. It was getting to me, so when Ong Tam sent word up that he needed some boats, I decided to take the operation along with Thanh.

"Chao, Ong Tam," I greeted him as I stepped off my boat at Golf dressed in my flashiest combat outfit: flak jacket hanging open with its upside-down bayonet tied securely on the left side and two hand grenades clipped on the right. A piece of captured Viet Cong camouflage cloth tied to the left shoulder fluttered as I walked.

On my belt, just a little back from my right side, hung my well-oiled untraceable .38-caliber pistol in its English World War II canvas holster, six extra rounds waiting in the cartridge holder sewn to it. An old aviation survival knife hung over my left buttock. My map stuck out at just the right angle from the right-side utility pocket of my starched jungle green trousers, which, of course, bloused neatly into the top of my polished boots.

The sleeves of my olive-drab T-shirt were rolled up two turns. I rarely wore a blouse—it wrinkled, destroying the image. My black beret sat rakishly cocked. I wore a cowboylike neckerchief of the same camouflage cloth as on my flak jacket. I let at least four inches dangle so it could wave in the breeze. Sunglasses and a cigar completed my costume. My men dressed more or less the same.

The coxswain, however, outdid us all with his low-slung, western holster carrying a .44 magnum revolver. The .44-caliber magnum was the most powerful handgun in the world, and the status symbol of the coxswains. They all wore them and, by unwritten convention, no one else did.

On the base we dressed as the paper pushers dictated, as the book said to. But I owned the Bassac; the only book we had was a scorebook to keep count of dead Viet Cong. We dressed as warriors; we dressed for combat.

"Chao, Thieu Ta," Ong Tam offered as we shook hands and hugged. His dress made the rest of us look like amateurs. An Australian bush hat with the left side of the brim turned up and a strip of Viet Cong camouflage cloth as a hatband topped his outfit. The cloth he used for his hatband had come from the same piece of material as mine—we had captured it on an earlier raid.

He wore a high-collared, open-neck dark green sport

shirt, an ascot of camouflage material, and sharply pressed light brown trousers rolled up just to the top of his brightly polished riding boots. The finest part of his haberdashery was his vest. It was made of small-mesh nylon net; its fitted pockets carried spare clips for his carbine, four hand grenades, two flares, one pack of cigarettes, a lighter, a knife, chewing gum, and a beer can opener. We admired each other laughing—a couple of kids whose mothers had let them dress up to play soldier.

"Good operation today, Thieu Ta. Kill many Viet Cong. Later we make big party," he said as he took my hand along with Thanh's and led us to his hootch.

"What's the plan?" asked Thanh.

It was a typical operation, same as we'd done many times in the past. Some Viet Cong had sent a challenge for Tam to bring the green boats in for a fight. It could have been a trap, and ordinarily we would have ignored it. By this time, though, our spy network was extensive. We knew within an hour the complete disposition of any enemy troops within twenty miles of Golf. It had cost the "9mm gang" plenty, but every dime was worth it. Ong Tam ran the show himself, becoming a damn big man in the area for it. The information we received proved to be almost ninety percent accurate—in intelligence, a phenomenal record.

In this instance there were only ten VC just bragging by throwing out the challenge to the neighborhood. They had no rockets or big stuff. A piece of cake.

A small, almost naked Vietnamese child about eleven years old ran up and whispered something to Ong Tam. "It is time," he said, giving me the note. We knew where they were as of twenty minutes ago. We rushed to get under way with twenty of Ong Tam's men. It was going to be a flanking attack. Marsh and his boys had set down at Tra On to alter our pattern.

We chatted as we tore headlong up the small canal. I put on my helmet. "I think Thieu Ta not too wise to fly red and white flag on top of boat. Enemy can spot leader easily."

"So can my men."

"That is true, Thieu Ta," he acknowledged.

"I think Ong Tam not too wise to wear that bush hat. Enemy knows you wear it and can spot leader easily."

He smiled. "So can my men."

"That is true, Ong Tam."

We laughed and hugged each other. Ong Tam was one of my very few friends on the Bassac. The man who said that command is a lonely profession knew what he was talking about. Sometimes I became so lonely for a friend that I could scream with the pain. But there were precious few people with whom I could afford the luxury of companionship. Captain Laske was aloof—he had the same problem as I—but Ong Tam was a peer, a fellow commander who understood.

"I sure wish you'd wear a flak jacket and helmet, Ong Tam," I said again for the tenth time. "You're too valuable to lose to some dumb sniper's bullet."

"Yes, it is true," he replied for the tenth time. "Can you get them for all my men?"

"No, they are very hard to get," I again answered.

"Then how can I wear them. Would you?"

I had no answer, just silently cursed all those brand-new, shiny flak jackets hanging unused in the hotel rooms of a thousand Saigon warriors.

At 0930, just as we rounded a bend where a Viet Cong flag flew from a tree, we made contact. The battle was like so many others of boat versus bunker. We traded rounds for ten or so minutes to allow the helos to join us, then landed troops on each side. We kept up our fire to hold the Viet Cong in position as the helos peppered the area behind them.

Thanh led ten troopers in from upstream; Ong Tam, ten from downstream. When they were in position, I lifted my fire. The Viet Cong, as they had done so many times, broke and ran from the bunkers. The cross fire cut them to pieces, but two of them made it to the jungle.

After beaching the boats, I walked toward the pile of bodies. The soldiers dropping concussion grenades into the bunkers chattered with delight. If anyone remained inside, this would finish them off.

Ong Tam was shouting orders that I couldn't understand. He saw me and gave me a wide grin, motioning me over. The sight of the bodies made me queasy. I swallowed hard to keep from throwing up. When I arrived, Ong Tam was searching one of them.

"These Viet Cong will never challenge Tam again. They—" A machine-gun burst transformed his words into a scream. He was tossed over the body and twisted down into the hard, mud-glazed clay. Blood gushed violently from his clutched stomach and from his mouth. He whimpered like a child.

Ten rifles answered the burst. Thanh leapt into the jungle with five men behind. The din of machine-gun fire wracked my ears.

"FIRST-AID KIT!" I screamed to Boats. A man was already on his way.

"Tam . . . Tam, you okay?" I cried, frantically tearing open his small-mesh nylon vest. The red ooze pumped through his shirt. I ripped it off him. Tam had no stomach, no chest—only a mangled mess of raw meat from his neck down. Two men tried to do something, tried to stop the bleeding, but it was useless; the clay beneath him was crimson from his blood. I cradled his head in my arms, demanding my men to stop the bleeding.

"You'll be okay, Tam, you'll be okay," I sobbed. His blood ran over my map, my pressed greens, my flak jacket, my cute neckerchief.

"You'll be okay, Tam. You dirty sonovabitch, you'll be okay."

He looked up at me, or at something, I couldn't tell. His muddied-over eyes didn't focus. I couldn't tell. It was important to me but I couldn't tell.

"Thieu Ta," he pleaded.

"C'mon, Tam, you're okay!" I rocked him back and forth as if he were a little child not wanting to go to sleep.

"He's dead, Commander."

"C'mon, Tam, you're okay, c'mon. Remember, we got that party tonight, okay? C'mon."

"Commander! He's dead."

"You're okay, Tam."

"Commander . . . he's dead!"

"YOU BASTARD, TAM! YOU DIRTY NO GOOD SONOVABITCHING BASTARD! You had to lead every raid, didn't you? Didn't let anyone else do it, did you? All by yourself, eh? You're a fucking hero, big man! See what it got you. You're dead, you're dead. Oh, Tam, forgive me . . . I'm sorry . . . I'm sorry . . . I'm sorry I killed you, Tam . . . I'm sorry."

I laid him down, placed his Australian bush hat over his face, picked up his cigarettes, and lit one. Thanh and his men came back, dragging the remains of a headless body naked except for a Chinese cartridge belt around his waist. Thanh dropped the body at my feet.

I raised my foot back and kicked it with all my might. I kicked it again and again. Its ribs crushed and dark brown entrails gushed out of its open stomach cavity as it rolled over and over and away from me.

"Commander, Commander," someone yelled, but I paid no heed, chasing after it, kicking and kicking until I fell in exhaustion. Tears filled my eyes as I emptied my .38 into the glob.

"Let's get out of here," I commanded.

I carried Ong Tam's body to my boat. I ordered his vest removed. I had his body wrapped tightly with several layers of battle dressing bandages and took my freshly pressed blouse from the radio compartment and put it on him. I put his bloody vest and bush hat into my combat bag.

The villagers gathered around as we tied up and I carried Ong Tam from the boat. The women cried and the men moaned. Their chief was dead. I laid him down gently in the village square.

"He's to be buried now," I ordered the village elders.

"It is not our custom, Thieu Ta," they replied.

I felt my eyes narrow and the blood drain from my face.

"It shall be now," I repeated slowly. Tam's body was not going to rot in this infernal heat for four or five days while a power struggle took place for his job.

"So it shall be," an elder pronounced.

Preparations were made. A plain coffin appeared; he was placed inside. I did not allow them to remove my blouse from his body. Before they closed the coffin, I triangularly folded my boat's battle ensign and placed it under his head. I covered his body with a silk Vietnamese flag and laid his hat and vest beside him. I put my black beret in his hands.

They nailed the coffin shut.

A Buddhist priest chanted over the covered grave. My men and I stood silently at rigid attention. The American flags on the boats hung at half-mast.

"People want Thieu Ta to say Christian prayer," Thanh said.

"I don't know any."

"People want, Thieu Ta."

> Now I lay me down to sleep,
> I pray the Lord my soul to keep.
> If I should die before I wake,
> I pray the Lord my soul to take.
> God bless Mommy and Daddy
> . . . Ong Tam . . . and me.

At the ops center the after-action spot report was simple to write:

A. Summary: Three PBRs of RIVSEC 512 attacked hostile position up small unnamed canal 10 kilometers southwest of the village, Phu Hoa, code name Golf. Engaged unknown number of Viet Cong firing from bunkers.
B. Casualties, Personnel, US: None.
C. Casualties, Personnel, VN: One KIA.
D. Casualties, Personnel, VC: Seven KIA.
E. Casualties, Material, US: None.

F. Casualties, Material, VC: Eight AK-47 assault rifles captured. No documents found.

I stared at the remarks section. What could I write? Tam fought because I cajoled, bullied, and shamed him into becoming a tiger. Tam fought because I gave him a few pieces of tin roofing and dirty sacks of bulgur wheat for his village. Should I write: I caused Tam's death because I wanted a high score of enemy KIAs to validate my own self-aggrandizement?

G. Remarks: None.

I waited at the ops center while the watch officer proofread my report.

"Hey, Commander, seven for one—not bad, not bad."

"Yeah, not bad."

I wondered if I still had any scotch left in my room. I'd have that party, but who would be my friend?

Sun Devil

———————————•———————————

Bong Bot Canal was a continuing source of irritation to me. I sent four more PBRs a little way in, and four PBRs came limping out with their tails between their legs. The SEALs went in and likewise stumbled out with three wounded.

A prisoner from the area in a "casual" conversation with Thanh admitted that the powerful and feared Viet Cong 306th Battalion staged out of this area, and it was indeed the terminus of supplies that crossed the Bassac. He also mentioned, much to my hidden joy, that the supplies were becoming fewer and fewer.

"I think we should destroy the area, Thanh."

"Thieu Ta knows that 306th have maybe one or two hundred men."

"Yes, I know."

For five days various plans crossed my mind. I flew into Cau Ke, the headquarters of the district through which Bong Bot Canal meandered, to talk to the district chief–subsector chief and his American advisor. I had flown in to meet them after Merrick and Martin had made their hit. Our conversation went easily.

The subsector chief had been asking for troops for the last six months to sweep the area. But Bong Bot was a long way from province headquarters, and ARVN troops were always too busy. I'd heard the story before. He was amenable to do anything we wanted to do. Bong Bot was the only canal that led to the Bassac from his town of Cau Ke. As long as the VC held it, they would heavily tax the sampans on their way to market, thus causing harsh economical hardships.

The first step in the plan was to declare the canal and five hundred meters on either side of it a free-fire zone. This he did and processed the necessary paperwork up the administrative chain. The Viet Cong would soon know of his action. I told the subsector chief that I'd keep him informed of the operation as planning progressed, but in truth I had no intention of doing so because of their poor security. The American advisors, of course, were to know everything.

Just to harass the 306th, I ordered the Seawolves to strafe the area two or three times a day and on every night patrol. The PBRs, every time they passed, were to fire their .50s at high elevation to strike way back along the canal. The .50s had a range of up to five miles. I moved 511's mortar up to 512, and for two days we mortared the canal. The 306th did not take kindly to our intrusion. On the third day they struck back. The boats caught hell and the helos couldn't fly through the ground fire. Several bloody firefights evolved. On the night of the fourth day I called off the harassment. Again Bong Bot had driven us out.

During the night I called in the LST, constantly guarded by circling PBRs, to take position outside the canal. At dawn and throughout the fifth day her 40mm guns bombarded the area. I moved her out at sunset. Knowing the efficiency of the 306th, they would have surely sunk her during the night. The T's 40mm rapid-fire, antiaircraft guns weren't very effective, but they did add harassment value.

I had previously requested that a five-inch, single-gun mount, such as the merchant vessels used during World War II, be installed on all PBR support LSTs. There must have been thousands still lying around in old warehouses, but I had no luck.

On the sixth day, four PBRs were sent to harass. The overzealous patrol officer roared into the canal, his guns silent, and before he rounded the first bend he had three wounded and hadn't gotten off a shot. Before he could come about, one more man was down and only the swift, low-level action of both Seawolf teams saved his ass. He came limping out with gun barrels cherry red. I had ordered all patrol officers to stay out of the canal—I relieved him on the spot for disobedience.

On the seventh day we rested. The next morning I called in my unit commanders. I even included the skipper of the T, who rarely got in on combat operations planning. "Gentlemen, I intend to destroy every village along the Bong Bot Canal from the Bassac to three miles inland of the Cau Ke Canal turnoff—a total of some five miles.

"The entire area is nasty Viet Cong territory and can no longer be tolerated. The subsector chief and American advisor at Cau Ke concur. I intend to burn every house, blow every bunker, and, if possible, level the area. All of you know that the Viet Cong 306th lives there and what it's used for. It must be accomplished."

"Are you saying that you want it returned to the stone age, Commander?" Don Rover asked as if on cue.

"That about sums it," I answered, adding: "This will be a maximum-effort attack."

The concept was orthodox—a tried-and-true maneuver for armies since men first started smashing each other up: Neutralize the area, then move in and destroy it. I had briefed Captain Laske. I needed his blessing for an operation of this danger and magnitude. "Sounds good, Interdictor," he told me. "Lemme know when you're ready. I was wondering when you were going to come up with it. I'd like to come along to observe."

We picked a name: Sun Devil. Martin's flamethrowers would be our key weapons. It would take four days, he said, to get enough napalm together for such an extensive show. Napalm was nothing more than jellied gasoline. A solidifying powder was poured into a barrel of gasoline and stirred until it looked like underset Jell-O.

We held the operation in tight security until the last moment. I didn't want a drunken remark made in some Can Tho bar to wipe us out. The 306th weren't farmers with rusty rifles. On the ninth day food tasted bad. I pored over aerial photos of the canal but could see very little. I kept looking because it seemed the thing to do.

I started having misgivings about the operation. Was it the right thing to do? How many casualties would we take for a plan I was losing confidence in? Would I be killed? Was I willing to sacrifice my life and the lives of my men for the chance of burning a few bamboo-thatched hootches? You've only got a little while to go over here, Sheppard, think about that. Call it off, idiot! It doesn't mean shit anyway. We don't have troops to occupy the area; the VC will be back the next day anyway. You can't win a war without a foot soldier on the ground. What are all those antiwar demonstrations in the States all about? Don't forget to bring that stupid bow and arrow.

Martin's pyro crews worked indefatigably at their trade, and within two days had amassed enough jellied gasoline and had equipped the base support mike boat to service and tend his greedy flamethrowers. The PBR MACE teams practiced their landings. Bill Marsh and his pilots worked out the complicated helo rotation required.

I wrote a message: "Sun Devil canceled," then tore it up. On the eleventh day it rained. I couldn't eat anything. I wrote another message canceling the operation—the weather was bad, a good excuse. The sun came out before I could send it. I burned it. Damn! Sheppard, you're crazy—you're grandstanding again. Give it up, give it up. I noticed my hands beginning to shake. I went to great lengths to conceal it.

During the afternoon the unit commanders reported early. I had continually run through all the various phases with each of them individually for the past three days. We gathered at my office and ran through the entire operation for the final time. At first light tomorrow, Sun Devil would go.

That evening I walked down to the pier to look at the boats. They were fearsome-looking things bobbing in the gentle current, their guns covered with canvas. Eight boats were there. We were maintaining one patrol on the river from each section just for appearance' sake. The rest of the boats were being finely tuned and honed. I wondered which boats we'd use tomorrow. I wondered which one I'd be on. Foolish thoughts; what difference did it make? A couple of engineers huddled over an engine. Their soft conversation in the dim light and the occasional clank of their tools were the only semblance of reality.

I looked down into one of the boats. With shock, I saw myself lying there covered with blood, my left leg gone, my stained hands trying to strike a match. "Good Lord!" I screamed, scrambling down into the boat to help myself.

"WHAT'S THE MATTER, Commander?"

I flinched at the sound of the voice. "Can't you see it?" I demanded.

"See what?" a voice said as a light flashed into the boat. It was PBR 127. "Nothing's there. You okay, sir?"

"Yes, yes, I just thought I saw something down there. I'm okay. A little nervous I guess," I apologized.

"Aren't you Reyes from the engine shop?" I asked.

"Yes, sir, I'm the pier sentry till midnight."

"Well, a beautiful night for it." The moon was full, rippling across the water when it wasn't playing tag with the clouds.

"Big operation tomorrow, huh, sir?"

"Yes."

"Begging the commander's pardon, sir, but are you scared?" he asked.

"Yes, I am, Reyes, damn scared."

"I hope you don't mind, sir, but some of the men were questioning whether this was the right thing to do. I mean . . . you know . . . wiping out a village and all."

"What do you think, Reyes?"

"I think it has to be done. I think it's the only way we can win. If you'll recall World War II, the prime objective was to destroy the enemy's homeland and supply routes."

"You don't talk like a seaman, Reyes."

"Well, sir, I have a bachelor's in political science and half my credits toward my master's." He paused as I looked at him under the swaying pier lights. "I got bored with school and volunteered for the navy and Vietnam. Ended up here—a pier sentry."

"It could be worse—you could be going with us tomorrow," I said, walking away.

"I am, sir. I volunteered for the mike boat flamethrower crew."

It was too dark for him to see my face flush. "Well, I'll see you in the morning," I managed to reply, walking away. "Good night, Reyes. Thanks, ah, for your support," I added.

I glanced down into PBR 127. I was gone.

I passed the EM club on the way back to my room. They seemed to be having a good time. The officers' club was as proportionately noisy. I thought I'd have a drink but gave it up. A few drops of rain started to fall. Tomorrow was going to be a chore—a nasty, unwanted chore. I wanted to go home. The rain fell harder.

At 0600 my alarm clattered me awake. My mouth felt dry, my stomach burned. I'd always felt this way before an operation but never this bad. I rang up the ops center. "Yes, sir, the T started her bombardment at 0453 and the helos have put in four strikes already," the watch officer replied. "No, sir, no word on any jet air strike from the air force. It appears that one fell through."

"Fuck 'em. Looks like we won't get any help from the Vietnamese." I'd tried to set up an air strike through the U.S. Army. They said they'd try but that the Vietnamese controlled the airplanes and used them only for their own operations. I had hoped for bombs, guns, and napalm.

"How about the Cau Ke artillery—are they lobbing in any shells?"

"Yes, sir, a few, but the major down there said they'd had

some trouble up north during the night and he can't spare many shells. Want me to bug him?"

"No, he'll do the best he can. I'll be in the mess hall."

A fine breakfast tasted like slop. I walked over to my office. "How does it look?" I asked Don Rover.

"Your boat's ready to go to the T. Four others'll be on station at 1045. Lieutenant Henry on the T reports all his boats are ready."

"Good. Which one of those dogs of yours did you give me today?"

"Number 127."

My blood coagulated in my veins. My head went light. I grabbed the desk for support.

"What's the matter, Commander?" Rover said, leaping to grab me.

I was silent, not answering for a second, not wanting to speak lest my fear betray me. "Oh . . . ah . . . nothing. Why 127?"

"No reason. Hell, it's one of my best boats. A little shot up maybe, but she's sturdy and has new engines."

"Can I take another boat?"

"It's the only one ready with all the extra ammo. I can have another ready in, say, twenty minutes, but the crews have already started their individual loading."

"No! Okay, shit, I'll take it."

He gave me an odd look. I felt like a fool—a stupid, superstitious fool.

Throwing my combat bag over my shoulder, I started for the piers, stopped to sign some papers Stills had prepared, then walked down to the river. The men, busy loading their boats, joked as if they were going to a carnival. The mike boat stood taller than any of the PBRs. Its cargo of highly explosive barrels of napalm could take out our entire base if it went up. I had to get it away from here. Ensign Martin sang "Old Man River" while directing the final loading and testing of his equipment. Idiots! Didn't they know what we were going up against?

I received good-natured jibes from the sweating troops.

No one talked about what would happen to the mike boat if a tracer tore into one of those fifty-five-gallon barrels of jellied gasoline. I noticed that Martin had plenty of fire-fighting equipment aboard. I stepped into the mike boat to inspect it.

"Well, Commander Nero, did you bring your violin?" Ensign Martin joked.

"Listen, Killer, if those toys of yours don't work, I'm leaving all your asses in Bong Bot."

"Don't worry, sir. These babies," he patted his vicious flamethrowers, "will do the job."

"Oh . . . good morning, Reyes. See you made it."

"Yes, sir," he replied, looking up from the engine he was wiping. "We'll have a good show today."

"Let's hope so."

Ensign Martin looked at me, his eyes penetrating my soul. "It'll be all right, Commander. It'll be all right," he said with a frightening insight into my thoughts.

I climbed down into PBR 127, stepping over where I had lain last night. Someone must have cleaned up the blood. My burgee snapped against the wind as we moved smartly away from the pier and downstream. The overcast skies gave no hint of sun.

"Rained last night, Commander."

"Yes, I know."

The trip passed in silence. We arrived at the T off the tip of Tanh Dinh about 0930. I went to the bridge to watch the shelling. Their barrage lifted five minutes after I arrived and three helos swung in for a strafing run. Their rockets left a dense white smoke covering the area.

As they pulled off target, the Cau Ke artillery laid in ten shells. I wondered who was spotting. Then the T started shelling again. My hope was to drive the Viet Cong away or at least underground. Firefights would hamper our effort.

I grew weary of the fireworks and headed down toward the wardroom. Bill Marsh had just landed his helo. We met at the coffeepot.

"Awfully quiet in there, Don," he murmured. "Damn awful quiet."

"You draw any fire, Bill?"

"No, didn't see a soul."

"Helos holding up okay?"

"Yeah, they're in good shape. But every one of them will be flying right into their periodic checks. You know you won't have any helos for twelve or so hours after this."

"I know it."

As I turned to sit, I saw Major Shellon from Tra On. "Well, Shelly, you come out to see how the senior service lives on board our luxury liners?"

"Yeah, Bill picked me up an hour ago. Say, sorry about the lack of shells from Cau Ke. I tried to transfer some of ours down there but I couldn't swing it."

"I know, the Vietnamese run the bullets."

"Don, I'd like to go in with you," he said.

"Christ, Shelly, you don't have to. It can get mighty dangerous in there. It's not your job."

"I think it is. I've been here eleven months and this is the first, the goddamned absolute first meaningful operation that's been put into effect. I've got to go."

A flash of his assistant, army Captain Gordon, lying dead in the bottom of my PBR with a bullet in his head because he too "had to go" on a previous operation slashed across my memory. Major Shellon wasn't needed; he'd get in the way. There was nothing he could do. I didn't answer; I just stirred my coffee.

"Okay! Damnit, Shelly, but I think you're an idiot. You'll have to ride in the battleship, the armored mike boat. I don't want to lose another soldier."

"Thanks, Don," he answered, and with a frown said, "Captain Gordon was doing what he thought best. He was doing his job." I felt like biting off my tongue.

I went up to the bridge again—1030, thirty-six minutes till I crossed the sill of Bong Bot. The clouds hung over our boats, smothering the sounds, denying clear vision. If it rained, I would abort.

Ten PBRs milled about, warming up their engines, checking out their equipment. The steel-hulled battleship and flamethrowing mike boat were in the middle of them. With binoculars I could see the SEALs lounging around, protected by their armor. They would be used if some real serious work had to be done on the beach.

I had 127 called alongside and took Captain Laske to the battleship. At 1050 I signaled all boats to form up. A few drops of rain fell from the black sky.

At 1055 I commenced the run-in, puffing heavily on my pipe to keep one hand busy, holding on with the other. The gunners swung their mounts back and forth. The coxswain's hands gripping the wheel were noticeably white. The boat captain uselessly rubbed an oily rag over his gleaming M-60.

At 1058, the LST's barrage lifted. The skies lightened. My legs felt heavy, my head rang, the smoke from my pipe suffocated me.

Bong Bot was a hundred yards away. The entire canal took the shape of a mammoth rattlesnake; the entrance was its huge, ugly, gaping mouth. The savage stare of its beady eyes burned into me. I must sail under the fangs.

It was 1101. I tapped the forward gunner. "Commence fire!"

We crossed the sill of Bong Bot at 1106. The sky cleared. I blinked from the glaring sun. "A good omen," I said aloud. The helos came in low ahead of us, chewing up the jungle on both sides.

We rounded the first bend and then the second. My gunners fired sporadically ahead of us. By now all thirteen boats—eleven PBRs and two mike boats—should be in. The first hootch appeared on the starboard as we turned the third curve. On the port another appeared fifty yards ahead.

"Pyro, Pyro, this is Handlash. First target my starboard side. Go to it. Out."

I continued ahead of the second hootch, two PBRs flanking me. The column came to a halt. The helos kept up their fire. My gunners were reloading. We carried four thousand rounds of .50-caliber ammunition aboard; fifteen hundred was the normal load. We even carried spare .50-caliber barrels.

The pyro boats moved into position. To the point of actual threats against the gunners, we had stressed fire discipline. In a winding, twisting, narrow canal such as this, the slightest misfiring could tear across the small fingers of land, devastating another boat. And worse, the boats receiving the fire might think it was the enemy and the resulting melee would destroy us all. There was no room for error or miscalculation. There was no margin of safety. This was my greatest fear. The danger existed, however, only for the first third of the transit. After that Bong Bot straightened out and each boat could fire at will.

The pyro PBR moved in close, sideways to the beach, their .50 calibers blasting away at the hootch. Their firing stopped as a pyro stepped majestically up on the engine covers. I could see the sparkling candle effect of the ignition flints as he pulled the trigger of the flamethrower. I could imagine the extremely high-pressure air ramming the jellied gasoline out of the nozzle into the arcing flints. I heard a deep WHOOSH! as the now-burning napalm's tongue of flame engulfed the house. The building disappeared.

We moved forward. An almost steady stream of 40mm grenades from the PBRs arched into the jungle about us. They could be fired with little danger of hitting another boat. Four more structures yielded to the pyros.

We continued. The first pyro PBR whipped about, coming swiftly alongside the support mike boat. Full tanks were swapped for his empties and barely forty seconds passed before he sprang forward again. The mike boat was the crux of the operation. Martin's crew had to refill and charge the empty tanks by the time the second pyro boat came alongside. They had practiced this entire complicated sequence for days. The second pyro came alongside and was away in seconds. Martin's plan was working.

We rounded the last turn in the canal. I could hear the

helos coming in behind us for their strike. I heard their rockets fire. The water off my starboard bow geysered in smoke and spray. The forward gunner screamed, grabbing his right arm.

"How bad?" I yelled.

He held his arm, looking at it. "Just a little shrapnel. It's okay, it's okay."

A Seawolf radio blurted in, "Ahh . . . sorry, Handlash. Any damage? Over."

"This is Handlash. Slight wound to the forward gunner. You're doing okay. Keep it up. Out."

All boats were now into the straight portion of Bong Bot. We'd had no firing incident from either ourselves or the enemy. Welcome though it was, the lack of opposition unnerved me. My mind played tricks. I envisioned rocket launchers and Viet Cong behind every tree, a Claymore mine on every branch. The pyros burned the hootches with ruthless efficiency.

About two miles into the canal a small factory appeared. The gunners played their .50s on its huge brick smokestack, intending to knock it down. The flamethrowers were useless here. Our three .50s chipped away at the base with little apparent damage. I called for the boat captain to break out the new rockets we had just received.

They were the M-72, light antitank weapons—LAWs, for short. A high-explosive, antitank round was propelled by a 2.75-inch rocket. Rocket and round together weighed a little more than two pounds and were launched from a twenty-five-inch disposable cardboard tube.

The boat captain pulled the safety pins and extended the inner tubing to its full thirty-five-inch length. This also cocked the round. Placing it on his shoulder, he looked around to ensure that no one was behind him. He aimed and triggered the round. A sheet of flame scorched out the rear as the twenty-inch-long rocket flew dead on to the smokestack.

The armor-piercing head crashed through the base of the

smokestack; nothing happened. Then a rumble. Then a full blast. The huge smokestack swayed, tilted, swayed more, stopped for a moment, then plummeted toward our boat.

The coxswain, watching the sport, yelled something and jammed his throttle forward. A second boat, which had come to help, backed out full. The chimney collapsed, bricks churning the water, bouncing off our bow, tearing up our sides. Five or six landed inside, one bouncing off the after gunner's helmet. Damn Viet Cong booby trap. They tried to get us but we were too fast for them. We laughed like idiots. Could you imagine the casualty report on a sailor wounded by a Viet Cong smokestack?

We fired six rockets into the main building with impressive results. I called in a MACE team to go ashore and destroy anything left with satchel charges. A satchel charge looked like an overstuffed canvas briefcase. It contained C-4 plastic explosives and a timed detonator. One simply set the time on the detonator, placed the satchel, triggered it, and ran. The charges destroyed the factory in six minutes. We continued upstream.

It was 1153. With several small villages burning behind us, we arrived at the main part of the Bong Bot complex. Here was the huge marketplace and the village hall. Here were the underground bunkers built of concrete. The Germans on the west coast of France on D day, June 6, 1944, could boast little better. We were the first government troops in this village in eight years.

The sense of urgency had left us. There was no enemy. I sent the SEALs in to search the village. Gunfire came from the beach. My after gunner yelled that he'd seen a man with a rifle run past an opening. The SEALs chased him but he got away. We found only a Viet Cong flag and a few propaganda leaflets.

"Destroy the village," I ordered, and the pyros, well covered by MACE teams, walked ashore and lived up to their name. They shot a blast into every tunnel entrance, the superheated flame consuming all the oxygen, suffocating those hiding inside. Each building got a kiss. We left to the intense heat of enormous fires and exploding satchel charges.

We had to use the same route out as we had on the way in. If an attack were to come, the Viet Cong would have had a long time to prepare for it.

Proceeding out, we finished off those hootches we'd missed coming in. Fear permeated the air and our firing was all the more intense for it. But only American bullets flew this twelfth day and the only casualties were a scratch on my forward gunner's arm, a few burns, and an after gunner with a bad headache.

As we crossed the sill at 1308, the adrenaline released its hold on my kidneys. I barely made it to the rail.

It was over. Mission accomplished and all that shit. We were safe but unsatiated. We had trained for the Olympics and taken the gold by default. The Viet Cong had cheated us. There would be no daring war stories on this one. I released the boats and headed for the T. Lunch would be ready.

Back at Binh Thuy there was little talk about the operations; there had been no heroic firefights, no opposition. Burning hootches was not considered dangerous or noble.

But other battles filled the days and new tales were told. New faces kept cropping up. Most of those who had preceded me had left. I was nearly the oldest gun in the delta. I was riding high. I now commanded close to three hundred men and thirty officers, including the SEALs. I reveled in it like a fat hog in mud. Each day saw us pull off more and more daring raids, driving deeper into Viet Cong territory with each cut. The thought that one well-placed sniper bullet could crush my megalomaniac existence rarely entered my mind, and never when I was on the river. I was invincible, as were my men. Though I was wounded four times, my faith remained. A protecting hand blanketed me.

At times, though, I felt my span of control spreading

mighty thin. It was as though I rode a tiger, guiding it only by a thin string through its nose.

RIVSEC 512, now transferred to the T, raised hell with Dung Island. They rushed through its myriad of small canals, viciously prosecuting any firing incidents. RIVSEC 511, back in its old hunting grounds, continued its harassment of the corridor. For the sake of safety, I tongue-in-cheek cautioned them of the danger. It was like being the coach of a winning football team. You give 'em their head and, though you personally might not have called a play the same as they did, you couldn't argue with success, and our ever-growing tally of dead Viet Cong attested to our success.

Such was the war, but what had been created? Quick-triggered green-boated gunmen? Were the targets always the enemy? I prayed so. It's a damnable situation—you have to keep your men pumped up for combat and always on the alert. They're taught, cajoled, and enjoined to draw fast, shoot straight, and roar into the very guns of the enemy. For what? Glory? Country? Honor? Self-preservation? I didn't know.

I did know that soon one can easily cross the line from boy next door to killer. Once the heady taste of blood is savored, an insatiable appetite for combat can follow.

The enemy is unknown, the target indistinct. Where do the bullets come from? Which old woman or child has the grenade? Which one of these people killed your buddy last week?

Who's to blame when the warrior crosses the line? His commanding officer who exhorts the combat spirit, the American penchant for hero worship, or our government, who sends these young men into battle?

To be there, to feel the power, to cross over into close combat is frightening. At the same time there is no greater thrill—no woman, no sunset, no music, no God—that can compare. You are Genghis Khan, Attila the Hun, and Caesar all in one.

How often we have drifted close to the bank or run a

canal, deliberately baiting the enemy to fire. You tease and tantalize. You play the game of here I am sweet angel, come kiss me, come play with me. It starts with the kiss of the gun and ends in a wild crescendo of violence—an orgasm of death.

And my men loved it.

Barbecue

———————•———————

The gas masks and antichemical protective suits were uncomfortable. Even though we'd been practicing for several days under actual gas conditions, I still didn't think we could fight with them on. The mask's narrow field of vision severely limited boat mobility, and our bodies, fully covered in the plastic protection, could not breathe. Fatigue came all too easily. We looked frightfully odd. Things were not familiar; movement was hesitant, unsure.

Romeo Patrol raced through the northern mouth of the Titi. Bill Norwick, with Yankee Patrol, was five minutes behind. The SEALs, in their battleship with Captain Laske aboard, followed as best they could. Marsh and his Seawolves sat at Tra On, their engines idling. Thanh, silent as always, stood at my side.

A slight cooling breeze blessed the clear midmorning skies. It was too nice a day for anyone to be killed.

I ignored the few desultory sniper rounds fired from around the fish stakes. We were looking for better game—machine guns. When we found them, we would engage while Marsh lifted off to bomb them with riot-control gas grenades. We hoped that the gas would immobilize the Viet Cong, allowing the SEALs to walk in and carry them out.

Another rifle shot greeted us from the church across the canal. We replied with ten LAW rockets and continued on. No more fucking around with that church. Norwick reported rifle fire. My boats took a turn around the first small island and headed back. I recognized none of the gas mask–protected men on Norwick's boat as we zoomed past him in the opposite direction. One of the masked creatures waved as we held on from the pitching wakes of the passing boats.

We passed the church at top speed. My binoculars scanned the jungle. How many times had I been back here? Too many.

"ROCKET!" screamed Bryan, the boat captain, cracking me across the back.

Willie, on the forward .50s, had ten shots in the air before the rocket round exploded in a harmless billow of black smoke thirty yards on the other side of us.

"Three Six, this is Handlash. Scramble two! Scramble two! We got one . . . am engaging now. Over!"

"Roger. We'll be there. Out." I could hear the whine of his engines over the transmission.

"Betray, this is Handlash. You copy? Over."

My words "we got one" popped back into my mind. What an odd thing to say. We got one? Who had who? Another rocket exploded behind my cover boat. The water around us splashed from a machine gun that joined the rocket launcher. We took three hits aft, but only holes.

We were on the second pass heading downstream as Norwick turned and headed back toward us. "Go Chinese," I yelled over the radio, and we headed directly for each other at a closing speed of about forty-five knots, all our guns on the same target. Going Chinese allowed us to keep the enemy under a cross fire. It was a bit dangerous, for if the outboard boats didn't lift their fire soon enough, the inboard boats would cross a damned inconvenient wall of .50s. It never happened though.

The gas masks were encumbering. I couldn't see worth a damn.

Just as we turned for the third run, the helos swooped in low, dropping their gas grenades, which looked like rabbit turds oozing from the sky. In seconds a thick, smoky, dirty-white gas cloud blotted the area. The firing stopped. The helos made a second pass. The noxious cloud drifted over our boats. I braced for the effect. Nothing happened. The clothing and masks seemed to work. It was said that without the masks the gas would irritate our lungs, causing violent, uncontrollable vomiting and convulsions. Supposedly, it would disable a man completely for twenty to thirty minutes.

We trolled up and down in front of the area until the battleship inched into sight. It seemed to give me a perverse thrill to stay immune to the gas. I wanted to take off my mask to see if it really worked. My irritated, bare gun hand told me better. The cloud dissipated. We eased away from the spot as the SEALs made their approach.

"She's all yours, Betray," I passed over the radio as we moved out and on to better targets. The gunfire faded into the background. Five minutes later I heard Betray call Mike One, the base support mike boat, into Titi. Optimistically, Mike One was to carry out all the prisoners that the SEALs captured. It had been standing by in the main river, loaded with a crew of volunteer gunners from base support.

Why did he call it in? Could the SEALs have been successful? We received no more fire as we passed the church, passed the little islands, and headed down toward the southern exit. I didn't know if it made me happy or sad. I felt bored. I'd never seen the sky so blue. We took off our gas masks; the moisture-laden air never tasted so good. Norwick was in the lead; I was in the number three slot, each boat separated by five hundred yards.

Norwick's voice came over the radio: "Handlash, this is Yankee. Couple of sampans pulled up on the beach. Request authority to blow 'em. Over."

I gave permission as he turned to port and dropped out of sight into the jungle. I heard the blast of gunfire and grenades. Five minutes later, when I got there, he was extracting.

"Hey, Bill, you missed a few back in there," I said, pointing to a couple of sampans pulled way up on the shore.

"A little too far in."

Cluck! Cluck! I mimicked, flapping my arms like wings.

"Nah! Just didn't want to get my boots dirty," he answered.

"Pretty boring day, eh?" I said.

"Yes, sir."

"I wonder if the SEALs got anything."

"Doubt it."

"Yeah, me too."

We just stood there like a couple of kids who couldn't decide what to play. "Hey, Commander," the boat captain on Norwick's cover boat broke the silence. "How about torching that hootch in there?"

I looked in at it. "It's Mister Norwick's play, ask him."

"Sure, go to it," Bill answered.

We watched them set a perimeter and move in to burn. They had learned to do this well. I was proud of them. It occurred to me that I was being a bit sloppy keeping these boats together out here. When the men pulled back, we soft-shoed out to the tune of the crackling bamboo.

I reported in: "Betray, this is Handlash. We're at the southern end of the big island heading back. How's it going? Over."

There was a delay . . . I called again. Surely no one could sink that chunk of iron. I signaled full speed; the boats jumped and battle ensigns sang in the wind. My burgee pennant had become all but shreds from the constant beating.

I called again. Marsh in his helo answered, "Nothing much, Handlash. They're in at the church. No contact, though."

"This is Handlash. Roger. I can't raise Betray. Tell him we'll remain down here out of the way. If he gets lonely, give us a call. Out."

We slowed to cruise speed. Norwick called, requesting permission to come alongside. As we joined, he pointed to a small canal leading inland from Titi. "Whataya think, Commander? The Viet Cong are probably bugged out by now. Let's take a look in there."

I stared at it. Why go in? We'd find the same old thing: nothing. Nothing but deserted hootches. It's too dangerous. Only a lunatic would take boats into such a narrow canal. "Whataya think, Commander?" he said again. "Hell, the VC are gone. Even if a few were still there, we could have a great fight and get our scores up." Bill continued triggering a Pavlovian drool response. I nodded toward the canal.

"Let's go," I answered and, leaving our two cover boats at the mouth, Bill and I took our boats in. The canal was narrow but no narrower than others we'd been in. But the jungle seemed thicker, blacker, more impenetrable than ever before. We proceeded in for eight minutes. My rapidly increasing heartbeat was telling me: Turn around! Turn around! Turn around! Get out of this evil, enchanted forest.

Deserted, somber-looking houses stared at me from behind ominous palms. Turn around! Turn around! Turn around!

Overhanging branches blotted out the sun. We snaked around a sharp bend. This was it. Screw it! We're getting out. I reached for the mike.

POW! POW! POW! POW! Norwick's after .50 spat.

The jungle behind him came alive with roaring gun crescendos, falling branches, and dancing tracer flashes. I watched helplessly; the canal was too narrow for me to bring my guns to bear. Then silence.

"Yankee, this is Handlash. Come about . . . easy. Over."

"Roger. Out" came his curt reply.

The boats could not make a complete turn. We had to jockey back and forth, taking a wretchedly long five minutes of aheads and reverses before our bows pointed out.

"Yankee, you ready?"

"Affirmative!"

"Roger. Hit it!"

White water shooting from our sterns, the boats bounded forward. The violent jet pump action and shallow water threw the boats far over to the side as we made our skidding, banking turns. Halfway out a light machine gun raked our port side, punching small, jagged holes, splintering the fiberglass. We fired back as best we could. "Yankee Two . . . Romeo Two, this is Handlash. Stand clear. We're coming out hot."

In three minutes we bounded across the entrance. Ahh! Safety, or relatively so. How odd to think of Titi as safe.

Norwick signaled he was coming alongside. "Commander, did you see the size of the hootch that fired on us?"

"Yes."

"Did you see all the sampans?"

"Yes," I replied, trying to be nonchalant. My heartbeat was settling back to twice normal.

"Let's go back and hit it!"

My heartbeat jumped up again. "You shittin' me?"

"No, sir . . . easy target."

I stared at the entrance to the canal seven hundred meters away. It looked so very small. It's stupid, Sheppard, don't do it. Risk versus gain? I picked up the mike: "Betray, Betray, this is Handlash. Have target for you. Over." Silence.

I repeated the call and waited. An out-of-breath voice I didn't recognize boomed back: "Ah . . . ah . . . negative . . . ah . . . Handlash, am engaged . . . ah . . . Over."

"Roger, Betray. Do you need my assistance? Over."

"Negative, Handlash. Out," came a much more professional reply.

"SHIT!"

"What about it, Commander?"

"Damn, Bill, I've only got thirty days left to go. It's stupid to go back in there," I answered.

"Hell! I'll go alone. I've got fifty-five left."

"I have all my life to stay," Thanh added.

I stared at M. Sgt. Nguyen Thanh from Soc Trang with his goddamned Cross of Gallantry pinned to his tiger greens. I was betraying him. I was betraying Ong Tam. I was betraying all I had preached and stood for. Thanh had only once before reminded me of my transient status. You bastard, Thanh, I cursed silently. Thirty days! Why risk it on a questionable target? Thirty days. You're a coward, Sheppard.

Willie mouthed, Gee, it'd be good fun, Commander.

A full minute passed in silent stares. My opposition wavered and failed. "Let's go." Our four boats wheeled around, heading for the tiny entrance. We crossed the sill at half speed, proceeding in and pulling up directly in front of the large hootch.

Bill Norwick took a hastily assembled assault team ashore. The rear boat and I took flanking stations up and down the canal and waited.

It seemed god-awful quiet. I waited, flipping the safety on and off my M-79 and checking continually to see that it was loaded. Five or six shots sounded from the other side of the hootch.

Willie's voice sounded from behind me: "Gee, Commander, I wonder what's going on in there."

"GODDAMNIT, DON'T SWEAT IT! Just keep your fuckin' eyes on that opposite bank!" I lashed back at him. Silence.

"Christ, I'm sorry, Willie. I don't know what's happening. I'm sorry, I apologize."

"Thieu Ta scared?" Thanh asked. Odd, he had never questioned me before.

"Yes, Sergeant Thanh, I am."

An M-16 fired six rounds. A grenade exploded. Silence.

"Take me in," I commanded.

"Mister Norwick . . . Bill . . . Sheppard here. Where the hell are you?" I yelled, kneeling on the bank in front of the hootch where they had gone ashore.

"Over here, behind the hootch," came a low reply. "Come around on the right side . . . low."

I started around, Thanh just behind me. I crawled. I hated to do that; it always hurt my knees and my greens got so damn dirty. I pushed my M-79 ahead of me. I'd never learned to do this properly. This was the finest hootch I'd ever seen. Whoever lived here must be a real wheel, I thought.

"Ouch!"

The twenty-yard-wide cleared area around the dull brown, woven-bamboo hootch was amazingly neat. Norwick, crouching, peered around the bottom of a large woodpile. He rolled over, looking up at me. "What's going on?" I whispered.

"Don't really know" came his clipped reply. "When we landed, four guys and some young girl came tearing outta this hootch here and made it into the jungle." He paused, catching his breath. Great beads of dirty sweat dripped off his face. His hands were shaking. "They're right over there, behind those big trees. No shit, Commander, what're they doing?"

"How the hell do I know. Where are your troops?"

"Three over there," he pointed to the left, then nodded his head to the right, "and two over there."

"Why haven't you zapped those guys yet?"

"Just waitin' to see what they're gonna do."

"Wait long enough and you'll be picking Viet Cong lead outta your ass. C'mon, we're getting outta here. Call your men."

A few quick commands followed by rustling branches started our extraction. The last man on the left eased back by the hootch on his way to the boats. Norwick kept his eyes glued to the jungle. I peered through a niche near the top of the woodpile. I heard the VC and detected their presence by the moving palm branches, but I could not actually see anyone. We were in too close for me to use my M-79. I didn't know where my own men were. I heard a man on the right ease by.

"That's it. C'mon, Commander, Thanh, let's make it," Norwick whispered.

We started back, Norwick and Thanh in the lead. Just before moving I glanced to the right and saw a tall Vietnamese step in behind the woodpile. We stared. His gasp for breath shattered my ears. His eyes grew tenfold, the slant disappeared. His pulse drove his temples in and out like a trip-hammer. Hanging around his neck, a Molotov cocktail bounced up and down against his heaving chest. He held a grenade in his left hand and a chromed 9mm German Luger in his right.

I stopped breathing. I stared. I floated my M-79 down, trying to squeeze the trigger. It wouldn't obey.

"HEY, they're coming. Hey, you guys, GET BACK. SONOVABITCH! Come back," Norwick's far-off voice drifted through the air.

I heard the slow, meandering, automatic pop of an M-16 way off in the distance. I heard men rushing around behind me. I squeezed the trigger harder. My gun wouldn't fire. I tried to crush the trigger. My finger ached. FIRE! FIRE! my brain demanded.

"Come on, come on." Bill's voice faded in and out.

The Vietnamese gently lobbed the grenade toward me. He was very tall. I squeezed harder. He was well dressed.

My finger turned white under the pressure. He needed a haircut.

I squeezed harder. My trigger finger burst, splattering blood slowly like lava oozing in front of me.

His grenade rolled languidly toward my feet. His feet were muddy.

Run, stupid! my brain flashed to my body. I squeezed the trigger harder.

RUN! RUN! RUN! STUPID, RUN! the panicked message flashed again. I tried to fire again.

The Vietnamese stared at me as if he had a million years to raise his Luger. His little finger was missing on his left hand.

My brain began to function. My God, the safety's on. My thumb flicked it off. The barrel pointed straight at his stomach. I pulled the trigger again—the M-79 fired with its loud characteristic blooping sound.

RUN! stupid, grenades kill! my mind demanded, trying to make my body work.

The man almost had the chromed 9mm German Luger leveled at me. His hand grenade wobbled slowly, then stopped against my boot. RUN! my mind demanded.

The dark green 40mm projectile, amidst black smoke, drifted slowly out of the barrel, sauntered across the five-foot gap between us, and crashed into his stomach.

Someone was yelling somewhere.

He doubled over as if hit by some gargantuan football. He lifted slowly off the ground and seemed to stay there, hovering over where he had stood.

"Thieu Ta!" I heard faintly spoken, as if through a long tunnel.

The man, still in the air, moved away from me, the gasoline from the broken Molotov cocktail around his neck floating gently down over his body. The jungle, framed by the huge gaping hole where his stomach and lungs had been, was a beautiful, virulent green.

He burst into flame.

With all my force I kicked the grenade away. Arcing into the air, it rolled once, twice, and coughed an anemic explosion. The low-order concussion smashed me against the woodpile.

I couldn't bring anything into focus. Thanh's voice was calling but indistinct, too far away. The uneven wood in the pile jammed into my back.

"Thieu Ta! Thieu Ta!" Thanh screamed, running toward me. A high-velocity, Russian-made steel bullet met him halfway. He went down clutching his leg and didn't get up.

An explosion resounded from behind the hootch. I jumped up, grabbing Thanh with my left hand and dragging him toward the canal.

"NORWICK! NORWICK!" I screamed. "I'm coming in . . . I'm coming in."

Hoisting Thanh over my shoulder, I stumbled past the burning man with the chromed 9mm German Luger. I nearly vomited from the stench. Three bullets thudded into a tree next to me. A slug hitting Thanh threw me to the ground. I crawled, dragging him behind me, while yelling to Norwick. Not a very cool way to do this, I thought stupidly.

As I made it to the corner of the hootch, two hands reached out and pulled me in. "Commander, where the fuck you been?" the beautiful voice of Norwick shouted.

"Thanh . . . I think he's dead" was all I could manage.

"We're in deep shit; we gotta get outta here," Norwick replied in a matter-of-fact voice.

I looked around as my eyes cleared. One badly shot up PBR had several bleeding men trying to plug it and get it under way. Its engines started and settled to a low hum. The other three boats, though badly holed, looked seaworthy. All engines purred, giving me sanity. We moved in, crawling under the cover fire of the .50s. The noise passed the threshold of pain. We were getting our asses kicked.

Bill, limping on a blood-soaked left leg, covered our retreat to the boats. I placed Thanh in the stern of my PBR, grabbed an M-16, and jumped back out to help Bill into his boat. Did I see Thanh move?

I counted; we had everyone on board. "HIT IT!" I yelled. I was in command again. As we leapt away, the flaming man with the chromed 9mm German Luger flickered and went out.

Once back in the wide, wide Titi, I called Betray. I couldn't raise him. I saw four Seawolves putting in strikes way ahead of us. What was going on? We raced for the area. I was dizzy, weak. My body rebelled against the slapping of the PBR hull. Thanh moaned. I rushed for his side. He slowly tried to sit up. "Head hurt . . . head hurt," he mumbled as I placed another battle dressing on his leg wound. "Don't remember, Thieu Ta," he managed to say.

"Ya got shot in the leg, Thanh. Twice. I guess you hit your head as you fell. You're okay, Thanh. We'll be out soon."

Finally an answer to my radio call: "Handlash, this is Betray. Under heavy fire. We are getting out. Over. Do you copy? Over!" I answered that we were on our way.

In ten minutes they came into sight. Explosions splashed

around them. The supply mike boat, Mike One, was catching hell. It was never made to fight. A jagged, four-foot hole violated its starboard side.

As we passed by the church, all hell broke loose. My after gunner fell. The boat captain leapt back, grabbing the .50s so fast that I doubt more than ten shots were lost.

I saw the helos dropping gas grenades. We put on our gas masks, but not soon enough. I got a slight whiff. My gut turned to fire.

We passed the plodding Mike One. It was a shambles. Two men lay on the coxswain's deck, but most of its guns were still firing. The battleship, delivering its maximum firepower, looked like a Roman candle from its muzzle flashes. We zipped past her on the nonfiring side, reaching for the Bassac. Water from a rocket explosion engulfed my cover boat. The gas cloud dimmed my vision. I could barely breathe in the gas mask. The suit pressed in on me, seeming to force my sweat back into my body.

The boat behind me broke through the spray, staying right with me. I could see the flapping fiberglass on its shot-up sides whipping violently from the bouncing and the wind.

A bullet ripped across the coxswain's station, smashing our radar. Shrapnel and shattered glass from its big tube sprayed the coxswain. He screamed.

The volume of fire increased, churning the water of Titi. Our starboard whip antenna was carried away. My hand dripped blood from the constant firing of my M-79. Willie was screaming incoherently as the concussion of his constantly booming guns wracked his body.

The gas cloud lifted. Yanking off my mask and grabbing the mike, I pleaded: "Three Six, this is Handlash. Get Pedro . . . get Pedro. We've got some bad ones here. Mike One looks worse. Get dustoff to Tra On immediately. Need Pedro now, now. Over."

The gas took its toll; a size twelve boot kept kicking me in the gut. Mucus poured out of my mouth and snot ran freely from my nose.

"Roger. Copy, Handlash. Hold in there, big guy. Out."

The boat captain on the after gun ripped off his mask with vomit pushing out right behind it. He kept throwing up, his face covered with it. The slop poured over his hands, his gun, onto the ammo belt. It squished into the .50's breech as a sizzling garnish to the pounding slugs. He kept firing and kept vomiting.

The staff holding our battle ensign took a bullet. It wavered, bent back, hesitated, and pulled the flag down at my feet. I stared at it . . . it didn't seem right. I stooped to pick it up. Three bullets jammed through our starboard side inches from me. I forgot the flag. My M-79 went back to work.

"Mister Norwick's been hit! Handlash! Handlash! Mister Norwick's been hit, Handlash! Handlash! He's dead, he's dead."

"You sure, Yankee One?"

"Yes! The top of his head is blown off."

"Yankee, this is Handlash. Roger. Out."

I vomited over the radios. What would I tell his wife?

We flashed across the sill of Titi and into the Bassac. The firing stopped. I held onto the side of the boat, fighting off the tears. "Handlash, this is Yankee One. Norwick is still alive. The bullet entered the eyepiece of his mask and whipped around his helmet, cutting him bad along the way. I don't think he'll make it. Over."

"Yankee One, control the bleeding if you can. Pedro's on the way . . . break, break. Three Six, you copy Yankee One? Over."

"Affirmative. Pedro's on the way, estimating ten, Handlash . . . break, break. Yankee One, head for center of the river."

"Anyone! Anyone! This is Mike One. We need help. Help us, please . . . for God's sake, somebody help us. Over! Over!" the radio cried.

My blood stopped circulating. A thousand daggers struck me. I stared at the radio.

"Help! Help!" blasted the plea again.

I wiped the vomit off the mike onto my once-starched

greens. I keyed the mike. My mouth couldn't move. The mike dropped out of my hand.

"HELP . . ."

I took the mike again, staring at it. My head cleared. "Roger, Mike One," I called as calmly as my spinning mind would allow. "This is Handlash. Hang in there. We'll be right back. Over."

"Please hurry. Thank you, oh God, thank you," came the panicked, broken reply.

"This is Three Six. Rolling in now!"

"This is Seven Six. Rolling in now!"

I touched the coxswain's stooped shoulder and pointed back toward Titi. A blank, robotlike stare answered as he swung his helm, pointing our bow back toward the canal entrance. The other two boats followed me around in smooth, gliding turns, but I stopped them with an order to remain clear and wait.

The canal loomed agonizingly small as our speeding PBR approached. My mind cleared. I could see forever. Romeo One's battered crew was ready. My body didn't hurt. Mike One came into sight. The enemy fire rivaled pictures of the invasion of Saipan. We were high on step, full out.

It was over. I wanted to go home. I'd played soldier long enough.

The boy in me disappeared and the man was born as we turned to take station behind the slow crawl of the churning mike boat. We slowed, firing our defense.

The battleship finally crossed the sill. Only a thousand yards for Mike One to go. I kept firing. Enemy bullets smashed into my boat. The compass disappeared. We kept going. The starboard whip antenna fell, carrying my burgee to the bottom of Titi. It didn't seem right. I couldn't hear anything. I kept firing. Thanh, lying in a pool of vomit, kept trying to fire an M-79. The coxswain kept slumping over his wheel. I noticed, but my eyes stayed glued to my target. And then I saw it.

"ROCKET! ROCKET! LEFT! COME LEFT!" I screamed, but nothing happened. Leaping into the coxswain's flat I grabbed the wheel, spinning it to port. The rocket missed but seared a burning path across my face.

An explosion threw metal from the starboard engine throughout the boat.

We continued on with the port. I could barely control the steering. Bullets hit us; a rocket passed through our bow, but there was nothing I could do about it. I tried not to notice, I tried not to hear the screams of my men. I tried not to be alive. We cleared the canal. I steered for the hovering Pedro. I saw other boats heading for Tra On to the waiting medevac helos.

Who was in command? I had no radios. I needed a radio. I must take command. My burgee; where was my burgee? Handlash, Handlash, this is Handlash, my mind repeated.

The 306th had won. We had paid our pound of flesh for Bong Bot. The VC owned Titi Canal.

Vietnam,
January 1968

———•———

The SEALs had captured a few VC and killed several others, but our wounded rate and amount of equipment damaged made our price far too high. Lieutenant Norwick was in the hospital in Japan with a fifty-fifty chance of survival. They were planning to put a steel plate in his head. Thanh was hurting and would walk with a limp for many years.

For the tenth time, I reread the letter that awaited me when I returned: "My name is Doug Patterson. I'm assigned to be your relief. I will arrive the end of December or the first part of January . . ."

"Doug Patterson," he said, extending his hand. Thousands of little gnats buzzed around our heads.

"Don Sheppard . . . glad to see you." I wore a black beret.

We piled into my well-banged-up jeep and drove down a dusty, poorly maintained road toward Binh Thuy, the small village some five miles up the Bassac River from Can Tho.

At Than Son Nhut airport in Saigon I sat silently on a hard wooden bench with other men in soiled and patched jungle greens, their eyes gaunt, tired, with a distant look of apathy. I was no different from any of them.

Civilian men in clean and pressed khaki bush jackets walked briskly by with no reaction. Women made up a fourth of the herd passing the hundred or so soldiers and one sailor. Only the most stunning called forth a hint of recognition. Army MPs attempting to keep everyone moving added to the confusion.

A major wearing a green beret sat next to me. After twenty minutes he said, "Intel boys figure the 1968 Tet cease-fire will be the most peaceful yet."

I grunted.

The wheels of the huge jet airliner folded neatly into their wells. Saigon fell astern.

What would I do without a gun in my hand?

What would I do with the rest of my life?

Mother, mother with my shield.